24 Chapters

Survivors' memoirs presented by:
Ever After Foundation

24 Chapters

24 Chapters. Copyright © 2024 Ever After Foundation.
Published by: Motivation & Success Publishing (Motivation & Success, LLC).

All rights reserved. No part of this publication may be reproduced, distributed, or transmitted in any form or by any means unless prior written permission of the author has been issued. This includes: photocopying, recording, or other electronic or mechanical methods. An exception may be granted in the case of brief quotations embodied in critical reviews and certain other noncommercial uses as permitted by copyright law. For permission requests, contact the author.

Table of Contents

Foreword - Casey Gwinn 7

A Note from Nancy E. O'Malley 9

Trigger Warning 11

Introduction 13

Chapter 1 - Annie Lagunas
Soledad 15

Chapter 2 - Amber Davis
Amber D 35

Chapter 3 - Andrea Lucie, PhD
Follow the Sun … All the Way to the Heart 53

Chapter 4 - Claudia Hinojosa-Torres
What's in a Name? 75

Chapter 5 - Anika Samone
Choosing Hope 89

Chapter 6 - Crystal Perras
Making Every Move a Step Forward 103

Chapter 7 - Dani G.B.
Breaking the Silence: A Path to Inner Peace and
Wholeness 113

Chapter 8 - Chantelle Pape
Giving Yourself Your Love 127

Chapter 9 - Damire Major
Letting Nothing Stop Me 141

Chapter 10 - H. Kress
One Chapter 153

Chapter 11 - DeAnna Thieme
Motherhood by Fire 169

Chapter 12 - Heather Marianna
Finding Myself 187

Chapter 13 - JoJo Rimmer
A Dance with a Hellion 201

Chapter 14 - Jennifer Hass
From Survivor to Thriver 219

Chapter 15 - JoDee Castello
Hopeful Roots, Humbled Growth 231

Chapter 16 - Misti L. Harrelson
Kintsugi—Fractured and Repaired with Precious
Metals 243

Chapter 17 - Shawna Rainwater Turner
Phoenix 261

Chapter 18 - Katie Meadows
A Path Worth Walking 279

Chapter 19 - Skylar Wolf
Father Not Like Daughter 289

Chapter 20 - Theresa Reyes
The Power of Closure 307

Chapter 21 - Kendra Trần
Unto Shore 321

Chapter 22 - Tiffany Winn
Rebirth: Naked and Unashamed 343

Chapter 23 - Lisbet Perez
Libertad! 359

Chapter 24 - Brenda Grisham
Life After 375
Gratitude and Appreciation... 389
Resources 397

Foreword
Casey Gwinn
President, Alliance for HOPE International

The first time I met Misti Harrelson, I was captivated by her passion, joy, and resilience. It was almost ten years ago in Oakland when she'd just escaped her abuser and came to the Alameda County Family Justice Center for help. I knew she had survived domestic violence and other force multipliers such as poverty, but she was already transforming her pain into power, her resilience into hope. I remember wondering what her future would look like as she focused her strength and inspired other survivors.

This book is the answer to that question. Misti, along with twenty-three other survivors whose stories fill these pages, has stepped forward in courage to share her journey to hope and healing. Their paths have not been linear, and each of these amazing women is at a different place in her own journey.

Their stories are raw. Their stories are, at times, messy and hard to read. But they are all worth reading. Whether you have survived violence and abuse or experienced the intersectionality of other types of traumas as each of them has, their voices deserve to be heard and elevated.

You cannot read this book without realizing that they deserve your respect and admiration. These women have rejected the shame and blame that society so often tries to place on them. They have boldly told the truth about the injustices they have endured, along with the pain, violence, and terror they have survived.

Bishop Desmond Tutu said "justice" is three things: confession, forgiveness, and reconciliation. Confession means telling the truth about injustice; forgiveness involves doing everything possible to repair the harm; and finally, reconciliation requires changing the conditions that allowed the injustice to occur. The stories in this book bravely reveal those injustices. Once we understand the challenges these courageous individuals have faced, it becomes our job to do everything possible to repair the harm and change the conditions that caused the injustice in the first place.

I strongly endorse this powerful set of stories. I have little doubt they will inspire many others as they have inspired me. May every reader fully absorb the authors' spirits and their longing for better lives and futures. As you read this book and witness the hope they have each found, reflect on your goals, the obstacles in your way, and the paths you need to travel to achieve your goals. Use their stories to motivate you to become who you want to be, love who you want to love, and do what you want with your life.

With great HOPE,
Casey Gwinn
President, Alliance for HOPE International
Lead author of the bestseller, *Hope Rising: How the Science of HOPE Can Change Your Life*

A Note from Nancy E. O'Malley

I read with fascination, intrigue, and utter delight the experiences journaled by the coauthors. Their writing styles are beautiful, almost melodic, and encourage the reader to keep going.

Each coauthor shares their journey honestly and openly. While some of what they recount must have been painful or uncomfortable to write, they nevertheless wrote heartbreaking and inspiring accounts that will empower and bring light to those in darkness. By doing so, the reader is hooked to keep turning pages, just as I was.

The stories within encourage me and others to reflect and perhaps challenge life from a place of awakening and authenticity. The selfless portrayal of experiences by these women inspires the readers to reflect with the courage of self-discovery while embracing life's many lessons.

Nancy E. O'Malley

*****

Nancy E. O'Malley served in the Alameda County District Attorney's Office for nearly thirty-nine years, during the last fourteen as the elected district attorney. The Alameda County DA had the first Victim Witness Division in the country, one of the reasons Nancy sought employment there.

In her time at the district attorney's office, Nancy created and supported nonprofit, nongovernment organizations that engaged victim advocates and she wrote legislation, now law, giving focus to the role of victim advocates in California and across the country.

As chief assistant district attorney, Nancy opened the second Family Justice Center (ACFJC) in the world, which focused on victim advocacy support and co-location of multiple agencies to provide more effective and comprehensive services to victims of crime. Even before attending law school in the 1970s, Nancy was a volunteer victim advocate in one of the first California rape crisis centers and domestic violence shelters.

Nancy continues to chair the California Office of Emergency Services (Cal OES) Sexual Assault Committee and serves as parliamentarian of the Domestic Violence Committee, remaining deeply involved in victim advocacy in each area.

*****

https://www.nancyomalleyforda.org/
https://cristoreydelasalle.org/people/nancy-omalley/
https://www.strongnation.org/people/nancy-o-malley
https://www.carondeleths.org/live/profiles/533-nancy-omalley-71

Trigger Warning

Within this book are stories containing detailed descriptions of physical, sexual, mental, emotional, financial, spiritual, and racial violence and traumas of all types. As you read, you may also experience a roller coaster of love, anger, fear, violence, grief, and every other human emotion, especially inspiration and hope.

Our authors have shared their most intimate experiences and the most vulnerable parts of their lives. Please be aware of these triggers and have a plan in place for you, our beloved and adored readers. Just like with life, this book may send you on a journey of brokenness and healing. Make sure you are in a safe place before and while reading it.

This book may challenge you. You may ask yourself hard questions and remove some masks you've been wearing. You may also learn new ways to heal yourself from each of our authors. That's why we encourage you to take notes as you read. Every life strategy and healing technique in this book has the potential to benefit you on your own journey. Listen to your gut—you know what's right for you. Get and stay in touch with your higher power.

Introduction

In a world where shadows and shame can often overwhelm, the path to healing and resilience stands as a guiding light of hope. Through this book, the Ever After Foundation and our co-authors aim to educate, inspire, empower, and enlighten readers about a subject that has been too often normalized throughout history. Our brave contributors have stepped forward to become the light that others need in their darkest moments. This book is an invitation to explore the transformative power of inspiration, revealing the stories of those who have endured profound trauma and emerged stronger, braver, and more determined on the other side because of hope.

Through their experiences, we discover the strength within each of us—the ability to rise, rebuild, and redefine our narratives. Together, we delve into the moments of darkness that often come before the light, illustrating how vulnerability and hope lead to growth and connection. As you read, prepare to confront both the deepest evils of humanity and the most awe-inspiring reasons for human existence.

These pages offer not just tales of struggle, but profound lessons of courage, hope, compassion, and the indomitable human spirit. We wrote this book to help others find their way out of darkness—with humility, kindness, and a deep sense of hopeful purpose. We are healers, Warriors, and protectors. We are your mothers, sisters, aunties, grandmothers, and other beloved family members. These courageous Warriors and co-authors are showing, through their actions, that we can do better for each other, and it all begins within ourselves.

Together, let's embark on a journey of healing, reminding ourselves that no matter how deep the scars, the potential for renewal and joy always remains. Your story is still being written, and hope is waiting to be discovered. We are our brothers' and sisters' keepers— you are too.

Chapter 1

Soledad

Annie Lagunas

Dedicated to the braveness of my daughters.

In 1989, after my husband was released from prison for the second time, he and I and our two daughters moved from San Jose to a ranch about twenty-five miles outside of Greenfield, California. We found a small community in Carmel Valley and ended up living on thirteen acres, a half mile between us and our closest neighbors. He'd suggested that moving to the country would be a nice change of pace from city life. It made sense to me, but moving also meant I would be far away from my family and my work. Just as he wanted.

Our marriage had been riddled with control and violence. The black eyes would just begin to fade before he made sure that they were bruised again; he no longer insisted that I cover them with makeup. I can still feel his cold, stark stare when he'd look me up and down and then slowly move closer saying, "Hmm, I can barely see that black eye anymore. I guess I'll need to freshen that up when we get home."

His words were so natural, as if they were something people said to each other all the time. The verbal and psychological abuse was constant in our relationship. But I did not come from an abusive household, and I didn't understand the elements of control.

My *normal* had become so skewed that I was surprised when a day passed when I *didn't* get hit. I wouldn't even flinch when he called out in public, "Hey, whore." His way of addressing me, a reminder that he had not forgotten or forgiven the affair I'd had. Mainly he did it so everyone would know I had betrayed him. As if he were the victim.

The Day Everything Changed
One day that particularly stands out, however, is July 29th, 2007. That Sunday seemed to be just another ordinary day in my life,

a life that was not so ordinary by most people's standards. In retrospect, something seemed off. The sun shone a little differently; the air was dry and hot. I felt extra sensitive to everything.

Over the years, many things had changed, yet so many remained the same. My oldest daughter had joined the Army National Guard and was at basic training, worlds away from the madness of our volatile home. The only communication we had with her was through letters. I wrote to her daily, needing the distraction from what my life had become—hell and darkness.

That Sunday, he, my youngest daughter and I got in the car for a trip to town. I knew exactly what awaited me once we returned home. I no longer feared the things he said he would do to me. Twenty years had a way of numbing the senses. I knew exactly what he was capable of.

I stayed silent most of the drive, unless he demanded responses to his incessant talking. He was always talking, telling me what I needed to do. How ugly and stupid I was. How lucky I was to have him because no one else could ever love me. How much of a whore I was. Telling me what *else* he was going to do to me. Telling me he could still take me someplace no one would be able to find me where he would torture me for the rest of my life if I continued being defiant and bringing these punishments upon myself. Or, I could be a better wife and listen to him and do as he wanted. But that day . . . That day he kept talking about the things he still needed to take from me.

There were five altogether: He was going to take out an eye, pop an eardrum, scar my face, hurt me to the point of disabling me, and cut off one of my fingers. He had already done three of these things over the past month when he took a mallet to my foot, burned my face, and cut off part of a finger.

By the time we'd driven the twenty-five miles to the town of Soledad, I was unsettled, a different kind of scared. I wasn't thinking about the groceries on my list. My only thought was, "How can I kill him? And if I do, would anyone miss him?"

It no longer seemed feasible to think about escaping, because my previous attempts had taught me that he would find me. Trying to figure out how to kill him had been my only thought over the prior weeks—it was the only thing helping me survive. Well, that and the Jack Daniels and Coke, which were always plentiful in our home.

As these thoughts cycled through my mind, I walked around a store I'd been in a hundred times before, and yet I felt lost. Something was different about him as well. Usually, he would be right by my side to ensure I didn't make eye contact with any men (or them with me) and especially to prevent conversation with anyone, pulling me close whenever he suspected a possible audience.

This afternoon, though, he didn't come near me, instead observing from a distance, just far enough away to make me feel like prey. The hungry predator stalked and circled, as if I were in a *National Geographic* episode.

As soon as we got to the car and loaded our groceries, he snarled at me, "Who did you tell? I didn't hear you tell the clerk you were a whore when he asked if you found everything. You know you have to tell everyone!"

On and on he went. The sound of his voice was quickly overpowered by my own pressing thoughts: "Can I kill him? I'm never going to get away from him if I don't do something. This has to end. I can't keep living like this!"

Over and over it played, like a broken record in my mind. I was so preoccupied that I hadn't realized that he'd given me the keys. He hadn't allowed me to drive for over a year—hiding my keys, disabling my car, and assuming the role of chauffeur, all to take away any opportunity for escape.

I drove onto the freeway, still hearing his malevolent babbling but not quite understanding that I was the one driving. I took the Arroyo Seco exit toward home, felt the steering wheel in my hands, and suddenly, my mind was spinning. I was driving myself home to a beating, the home that had become my prison.

I snapped back to the present when he turned up the radio. A song he'd dubbed *my* song was playing, and he said, "Oh wow, your song is on, you coldhearted snake." He resumed calling me names, describing the punishments he still needed to inflict. He talked about splitting my tongue so I would physically be the snake he continually said I was. Part of me felt paralyzed as my mind raced, my knuckles white around the steering wheel.

He repeated what he was going to take from me. I was barely hanging on. It was then I realized this would be my opportunity for freedom. I prayed, like so many other times before, and found myself turning the car around on this two-lane road. I had to try something because going home meant there would be no escape.

At that moment, I knew I couldn't go back to that house.

We were only a couple of miles from town. I didn't know what I was going to do if I made it that far; I just prayed that I would. And I was running out of options. If I tried to kill him, I knew I might be the one who ended up dead.

I was halfway through turning the car around before he realized what was happening. He yelled, "What the fuck are you doing?"

I yelled back, "I'm done! I am going back to town."

Suddenly, I was more scared than I had ever been. He yanked the keys out of the ignition and the car stalled. It sat dead, blocking the road. I struggled for the keys, yelling and screaming. If he was speaking, I couldn't hear it, too caught up in my own fight. I saw a vehicle coming toward us, getting closer and closer. I finally screamed, "That car is too close. Give me the fucking keys!"

He finally released the keys after realizing that the car would need to stop since it couldn't get around us.

With the car restarted, I finished turning and pulled onto the dirt shoulder. The SUV passed, and my heart sank, though I'm not really sure what I was expecting them to do.

I jumped out and started to speed walk in the direction we'd just come from. It was all reactionary. I was so scared of him catching up and dragging me back to the car, I didn't even think about my twelve-year-old daughter still sitting in the back seat. Everything happened within seconds, yet it seemed as if everything was in slow motion. I was so focused that I hadn't noticed the passing SUV had also pulled onto the shoulder up ahead.

I was confronted by the driver—a woman, small in stature, but still taller than I, and the passenger, a man who towered over me. They blocked my way and the man said, "Hey, we're off-duty deputies. Where are you going?"

I stopped dead in my tracks, not believing what I'd just heard. Was I daydreaming? Or were my guardian angels really standing in front of me? I didn't know. I was both elated and numb.

"We know something was going on. We saw the struggle in the car," the man continued.

My heart pounded so hard, it felt as if it might leap from my chest. The man tried to make eye contact. *Will my prayers finally be answered?* I was so scared, knowing the fate that awaited me if this was a hallucination. Even worse, what if I told them and they didn't believe or help me?

They both took a step closer and asked again, "Are you OK? Where are you going?"

This was it. I realized I would never have another opportunity like this, so the words came flooding out: *I am going to town. I can't do this anymore. Look at this tattoo and look at this one and he calls me* whore *and he burned my face and I can barely walk because he hurt my knee.*

My almost incoherent, manic rambling continued as twenty years of abuse spilled forth in a few seconds. Then I heard the male deputy say, "OK, OK, OK." He then told the woman to stay with me while he went to talk to my husband.

I was suddenly aware of my surroundings. Little heads bobbed around in the deputies' SUV.

I looked in the direction the officer walked and saw my husband outside our car, on the front passenger side. My daughter was also out of the car, on the driver's side. She seemed frozen. I had a sinking thought that the deputies obviously had no weapons on them, and we were in an area with no cell phone reception. There was no way for them to call for assistance if they needed it. Would they need it?

The deputy walked toward my husband, but before he could get close, my husband calmly said, "Oh, I am so sorry about this, officer. You see, my wife has already been drinking and she is a little crazy. I should get her home. If you can just help me get her into the car. . ."

My daughter had made her way to my side, and the deputy stood close enough to my husband now that he had to have been able to see the buck knife on his belt. Then the male deputy returned and said, "These are your options—you either need to get in your car and go home, or get in our car and we'll take you somewhere safe."

I had prayed for this moment during so many dark nights filled with blood and pain. Each attempt had left me with only bruises and more prayers. My faith in God had been the only thing he hadn't been able to beat out of me. My guardian angels were finally here, waiting to take me away, and I stood frozen.

The deputies' words echoed in my mind. Could they really get me somewhere safe?

I was empty. I was so broken and shattered that I barely felt human. The stakes had dramatically changed. *If* I went home, it was no longer just a beating and a black eye that awaited me. I don't know how long I stood there, unable to move or speak. It felt like hours, until I finally blinked and saw my daughter standing directly in front of me. "Mom," she said.

This was my chance. This could be the end! *This* is why I was turning the car around.

Yet my mind bounced back to the most important question: What if they can't take me somewhere safe? The consequences of being found again were unimaginable. This time, he would take me to the middle of nowhere so that no one would ever find me. He would torture me to death. He'd been telling me this for months, and I knew all too well his were not empty threats. He was waiting for me to "make him do it." If this failed, he would end me.

I couldn't move. I could barely breathe. I felt my daughter's small hands on my shoulders, and she shook me as hard as her little body could, shouting, "MOM!" When she finally saw life staring back at her, she whispered, "We have to go with them because if we go home . . . he is really going to hurt you this time."

She didn't say what she really meant, but I knew what she was trying to save me from.

Even with the desperation in her voice and the tears in my eyes, I remained immobile with fear over making the wrong decision. I fully understood what the consequences would be *if* this escape attempt didn't work. It was so hard to imagine us being free. And either choice could lead to death, or worse.

My daughter was not giving up. She turned to the male deputy. "We have to go with you. Please don't let him take us home."

I don't recall hearing his response. I just remember seeing the female deputy rush to the SUV, open the passenger door, and motion for us to get in. My daughter clutched my arm as the male deputy maneuvered us toward their vehicle. "Get in," he said. Once we were seated, the door closed and locked, and the little ones who had cleared the seat for us were now in the back of the vehicle.

I don't know if anyone spoke when we drove away. I kept looking forward. I was terrified of looking back. I thought about everything that suddenly was behind me: my purse with my driver's license, my cell phone (deliberately), my car, house, and job . . . and the man who swore he loved me with every other breath but never hesitated to beat me black and blue.

The drive back to town took forever, probably because I wasn't breathing. We finally pulled into a gas station, putting us back almost where we'd been not even half an hour prior. Again, I sat paralyzed, except for the pounding of my heart and the tight grip of my daughter's hand in mine. My thoughts raced: What if he followed us? Was he watching us from the other parking lot? He was so diabolical that I half expected a shootout, like a scene from the movies. He would not let me go this easily.

We waited for the Soledad patrol car to pick us up, and I thought about what had just happened. I was so close to freedom. My prayers had finally been answered on a country road on a Sunday afternoon. I didn't know if this was the beginning or the end—it turned out to be both.

From Trauma to Freedom
While my memories of the exchange are cloudy, I know the deputies recounted the ordeal to the officers picking us up while we anxiously waited in the SUV. I don't know if the deputies said anything to us or if we shared a goodbye and/or thank-yous or even if hugs were exchanged. I like to remember it as if there were. I only know that as we drove away in the patrol car, I thought I would never see my guardian angels again. I didn't even know their names.

The following days and months became about realizing that I had experienced *trauma*. I couldn't name it, and I didn't know what to do with it. I struggled with everything and was barely functioning. How would I ever move forward? Would I ever feel human again, have my own thoughts, and be able to care for my daughters? They had taken on the job of caring for me because I was incapable.

I still could hear his dialogue nonstop: *You're a whore. You're fat. You're stupid. You're ugly. You're nothing without me. No one will ever love you.*

I was trying to get from one day to the next. I needed to heal from things I could barely acknowledge, much less say out loud to anyone. I still couldn't understand all that I had been through.

The long journey to healing has taken different forms during different times of my freedom. It began with regaining my literal voice, discovering that, for a long time, my thoughts had not been my own. I had to figure out how to silence or tone down my abuser's voice so mine could resurface.

I was finally able to write as I began to process my life, but I still didn't trust it. In those early months, it was so hard to quiet my thoughts and fears. Fuzzy art became my best friend. I would sit for hours coloring these fail-safe posters in silence, deep in my own head.

Sometimes my mind would not settle enough even for coloring, so I would watch *Top Gun* or *The Passion of the Christ*, over and over again. I sought comfort, something I didn't know how to find.

During the day, I attended church and read the Bible and prayed every moment my mind allowed me to. Church became the one place I felt safe.

I didn't know it then, but coping happens before healing. What I also didn't know then is that coping is not healing.

In August 2007, I created for myself (but also with other survivors in mind, acknowledging that there must be other women out there in the same position) what I called the Freedom Time Capsule. It was a series of questions to be answered over a week, once a month, questions that I believed would help me look past my current situation and force me to think about the future.

The questions were:

- *Day 1. How do you feel today, right now? How do you feel about getting out and where you are in your situation?*
- *Day 2. How do you feel about yourself and your life at this moment?*
- *Day 3. What struggles are you going through today?*

- *Day 4. What do you want for tomorrow?*
- *Day 5. What do you want for next month?*
- *Day 6. What do you want for a year from now?*
- *Day 7. What do you thank God for? Including giving you the courage, strength, and faith to get out and stay out.*

When I reread the questions recently, it was hard to believe that in my fragile state, I'd managed to put this into words and into practice. How did I have the state of mind to make this exercise so intentional? Calling it a time capsule was very deliberate. For my entire marriage, I believed I was the only one experiencing this kind of abuse. I felt so lonely. Yet after becoming free, I knew almost instinctively that I wasn't alone. Others needed to heal too.

But just because I needed to heal didn't mean I knew how. Also, you can't begin to heal from one trauma when you are experiencing others. Within nine months of gaining my freedom, I lost both my mom and my sister. The compounded trauma sent me into coping mode. My body was unable to handle all the emotions bombarding it. I would go days without sleep and then my body would shut down and I would sleep for days without waking.

I turned to unhealthy coping mechanisms to keep me going until two years later while walking on the beach in Aptos. Something shifted in me, and I suddenly felt peace, a peace I didn't know I was capable of. I wanted more of that feeling and often returned to the beach for long walks with myself and God. During those times, my mind cleared enough that I began to write. I'd always loved poetry, and it was during this time that it finally came back to me.

My voice, stifled for so long, was finally resurfacing. It was so empowering to use my words in this way, allowing my feelings to seep out of me. This became a pivotal step in my healing journey. No one could take this away from me, and the poems and words flowed. It felt so good to finally have my own voice back.

My creative nature also began to return, which allowed me to have quiet, intentional time making jewelry. When things became too stressful, I turned to creating.

Working Toward Recovery
The following year, I enrolled in community college and began seeing a therapist. Honestly, both were scary and it took every ounce of energy for me to do these things. The first few weeks, sitting in a room full of strangers felt daunting. I had to be very persistent and patient with relearning how to learn. I did not understand it at the time, but this is when my healing journey took a real step forward.

I was immersed in an environment where it felt like I was relearning everything, like a child. I was building up my own self and identity one block at a time. I had to trust myself and others, and that took time and patience.

Therapy was overwhelming in so many ways. I met with my therapist once a week and at the beginning, I cried more than I talked. Understanding that the process would be difficult was one thing; living it all out again was something I'd been completely unprepared for. Working with the right therapist made a huge difference.

Healing for me was slow and painful, but worth it. I've realized that healing may take many more years, but it comes in waves, and once I get over one wave, I can move forward until the next one arrives.

I began to live and not just sleepwalk through life. I began to understand the complexities of domestic violence, and I wanted to share my story so others wouldn't have to live through what I had.

A couple of my professors at Cabrillo Community College would eventually become my mentors and were instrumental in helping me move from healing to helping. I remember standing in front of the classroom and talking about my abusive relationship. When I finished, one student came up to tell me that she recognized she was in an abusive relationship; another student told me she had just gotten out of a toxic relationship. At that moment, I knew why I'd survived all that I had—to raise awareness by using my voice and sharing my life experience. It was a catharsis I never knew I could have.

It was amazing to see how my first time speaking in class affected others on campus. Students who'd heard from someone else about my story would come to me to share their experiences or ask me questions about getting out. Professors requested that I speak to their classes. Eventually, with the support of the campus counselor, we started the college's first peer support group for survivors of intimate partner violence and domestic violence (IPV/DV). It felt good to know that I was making a positive impact.

Even though it may seem like I was doing a lot toward my healing, it was still not enough. I often found myself on the beach for hours at a time, writing thoughts and poems. The journaling that I'd begun was intentional writing, with questions either from counseling sessions or about my future.

After graduating from Cabrillo with an AS in Human Services and an AA in Communications, I moved from Aptos to

UC Berkeley. The safety net I'd built and developed would be left behind, and I was starting fresh. Thank God I had a solid group of friends and family who supported me so that I didn't feel completely alone. I decided that I would make the best of being a college student, even though I was forty-nine years old when I started my first semester at UCB.

The Ebb and Flow of Healing
I was attending a top-ranked university, making friends, and moving forward, until about a year and a half in when I realized that I wasn't. Trauma reared its ugly head as my coursework for my double major stirred things up. I didn't have time to struggle with trauma—I was too busy with homework and trying to graduate. I returned to my intentional journaling, which led me to more poetry writing. That and my friends helped me make it to graduation in 2016, with majors in both Gender & Women's Studies and Chicano Studies.

Even with that huge accomplishment, I was far from successfully managing my trauma. I was moving through it, functioning much better than I had years before, but I was still not emotionally healthy.

Healing is like my own ocean rushing inside me, lots of ebbs and crashing waves. My healing journey has taken many twists and turns. I've used conventional and unconventional methods, like when I gave into my faith and returned to church, not just as an occasional guest but in giving my life over to God.

I was growing as a human, as a woman, as a survivor, and with that came understanding myself well enough to know when the tools I'd built up were not enough to get me through a particular season or challenge. I turned to painting, moving from my original fuzzy art to actual paint and canvas. There was something soothing about a blank canvas that I could turn into whatever I wanted.

It would be another year of intentionality and prioritizing my needs before I could function in other areas of my life. It was important to me to be functioning as close to 100 percent as I could because I was working with survivors who came to me in various stages of freedom and healing. I did my best to be an example that moving forward and accomplishing goals was possible.

When I was back in my rhythm and groove, COVID shut everything down. I fully expected to be fine, to continue happily working from home. But like so many others, the isolation got the better of me and swept over me like a tidal wave! All the healing I had done, all the forward momentum, all the accomplishments felt like they were receding with the tide. I knew what it felt like to be completely empty, and I was slowly feeling that way again. And just like all drowning victims do, I flailed.

It didn't matter that I had fabulous tools in my healing toolkit. I didn't have the motivation or desire to use any of them and instead reverted back to my unhealthy coping mechanisms. All I wanted was to self-soothe and survive one day to the next. Healing seemed so far away, and even my faith, which had always been my stronghold, felt like it was slipping away from me. Despair and depression set in fast, to the point that I didn't know how I would emerge from it.

After months of sinking deeper into the abyss, I was desperate. I reached for any and all lifelines I could find. I got back into virtual therapy, painting, writing, connecting with friends, and exercising. I went from doing nothing to doing it all. I had to do it all, even when I didn't have the energy or desire, until the weariness started to leave me. I was finally coming out of the darkness, which had felt so debilitating, and I was fiercer than ever.

I wrote and published a book and continued my full-time job on a hybrid schedule. Life was good! I'd survived again and learned more about myself and my healing; I learned that the desire to be healthy was in my hands.

Unfortunately, I got COVID midyear in 2022. Even though I was vaccinated and had high hopes that I would recover quickly, I suffered further traumas as I navigated long COVID and related complications.

The year since has been a roller coaster. Staying focused on health, emotional and physical, remains my daily work. For me, staying healthy and healed is like being in recovery.

This journey of healing is mine and mine alone, and although others may have similar tools, every healing journey is individual. We are all different with different needs to reach wellness and stay there. Let's keep walking toward a happy, healed heart and mind.

*****

About Annie Lagunas:
Annie is currently working in a DV/IPV agency in the Bay Area. She is a survivor of nineteen years of horrific violence and control imposed by her husband during their marriage before she found freedom.

Hers is not just a story of pain and suffering, but a story of survival and victory. She was able to testify at her ex-husband's trial, where he was convicted of twenty-eight felonies and is currently serving four consecutive life terms.

It is a story of the future, after walking away with only the clothes on their back. Now a graduate from Cabrillo Community College with an AA in communication and an AS in human services, before attending UC Berkeley, also graduating as a double major in gender and women's studies as well as Chicano studies.

Annie is a public speaker, poet, author, advocate, educator, and the proudest military mom with both daughters serving our country in the Army National Guard and the US Air Force. She is a California native and has Mexican roots, which highly contribute to who she is.

Her story is far from over as she continues to use her voice in all spaces in order to raise awareness for all women who still have no voice of their own.

Instagram: Spreadingfreedom_
Tiktok: @reasons2bfree
Books available on Amazon:
Brand New Peace: Poems and their Stories
I am Under Construction - A personal journey to regain self after abuse
Walking into Wholeness - A personal journey to regain self after abuse (revised version of I am under Construction)

Chapter 2

Amber D

Amber Davis

Amber D

I dedicate all my success and knowledge to my son, Avery.

Part 1

No one ever asks to be born into this crazy world, especially under shitty circumstances.

I guess that's the circle of life, right? Whatever it is, you are expected to grow up, be a strong, hardworking person, and overcome anything thrown your way. My name is Amber D, and so far, I can truly say as hard as it is at this moment and has been in my past, I CANNOT give up. I am STILL HERE to tell my story.

I was born in 1992 at Sutter Hospital in Oakland, California. Some woman who was high on cocaine and methamphetamine gave birth to me. She left me at the hospital, where I lived for a few months as "Baby Girl" before I was handed over to the foster system.

Luckily for me, I was adopted by a wonderful couple who raised me as their own, at least in the beginning. Two years after adopting me, my parents received a call from Alameda County, informing them that my birth-giver had delivered a baby boy. I can't believe this woman brought not one but two people into the world while pumping her body full of damaging drugs, only to surrender us both to the state. Alameda County CPS asked my parents if they would adopt my brother so we could be raised together. They agreed, thankfully. They had a son and a daughter, like they'd always wanted, and my brother and I were able to grow up like siblings should.

Part 2

In 1999 my mom gave birth to her own biological child—a baby boy. My second younger brother! By 2001, my sister was born, and we became a family of six. I was old enough to understand my parents had hidden financial concerns at this point. With three younger siblings and financial issues, I ended up babysitting *all the time*—and I hated it. I loved my siblings, but I didn't want to be responsible for babysitting constantly.

Our family started attending church when I was a little girl. There, my mother befriended another woman who I dislike to this day. She significantly influenced my mom's behavior, changing our family dynamics forever. My mom's "friend" was rude to everyone. She spoke disrespectfully, name-called, and punished her children cruelly for minor offenses.

My mom picked up the name-calling habit and forced me to wear skirts because her friend made her daughters wear them. I'll never forget my own mother calling me a *cow* and a *slut*, the same names her friend called her own children. Then my mom started calling my biological brother names every time he did something wrong. Like, WTF? We were just kids. We didn't deserve the abuse.

Part 3

In 2003 I was eleven years old. Puberty proved challenging. On top of the physical and emotional changes my body was going through, my mother turned her back on me. Her "friends" from church were always in her ear.

There is no parenting handbook, but if there were one, destroying your child's self-esteem would not be in it. I wish my mom had come to that conclusion on her own. Instead, I suffered through horrible punishments and developed negative feelings toward my mother. It wore on me. She didn't see any value in what I had to say.

One day, I ran away to my grandmother's house the next city over. It took over an hour to walk there. My granny listened to my feelings about my mom and the struggles I faced. Though she let me stay for a few hours, deep in my gut, I knew she'd relay everything back to my mom. My parents picked me up that night.

I was embarrassed and terrified that I would get the beating of my life. They were upset. I was a smart, independent kid who made mistakes and learned from them, but to my mom, mistakes may as well have been war crimes. She flipped out when we came back with C's on our report cards or with any number of tardies or absences. More than once, she accused me of skipping class, and when I explained my side of the story, I was whooped and punished.

When I started middle school, she said, "If I were your age, I would be beating you up, so you're going to learn a lesson." Who tells their kid that?

When my mom forced me to wear a uniform to my public school, I snuck clothes into my backpack to change into. She figured it out one day and consequently mandated bag checks before we left home in the morning. I hated my life. But I didn't get into any fights in middle school. I made lifelong friends there.

Part 4

In seventh grade, I joined the Girls Inc. of Alameda County Eureka program my school offered. We went on field trips, took swimming and self-defense lessons, played flag football, and learned about workplace etiquette, internships, and occupational skills to give us a head start. The program required a four-year commitment, which was the perfect opportunity to get me out of the house.

It took some begging, but my parents relented and signed me up for Eureka. We were required to wear shorts and pants, which meant persuading my mother to stop forcing skirts on me. Through this program, I met some of my closest friends.

Our motto was, "Be strong, smart, and bold." At twelve years old, I didn't take that seriously, but in my later years, I understood and I repeat it to this day. It reminds me of my durability.

By eighth grade, my relationship with my mother was in shambles. She didn't trust me. If I asked for permission to visit friends, she accused me of lying. In response, I would sneak out. My friends lied for me, claiming their parents were taking us to our destination. We went to the movie theater, the mall, and other normal teen hangout spots, but my mom was convinced I had a hidden agenda. She'd claim, "All the boys know the color of your panties," even though I was still a virgin and nobody had that information. I hated it when she said dumb shit like that. Seventh grade sex education was as far as my knowledge on sex went, but my mother repeatedly accused me of sexual behavior. Her belittling attitude hurt me and widened the chasm between us.

Part 5

In 2006 I was preparing for ninth grade at Oakland High School. At fourteen years old, I'd hoped that I'd earn more freedom, that I'd get to participate in school activities and hang out with my friends without such a tight leash, but my mother's treatment of me worsened.

According to my mom and her church friends, if I played basketball I would become a lesbian. Funny how being part of an all-girls' activity program didn't have that effect.

By tenth grade, I skipped classes and did whatever I wanted. If my mom refused to give me an inch, I'd take a mile on my own. My friends and their parents thought my mom's strictness was strange, which was validating.

Years of mistreatment reached the surface. I became more vocal to my mother about her behavior and how it affected me.

One day, she said, "Get out of my house."

I had no idea where I was going, but I got the fuck out of there. I trekked two miles from 73rd Street to High Street.

In Oakland, you're bound to run into someone you know whenever you're out. God's angels sent one of my closest friends to bump into me on the street. She knew the gist of what my home life was like. Her mother agreed to take me in. My friend, two years older than me, and I clicked like sisters, and that's what we became.

I spent a few months living there before my mother reached out to my friend's family, threatening to tell the police they were hiding a minor in their home if they didn't agree to kick me out.

Terrified, my friend's mom said I couldn't stay with them anymore.

At fifteen years old, I was homeless.

That same friend snuck me into her house while her mom worked, gifting me a safe place to sleep, and then we'd tiptoe through the house while getting ready for school the following morning.

I went to school every day never knowing where my head would lie that night. Sometimes, I rode the public bus around Oakland to nap. In my most desperate moments, I slept in strangers' unlocked cars (thankfully, no one ever caught me) and stole clothes and toiletries from department stores.

Before classes began, I cleaned myself up to the best of my ability in the girls' bathroom so no one could tell I was homeless. Some friends brought clothes to school for me. They were so kind, helping me every step of the way. That's rare at any age, but especially in high school.

Part 6

During the summer after tenth grade, I was looking forward to an internship with the San Leandro Fire Department through Eureka. I transported myself to the fire station from whoever's couch I was sleeping on.

Staying committed to a four-year program at fifteen while living on the streets of Oakland was challenging. Couch surfing became normal. My boyfriend helped me make it through the summer.

When the new school year rolled around, my mother refused to help with enrollment. I asked my uncle to enroll me in school, and he agreed. I was living with my grandmother, thankfully out of the couch-surfing scene for a while. My then-boyfriend got into trouble and wound up in jail, so I broke up with him. I couldn't support someone in jail, considering my position. I had to be on my best behavior.

My uncle filled out the forms as my guardian and I was able to attend Oakland High School for my eleventh grade year. My mom was pissed when she found out. She couldn't stand that I was determined to make a life for myself. I had to be strong, smart, and bold, no matter what she said or thought of me.

Meanwhile, my mind and body were feeling the effects of trauma. My mom had never supported or understood me. Homelessness and loneliness had taken their toll. Sometimes she'd lure me back home, only for me to be out the door in no time at all.

Part 7

Junior year was difficult. My focus in school whittled away, and I grew irritable, picking fights, skipping classes, and falling behind. I did enough work to stay on the cheerleading team, but I was eventually removed due to my behavior.

That year, I attempted suicide. I felt lost and alone, stealing from stores to survive. I drank alcohol and smoked weed with my new boyfriend. Later, we tried ecstasy together.

I was exhausted. Two people I'd considered friends sexually coerced me. Because they gave me a place to stay, they felt entitled to "get what they wanted" from me. Every time I said no, they escalated. Fearing being beaten and raped, I relented.

But I had goals. I had a future ahead of me.

I did not want to become a teen mother. My mom spoke down on me so much, calling me a slut and so many other horrible things, and I needed to prove her wrong.

During the spring of my junior year, I moved in with my boyfriend's family. He was my best friend. He knew everything about me, and he had my back. My safe space. His mom was understanding and gracious in allowing me to live there, but she and other family members expressed concern for whether I would get pregnant. I reassured her that I was determined not to become a mother until later in life. I became part of their family.

At the end of the school year, my guidance counselor informed me that I would be held back because of my poor grades. I wasn't having it. I'd entered that school determined to be part of the class of 2010, and I worked my ass off to make up work and boost my grades.

Part 8
Throughout my senior year, I was still stealing to survive. On February 15, 2010, my boyfriend and I were out of money after celebrating Valentine's Day. My period started and I didn't have any menstrual products left.

My boyfriend drove me to a store I'd never stolen from before. My methods were tried and true: I grabbed menstrual products, a painkiller for cramps, and juice, threw everything in my purse, and walked out like nothing happened. Loss Prevention met us outside. They knew I was the perpetrator, so they focused on persuading me to remove the stolen items from my bag. My boyfriend grabbed my purse and told me to run.

They didn't catch me. When I looked over my shoulder, several employees were wrestling with my boyfriend, so I went back to help him. I grabbed one employee's dreadlocks and swung him into a car. He yelled, "You stupid-ass bitch."

After the altercation, the police arrived. They took me to juvenile hall. I was still seventeen years old until September of that year. My boyfriend was nineteen, so he went to jail.

That was one of the worst months of my life. When the authorities contacted my mother, she threatened to leave me in there until I was eighteen. I kissed her ass until she agreed to pick me up. I wore an ankle monitor for three months under the supervision of my parents.

While making up for school assignments and keeping my head down, I worked at a grocery store. Once the ankle monitor was removed, I moved back into my boyfriend's house.

Through all that bullshit, I made up two school years' worth of work and graduated on time. I was so proud of myself. Only four people came to my graduation ceremony: my boyfriend, his mom, my birth sister (surprise, my biological mother had another!), and her boyfriend. My mom didn't care enough to see me walk across the stage, and that fucks with me to this day. It really hurt. I was chosen to do the class speech, and sometimes I reread it. It reminds me how far I've come.

Part 9
After graduating high school, I buckled down and mapped out my future. My boyfriend's mom told me I would have to move out by the time I turned eighteen. They weren't my family, and that was OK. I took it on the chin, swallowed my pride, and moved out on my own. Though it felt like I was being abandoned again, I reminded myself that they weren't obligated to help me, and that I needed to be grateful for how much they'd done for me.

My boyfriend and I tried maintaining our relationship, but deep down, I was angry about being kicked out, and our relationship didn't last long. I focused on leveling up in life, but he was comfortable with where he was. His family came between us too, and that was the final straw.

After three and a half years together, I was free and couch-surfing again. I loved it. I worked for a well-known financial services company, and I started strip-dancing on the side. The money was good, it was fun, and I avoided the wild side of the industry that people assume every stripper dips into.

Part 10
I needed to find somewhere else to live. I stayed on a friend's couch, shared in rotation with five other people who had nowhere else to go. I called it the party house. Then, I got an apartment with a roommate and we both paid rent.

By 2015 an apartment opened next to my grandmother's apartment. A friend and I rented it and got back on our feet. We were proud of ourselves. Living next door to my grandmother was good.

I took classes to become a phlebotomist while working security jobs in San Francisco to pay for schooling and living expenses. I always had a job, but it was time to build a career.

In May 2015 I graduated as a certified licensed phlebotomy technician.

Despite my achievements, my mom didn't support me through school or offer encouraging words. Either she didn't care or she didn't believe I would succeed on my own. After I received my license, she started helping me out. I gave her something to believe in, I guess.

No matter what happened between us, I loved my mom. I wanted to have a relationship with her. I did my best to be a hardworking daughter so she could tell others I was financially independent and taking good care of myself. I felt resentful, though, like I had when she refused to attend my high school graduation.

Part 11

At twenty-three years old, I was in a career that I loved, and I was on my big girl journey.

Over the next four years, I lived my best life. I leveled up in the phlebotomy world, adopted my dog Tater Tot, bought a brand-new car with only three miles on it, started modeling, and more.

In 2019 I took my first two trips out of the United States. The first was to Mexico for a friend's wedding—I was a bridesmaid! Later that year, I went to Phuket, Thailand, with a group of friends. There were twelve of us altogether. It was an amazing trip, and I want to go back someday.

By the time we returned to California, the COVID-19 pandemic had begun. Before our trip to Thailand, I came down with a nasty flu with strange symptoms: my nose was clogged for over two weeks, and I couldn't smell my dog. I almost missed the trip but recovered just in time.

Between uncertainties around COVID and the severe wildfires raging through California, it was a scary time to come home.

Part 12

As a phlebotomist, I was an essential worker. I hated going to work during the height of the pandemic. It was terrifying, never knowing if I'd get sick.

Since I had a nice safety net of savings, I left my job during lockdown and spent time with my dog and worked on an entrepreneurial venture. Entrepreneurship had always been in the back of my mind, but it was hard to settle on a starting point. Lockdown gave many people time to think about what they wanted. I used that time to research natural body care products and skincare. I learned about skin types, oils, chemicals, and the effects of what different products can do to different people's skin.

I started making body products by hand. There was a lot of trial and error, but I put my heart into my business.

On January 4, 2021, FREE•LY by Amber D was born. We sell body butter, exfoliating scrubs, body oils, soap, beard oils, and exfoliating lip scrubs.

Later that year, my friends and I started traveling again. We went on multiple trips, met new people, and I even went on a trip by myself, all while growing my business.

Part 13
My grandmother was diagnosed with cancer. We'd been neighbors for seven years. She refused treatment and didn't acknowledge her diagnosis. She lived like nothing had happened. I spent more time with her. She loved my dog, and since I don't have kids, she loved him like a grandchild, and he loved her too.

I watched her deteriorate. Seeing her decline in real time was devastating. She was older and I knew this day would eventually come, but no one can predict death. My mom stayed by her side the whole time, even when my grandmother couldn't speak anymore. I helped my mom with anything she needed while she cared for her mother.

On September 14, 2021, at around 8:00 a.m., my mom woke me up and told me to come to my grandmother's apartment. She was taking her last breaths.

Heartbroken doesn't begin to cover how I felt.

Seeing my grandmother take her last breaths and hearing my mom cry when Granny's body was removed from the building left me in a daze. I lost one of my best friends that day. We'd had our disagreements over the years, but she knew she could call me for anything, and I would pull through every time.

I would trade anything in the world to have Granny back.

It felt eerie staying in that apartment. My grandmother had lived in that building since 1992. Living there was too weird after her departure.

I reached out to people to figure out new living arrangements. I wound up back at my ex-high school sweetheart's house in October 2021.

What was once a safe space in school was no longer safe in adulthood, a lesson I quickly learned after moving in with him. We became a couple again after a few weeks, but he needed to do better. I deserved better because of what I had accomplished.

But I proceeded with him regardless of my gut feelings, rekindling our relationship in our thirties, thinking things would be different.

Part 14

Things were not different. He wasn't working. I came home to a filthy house while he played video games. I wasn't used to that. It fucked with me, and I acted petty. He was lazy, irresponsible, and content with living in filth.

If he didn't have to work, I didn't have to work. I job-hopped for a while before giving up on work completely. Eventually neither of us were working. That was a bad idea. What the fuck was I thinking?

I know now that my brain was trying to mourn my grandmother, but I wasn't letting it happen. I quit my job because my emotions overwhelmed me. I wasn't there mentally, but I tried showing up.

When 2022 came around, I decided it would be a good year, that I'd bounce back, and good things would happen.

Boy, was I wrong.

My boyfriend's older brother visited often. He felt like a brother to me, and we had a good bond. I came home from work one night when my boyfriend's brother and cousins were visiting. I ragged on his brother before he left, because I disliked his girlfriend.

He grabbed me, hugged me, and said, "Sis, stop playing. I love you."

He died a few minutes later in a car crash on the freeway.

Putting my emotions aside, I supported my boyfriend through his brother's death. I didn't expect to mourn for someone else while working through how to grieve my grandmother.

Months later, my boyfriend and I became homeless. After building a solid life for myself in adulthood, hitting another rock bottom devastated me.

Part 15

The years 2021 and 2022 beat my ass, so when 2023 rolled around, I didn't promise myself that it would be a good year.

Mental health troubles forced me to step away from my business for a while. I participated in beauty pageants and won two awards, but those achievements didn't come close to breaching the dark place I was in mentally. I saw no way out.

Despite his desperate attempts to seem OK, my boyfriend was drowning in grief over the loss of his brother. Neither of us were OK. I wanted to break up with him. He thinks he's never wrong; even seeing him cheat with my own eyes didn't sway him from that position.

The day I gathered the courage to break up with him was the day I almost died in a car accident. I got away with a broken spine, a break in my chest cavity region, broken ribs and neck. My car was split in two.

While the EMTs rushed me to the emergency room, the police and medical staff said they had never seen anyone survive that type of crash. According to them, I should've been dead or paralyzed, but God decided it wasn't my time yet.

Since we were homeless, I kept most of my belongings in my car, so in that accident, I lost all but my cell phone and the clothes on my back.

Everything happens for a reason, and I spent my recovery time pondering the lessons I could take away from the crash.

My mom lived out of state and my dad was visiting her, so my ex-boyfriend took care of me by himself. I wanted to die, but God let me survive because I still have purpose.

The week I spent in the hospital was miserable. I slept with a neck brace for three months and wore a back brace to correct my fractures for four months. The doctors warned me about depressive symptoms being common after severe car accidents.

I thought, "I already deal with depression, so this should be fine."

Wrong. Those months spent recovering, living in Oakland with my boyfriend, were the most depressed I've ever been. I couldn't do anything for myself. Working, grocery shopping, showering—all out of the question as solo activities. I had a petty partner, no car, and a lot of pain. It took me back to being eighteen years old, trying to move out of his mother's house, to get away from a man with no motivation to be a provider but who wanted a wife and kids.

Part 16

In 2024 I'm focusing on bouncing back and getting my own place again. Recently I've spent a great deal of time in physical therapy, but I'm struggling. My pain feels worse now than before I healed.

The details of my life could fill a book. Anxiety and ADHD made writing this a steep challenge. But overcoming these adversities, trying my best every day, and nurturing my faith in God have toughened me. I will live the successful, wealthy life I have always dreamed of, no matter what curveballs come my way. I refuse to let anyone drag or hold me down.

2025 will be better than the last few years. I'm optimistic and excited for the future, even if that means leaving some people in the past. No more settling.

Maybe God brought me all the way down to show me that the path I was on wasn't good. Sometimes, we have to start over in life.

I have much more to say, but I'll save that for when I discover my purpose.

*****

About Amber:
Amber Davis was born and raised in Oakland, California. She says, "Life is full of ups and downs; and I manage to get through it all with God on my side and my dog Tater Tot." She also has a whole new reason to keep going and to never give up—her soon-to-be-born baby boy.

Chapter 3
Follow the Sun ... All the Way to the Heart

Andrea Lucie, PhD

To my mother.

I was born in Chile to a young single mother. At the age of five, because of economic hardships, I was sent to stay with my grandparents. They lived in southern Chile in a small village situated in the depths of the Andes Mountains where they served as healers. They performed an array of healing practices to reinstate the well-being of the people in their community. They knew how to cure *mal del ojo* (evil eye), *mal del viento* (wind scare), *mal del susto* (fright sickness), *empacho* (gastrointestinal problems), *santiguear* (give the sign of the cross), and *correr ventosa* (cupping glass). They also had an extensive knowledge of the use of native herbs and plants.

I grew up witnessing native medicine, and I believed it was the standard form of healing. In these practices, there was no separation of mind, body, or spiritual illness; the healing practices were all-inclusive.

A few years later, I moved back to live with my mother in Santiago. I learned quickly that the simple life I had with my grandparents was starkly different modern life in the city. Inept in my adjustment to a life far from the farm and the sacred, I immersed myself in books and in a world of creativity that still serves me today. My father's absence was never discussed; my mother avoided the subject by saying she was both mother and father.

My solitude shielded me from comparing our socioeconomic situation with that of others around me. I grew up happy with the few resources we had. Our life was occupied by moving from one place to another in the middle of the night to avoid paying the rent we could not afford and finding creative ways to survive. Because of these experiences, I grew very resourceful.

Food was scarce, and restrictions were abundant. Afraid that I would follow in her footsteps of single motherhood, my mother imposed strict rules for socialization. She was an authoritarian, at the same time caring and overprotective. Because of this, my circle of friends was limited to my relatives and a few family friends.

The Beginnings
In 1992 I immigrated to the United States. Chile was far away; even farther was the farm life I left as a child. Like any new immigrant, I struggled to adjust to the new country and society. The language, food, and cultural differences kept me in a constant state of shock for at least the first year. Quickly, I learned the American way of living: effort equals improvement. Everything one might dream of is possible, and the American dream became my dream.

My professional career began with cleaning baking trays at a doughnut shop, followed by a short tour as a hotel housekeeper. Two years after my arrival in the US, I found the path that would take me to where I am today—I began to work at a military base. The majority of my first twenty-five years in my adoptive country, I worked at a military base; I also studied to obtain my PhD, dated, and married (and subsequently divorced) a military man.

In my life, I had everything an ordinary woman could hope for: a marriage to a wonderful man, a house in an affluent neighborhood, a profession that allowed me to fulfill my path, and a position of privilege. At the pinnacle of my career, doing what I loved most, I felt uneasy, misplaced, and restless. I had an abiding sense that I was missing something.

Though my days were filled with continuous expressions of gratitude, my restlessness required attention. Helping others find their own path to healing was both exhilarating and fulfilling; I was only content when helping others, and I could lose myself in those moments. Still, away from my therapeutic setting, I was sad, angry, and unhappy. Something was not aligning. I found myself both liking and regretting my success. The identification with my ego was a powerful reason to continue that path and the life I had, but a voice in my heart kept screaming to let go, surrender the ego, and search for something that had been, until then, unknown to me.

As the veil of ignorance began to lift, I became aware of my internal states, my identification with the ego, and my unhappiness in knowing there was something else I had to do. I was no longer content with a mundane life; I needed to find my wholeness, my oneness, my connection to the universe. I felt a call to conduct a search that I could no longer ignore. The voice in my heart would not let me turn a deaf ear as the need to leave strengthened.

When one answers the call to surrender ego, it happens with an abundance of pain. The Great Spirit had guided me to this place to detach, to surrender all ego properties and become a whole person ready to learn and receive the ancestral medicine.

"She has gone off the deep end or she must be going through a midlife crisis," said my ex-husband. "You have lost your mind," said my mother.

I was glad I had "gone off the deep end" and could clearly see with my heart's eyes. I was glad I had "lost my mind" to see both the surface and the bottom. Everything in between was where I'd lived until then.

How did I get here?
In 2011 I met Uncle Henry, a Native American healer of the Lakota Sioux Nation. Uncle Henry, an elder and a wise man, probably heard from my heart what I could not. Soon after we met, he extended an invitation for me to learn from him.

I spent many weekends at Uncle Henry's place observing, listening to his stories and teachings, and participating in his sacred Native ceremonies. Sitting in a circle around the fire during council nights, I finally found my tribe, at a farm in Maryland, thousands of miles from my grandparents' farm. Uncle Henry spoke their same words, he described their same world, and he began to unveil my heart's desire.

Inside the sweat lodge, I experienced the cathartic effect of this sacred ceremony. This awakened an intrinsic curiosity to explore deeper Native healing and shamanism. I thought of myself as an American woman with Chilean roots, completely westernized by my education and experiences in the US. Somehow, working with the wounded military personnel exposed the true identity and desire of my heart. I longed to reconnect with my own *curandera* roots (medicine woman) and to find my healing place.

In July 2014 Uncle Henry invited me to attend a sun dance in his land. At Uncle Henry's sun dance and during the healing ceremony, I asked the Great Spirit for guidance: "What should I do about the sadness? Do I need to leave? Where should I go?" I pleaded. As the clouds moved past the Sacred Tree and cast the shadow on the ground, the answer was as clear as a neon sign on a dark night: "Follow the sun."

One by one, the elders passed in front of and blessed the participants as the sun dance came to an end. In a mystifying combination of bliss and confusion, I was left with a clear message that I must face and decide if I should follow. The Spirit had answered my questions and commanded action.

My life needed to change. All that I had, and what I believed to be me, needed to be released so I could create space to find my true self.

Uncle Henry, at eighty-nine years old, was the leader of forty-five sun dances, the spiritual leader of his small Lakota community, and my precious mentor and friend. He once told me, "It is OK to be afraid. Just don't let the fear paralyze you." His words resonated as I drove away from the sun dance and back to Old Town, Alexandria, my then home, where my life, suspended in limbo, awaited me.

In its infinite wisdom, the Great Spirit was telling me to turn away from the compliments because I was beginning to like them. In an environment where success is measured by public appraisal, I was enjoying the recognition too much, even if it came from those under my care. My work, or any true healer's work, should come from compassion and unconditional love where there is no place for the ego.

As a shaman, a true healer is a man or woman of service to those in need. The healing mission must be one of love and respect for humanity. That is what I saw in my grandparents and that is what my heart wanted to find.

Back To Your Roots
Thirty-five years and thousands of miles away from my childhood, I heard the call to reconnect with my roots and search for this ageless healing practice. Although I held a deep love for my work with my military family, I still felt alone, misplaced, and disconnected. The discrepancy in my life required attention.

The desire to explore native spiritual practices grew stronger and prompted me to search for the shaman within.

In September 2014 I stood in front of my colleagues and announced I was leaving. Some of my friends praised my courage for leaving everything behind to "follow the sun." In my heart, I knew the sun was leading me west and south, closer to my indigenous roots, and I was eager to follow.

I had practiced letting go and letting be during my countless yoga and meditation practices but never understood the true value of this statement. Letting go and letting be is about surrender and acceptance and about pursuing the heart's desire, even at great cost.

In October 2014 I bid farewell to the job I loved and all the things I once considered mine, and I moved to Mexico in search of shamanic healing practices.

Once in beautiful Puerto Vallarta, still unsure of the meaning of following the sun, I marveled at the beauty surrounding the town. Each morning and evening, I walked the beach, thinking about how to make sense of my trip south to follow the sun. What was I supposed to do? How could I find my true self? What was it that I really needed to let go?

A couple of months went by, as did a few failed attempts to connect with an indigenous group. Disappointed about how things were unfolding, I walked on the beach. As I had many times before, I saw the group of Aztec dancers with their beautiful feathered attire, dancing in ecstasy under the sun. From afar, I observed and then kept walking. I was intrigued by these men, their dances, and their music, but mostly, I was intimidated by their masks and my inability to see their faces.

This day in particular, I was feeling disheartened and lost. Too much had happened in the prior two months, and nothing made sense. I felt as if I had reached a wall with no place to go. During those walks, I watched the Aztec dancers, but I never dared to talk to them.

Until one day, while I slept at the beach, the sound of the drums abruptly woke me. Embarrassed to be seen as rude, I didn't move away from the group playing and dancing for the tourists. The dreamlike sound, dance, and colorful customs felt as if I were dreaming while being in the middle of their performance. The surreal sensation wasn't complete until the end when a man approached me.

Reaching for my bag, I anticipated he was looking for a donation. Instead, he kneeled and asked who I was and what I was doing there. His skin, leathered and darkened by the sun, was framed by a mask of an unidentified animal. His long black hair was adorned with a voluptuous headpiece made of feathers. His dark brown eyes were encircled by black paint and his mask left only his mouth uncovered. I questioned if I was still asleep.

He asked again why I was there. As someone who had just awakened, I said, "The Great Spirit instructed me to follow the sun during my sun dance last year, so here I am." As the last word was spoken, a sense of panic overwhelmed me. I wanted to rewind and take back what I'd said.

While I looked for a way to backpedal, matter-of-factly, he said, "Oh! We are having a sun dance next month. Would you like to come?" There was no question about *who is the Great Spirit* or *what is a sun dance*, or *what did I mean by "following the sun."* The search for my tribe had ended and my journey to search for the shaman within and my own healing path had begun.

Death of the Ego

The clan was composed mainly of members of the same family. They traveled throughout the country, leading and attending ceremonies. To support their travels, they performed ancient Aztec dances for the tourists; they were solely dedicated to *El Camino Rojo* (the Red Road). Their purpose in life was to walk the Red Road. Sacred ceremonies, including music and dances, were their means to a spiritual life in an effort to honor Mother Earth and the ancestors and to align with the energy of the universe. It was not something they did; instead, it was who they were.

In their company, I experienced and witnessed powerful sacred healing ceremonies that brought me back to my roots. Clan members became my family, friends, and teachers. Furthermore, they became intrinsically invested with my own processing and healing. Under their guidance and support, I withstood the intensity of ceremonies that became catalysts to my own healing.

After a few weeks in Mexico, I felt violently ill. Local doctors suspected it was the dengue virus. Without warning, one morning I felt weak and my body ached intensely. I could not leave my room. I lay in bed, and in a matter of minutes, my body began to shake. Scared, I waited a few minutes, trying to make sense of this assault before I reached for the phone. I was unable to dial the numbers as I could not stabilize my fingers. My teeth chattered uncontrollably. My mind raged with fear, my head on fire, my body in horrible pain, and my back freezing.

When I finally reached somebody for help, my temperature was over 103°F. The pain was unbearable; even my skin's contact with the bedsheets hurt. The visiting doctor was able to control my temperature and I got a couple hours' rest, but this cycle of convulsive fever and pain lasted for days.

The high fever and pain punished my body while the loneliness battered my heart and soul. Alone with my little dog, Jenny, I cried for all the things I had let go. With indignation, I screamed to the Great Spirit, "What else do you want to take away from me? What else do you want me to give up?" Following my heart's desire, I had left everything and drove to Mexico to search for my path. In my car, my material life was summed up by two suitcases, my laptop, a sewing machine, and my little canine companion of thirteen years. Images of my home, my ex-husband, and a comfortable life passed through my mind as if the ego intended to suffocate the voice in my heart. I had left everything behind, and I felt so alone.

A few days later, and while I was still sick with dengue, my little Jenny's health began to deteriorate. Pancreatic cancer had gone undetected by her veterinarian. Jenny succumbed fast to the illness. Witnessing her wasting away brought one of the most intense pains I have experienced, or so I thought. I had to let go of the most precious part of my life and the only real possession I'd carried with me in my journey. Letting her go reminded me of all the people I'd let go of in the past. I grieved the loss of my father, the loss of husbands, the loss of my childhood, my innocence, the loss of a baby, and the loss of my trust.

Christmas 2014 came and went, and through sunny days, I lay in the darkness of my room. With unopened windows, I grieved Jenny and everything her death signified. Holding on to her blanket, I cried. I blamed myself for keeping her alive too long, unable to let her go when she was probably in pain. Intrusive thoughts inundated my mind: "She probably needed to leave sooner. She was probably in pain all the way from the US . . . The trip was too long for her and she must have been in so much pain."

Clinging to those I loved was how I coped with my insecurity and fears of abandonment, and Jenny was no exception. Now, all the pain accumulated over years poured out of me with the tears. For days, I felt her absence in my arms. I needed her.

Jenny was the catalyst to my truly beginning to let go. Leaving my ex-husband, my job, my house, all my material belongings—this was just the superficial layer of possessions I still carried with me. It was the deeper layers of memories and pain that I also had to let go.

Cognitively, I understood letting go and detachment, but in reality, my anxieties and suffering were because I had not let go of deep-rooted pain I'd experienced in the past, and until I acknowledged that, it would not go away.

Did my illness, Jenny's death, and my solitude mark the beginning of my ego death?

For the following months, I participated in sacred healing ceremonies that allowed me to explore and process painful life experiences to which I was still clinging. With each event, I took notes about my internal state, including my reaction to the ceremonies, to the environment, and to others. Participation in these ceremonies allowed me to become painfully aware of how broken I was and how much I needed to find my own healing.

As a result of this ten-month journey, I uncovered the source of deep-rooted pain and unresolved issues that prevented me from knowing my true self. In addition, I hoped to equip myself with the ancient knowledge to help others find their healing paths. To do that, however, I had to allow myself to heal.

A few months passed and the clan invited me to attend a massive gathering in the mountains of Nayarit, about five hours from Puerto Vallarta. There, several tribes and groups from different parts of Mexico and other countries were honoring the Spirit with different ceremonies. During this event, I attended the Bear Clan dance, and for the first time I experienced an altered state of consciousness.

After a purifying *temazcal* in preparation for the ceremony, the ritual started at dark. Nearly 100 participants lined up to be cleaned by the *ahumadores* and slowly entered and took positions around the large circle drawn around the firepit. On one side was the drumming circle. The chanting and dancing intensified as the fire grew stronger.

The full moon had a glowing halo around her, providing the ceremony a mystical tone. The men, covered with full bearskins, entered the circle in crouched position, dancing and growling like bears. The rhythmic sound of the drums and the monotonous cadence of the dance quickly induced us all into an extraordinary state of consciousness. A combined heartbeat followed the drum, and the energy grew stronger as the bears danced around the fire.

The bears teased us by getting close enough for us to touch their skins, which created a sense of exhilaration. The drumming and chanting intensified as the bears invited the participants to connect with them and dance around the fire. Everybody wanted to touch and feel the skin of the powerful animal. Holding on to one another, the participants and the bears danced around the fire.

I looked up to the moon and felt the overwhelming bliss of being a part of something sacred and ancient. The bears growled as we moved. In front of me, the bear-man's skin became soft and alive. The bear-man was no longer a man with a bearskin covering his body; bear and man were one. At that level of consciousness, I was a part of the whole; there was no individuality, no beginning nor ending, and no distinction between human or animal.

Time and space disappeared, and I experienced an overwhelming peace and love that is impossible to describe without indulging in literary terms. I accessed this deep spiritual experience several times while participating in the ceremonies.

I felt ecstasy. In that circle, it was as if my body no longer belonged to me. Instead, I was a cell of the whole organism of the creation. I felt connected to the other humans, to the large tree beside the circle, to the drum, to the moon, to the stars, and to the bears. I was equally a part of and an extension of the others. That night, those men were not humans dressed in bearskin; they were bears. The bear spirit ascended into their bodies, took over, and danced with us.

In that circle, I was a part of the whole universe. That night I felt an ecstatic, effortless, and spontaneous sensory awareness and attunement to others.

Once I surrendered my need to control all aspects of my life and accepted this new way of living, my path began to unfold in such a beautiful way. Freedom was knowing that anything I needed was already provided; the universe was in alignment with my inner world.

During my time in Mexico, I met the man who is now my husband. For the first time in my life, I fell truly in love. Four decades had passed since my first marriage, and too many failed relationships had left me confused about love. Then one day, the universe spoke and there he was, this dark-skinned, bright-eyed, skinny and shy Mexican, smiling at me. It only took a couple of days for us to know we were partners, and our romantic adventure began spontaneously by creating a home together.

After almost a year in Mexico, my heart told me to go back to the US. There was something I needed to conclude, one more step I had to take. Although I couldn't make sense of this command, I knew better—when the Great Spirit talks, the heart better listen.

One Final Step
We packed the car and together we went back to the US to my old home in North Carolina. For the next three years, I worked at the military base. The greatest opportunity led me to Colorado to work at the university in a new program for veterans. Back in a clinical setting, it was again my military family who brought me to the awareness that I needed to break loose. I needed to again let go of the conditioning of the system and surrender the construct still ruling my decisions. Yes, I was happy with my husband and my professional life, but my heart again whispered that I was ready now to embark upon my true path, and this was the time to let go for good.

I had taken the last step, and there was one giant leap to my true path. This path was not in the US; the curandera work needed to be done in a new environment, closer to the heart of the Mother. The earth, the jungle, the ocean, the mountains, the clan, the Red Path was calling me to let go of all and dedicate my life to traditional shamanic healing.

In October 2020 I packed my car with my two dogs, a few bags of clothes, and my beautiful Mexican husband, and we drove back to Puerto Vallarta. Each mile closer to my paradise was a step closer to my true path, my true home, my true self.

For a few months I worked on deconditioning my mind and resetting my beliefs by doing what I always ambitioned to be—a beach bum. Sometimes the fear sneaked up on me and I panicked, convulsively looking for jobs that would allow me to have a salary or a way to "make a living." Each time, the universe imposed its command to stay the course and to listen to my heart.

As I continued attending sacred ceremonies, I regained a clear awareness that to be of service and help others to heal, I had to complete the "work" on myself. Although not as often as before, my main symptoms—anger, anxiety, and fear—were still there. I was ready to confront all the unprocessed pain inflicted during childhood.

Up to that point, I'd experienced many shamanic ceremonies and altered states of consciousness but without any sacred medicine. The Grandmother called me first, and for a reason I would later discover. I attended my first ayahuasca ceremony with a cast on my right foot. In an angry outburst, triggered by a fight with my mother, I had lost a fight with a closet, breaking a couple of toes. Why was my mother the catalyst to such intense angry outbursts? I knew now . . . but was I ready to face the traumas that led me to resent her?

The offering of the *rape* (Amazonian tobacco) prior to receiving the Grandmother sent me into a two-hour purging spree that manifested in uncontrollable shaking similar to what had happened with the dengue virus. The sweat, the tears, the bowel evacuation was just a prelude to my first journey with the Grandmother. I pleaded for her gentleness as I was in such an exhausted state. The Grandmother listened, and that night she rocked me in her arms until I felt loved, at peace, and safe.

Thinking now that I could ask the sacred medicine for what I needed, I went to my second set of ceremonies in Costa Rica with "clear" intentions: to release the emotional attachments to the physical and sexual abuse inflicted as a child. Now I could acknowledge it, and although so much work had gone into accepting these events, I still thought that my reactions were still triggered only by these traumas.

But the Grandmother had her own plans for me; she knew better what I truly needed. I had buried a deep-rooted traumatic event in my subconscious, and although I knew very well what it was, I'd never faced it. During my first night, the Shipibo Maestra Maricela came to my mat and sang her *icaros*. As if she was seeing my visions, she sang to the baby I'd lost at age eighteen.

A day earlier, while walking to dinner with colleagues, I saw a pair of small tennis shoes on the sidewalk. My group joked about who could have lost them and who should take them home. During my first night of ceremony, feeling so sick and *mareada* (dizzy), several visions manifested. Many of these visions were of scary creatures I dismissed by forcing myself not to follow them. Then a harmless vision showed me walking along a path where a pair of tiny shoes, like the ones I'd seen a day earlier, were on the side of the road. Feeling safe to follow that vision, I let myself go by picking up the little shoes. As soon as they were in my hands, a force gripped and took me down a rabbit hole, not allowing me to turn back.

Within this labyrinth, I saw horrible visions of the death of that baby. Lying on a surgical table, my belly was cut open. Forceps held my lower belly muscles apart while piece by piece, the baby was pulled from my womb. As a witness to my suffering, I stood feeling the grief, pain, desperation, loss, and guilt. In that nightmarish scene, I was the girl on the surgical table, and I was also her witness. I felt so much love and compassion for the girl and for all the forces that led that young girl to the table. I embraced her grief, her pain, her loss, and her devastation. I could do nothing but observe and accept.

This unbearable horror was abruptly interrupted by a small, beautiful toddler with rosy cheeks who, smiling at me, held my hand and walked me away from the scene. I knew it was Sebastian, the baby who was never born. He was wearing coveralls and tiny tennis shoes.

The Maestra sang the *icaros*, a soft, lullaby-like song that I could understand, although the language was foreign to my ears. She sang to the baby, she sang to the girl, she sang to me, she sang to my pain and for my forgiveness. For the first time, I grieved the loss of the baby and cried for the next twenty-four hours, and days after.

The second night of the ceremony, I sat outside the *maloca* still crying, unsure if I could go back in, but I also knew I had to as the work wasn't done. This time, the Grandmother allowed me to rest and find peace. During the third night of the ceremony, the sacred medicine had a special agenda for me. I had to complete the work of letting go and forgiving those who hurt me.

During this journey, the visions came at me strongly, I embraced myself by grabbing my pillow, lying "safely" on my side. Suddenly, the pillow took the form of a man dressed in a suit and tie. His arms wrapped around and held me tight, incapacitating me. Paralyzed, I tried screaming for help, but no sound came from my mouth, just a primal growl I didn't recognize. No one came to my rescue.

Although this man's face was unfamiliar, I knew he was all the men who had touched and abused me as a child and teenager.

During this fight to release myself from this pillow/man, the panic and anger transformed into an intense sense of compassion, and peace overflowed me. Exhausted from fighting, finally, I was liberated. How could one explain this sense of forgiveness, acceptance, and letting go? It can't be explained.

Many ceremonies followed these and not always with the Grandmother. Other sacred medicines had a part in my healing process. Each one in its unique way allowed me not only to release attachments to trauma and pain but also gifted me with the most profound unconditional love, compassion, and forgiveness. These ancient medicines are sacred, and they need to be served with the respect and reverence they deserve.

In 2014, a year before Uncle Henry transcended, he wrote a book titled *The Medicine Is Sacred*. His teachings and wisdom were a prophecy to my experiences years later.

Today I see the world with intense colors, with a daily desire to sing, dance, laugh, and express gratitude for all the blessings I have received. Even those painful experiences were blessings. As I know now, those experiences do not define who I am, do not dictate my behaviors or guide which path I walk. I walk the Red Path, the path of the heart and the path of service. I am grateful to those who inflicted pain as they are my master teachers. I know they acted without consciousness and for that, they are at no fault. Including myself.

In 2020 I offered my first sacred medicine retreat. My intention was to bring the sacredness into the therapeutic space and offer the medicine with the respect and reverence it deserves. Following my grandparents' steps and Uncle Henry's teachings, I honor them by guiding others to find their own healing. By finding their inner guide, they can find their own path to wholeness. We all know at heart who we are; we have just forgotten.

With love and compassion, I understand their pain. With each embrace I give, I honor my tribe, my ancestors, I honor

Sebastian, and I honor all the healers and curanderos and those who, in silence, work to bring true healing to humanity.

The work is not done. There is still so much to do. The path to wholeness is a long one.

While surrendering my ego identification and letting go of the construct of my life, I followed the sun all the way to my heart. I gained true brothers and sisters with whom I share El Camino Rojo. I searched and found the shaman within; she was always there, waiting to embrace me. I found and confronted the source of pain and forgave those who hurt me. *El trabajo* is not done; it is in progress. That is my path.

O Meteo, Okahe! Each day we die and are reborn; life is a cycle.

*****

About Andrea Lucie, PhD:
For the past thirty years, Andrea has worked with the military community including for the Department of Defense at Marine Corps Base Camp Lejeune, Walter Reed National Military Medical Center Bethesda, the National Intrepid Center of Excellence (NICoE), Marine Special Operations Command (MARSOC), The Marcus Institute for Brain Health at the University of Colorado and lately as facilitator of traditional medicine retreat for veterans, their families and first responders.

Andrea grew up in the south of Chile and at the hills of the Andes mountains. She learned from childhood the value of traditional medicine while observing her grandparents perform traditional healing rituals. Her knowledge is drawn from traditional educational institutions in the United States as well as from mentors from the Lakota community, and Mexican healers.

An advocate for integrated medicine and a holistic approach to healing, Andrea has specialized in the holistic treatment of post-traumatic stress disorder and traumatic brain injury.

Following her desire to continue her service to the military community, Andrea moved to Mexico to facilitate sacred medicine retreats in Mexico, Costa Rica, and Jamaica. There, she founded The Red Path Retreats, LLC, an organization dedicated to providing sacred medicine retreats to non-profit organizations helping veterans, their spouses and first responders.

Honoring the sacredness of the medicine, she has worked with traditional healers from Peru, Brazil, and Mexico. Now she is a full-time retreat organizer and facilitator.

The Red Path Retreats
https://redpathretreats.org

Chapter 4

What's in a Name?

Claudia Hinojosa-Torres

I dedicate my chapter to my children Monique, Danté, Kalen and Lincoln. Each of you has a part of my heart and reflects the blessings of my life. To my father for always being the voice in my head, reminding me how much you loved me; separate oceans, but we had a connection like no other. My mother, who came to America with a broken heart yet has been the basis of my dreams, I love you for fighting for me, never giving up, and teaching me the power of prayer. My faith is part of you and will always live in me. You are what magic is made of. #FaithMadeMe

The first thought that pops into a new mother's head is her baby's name, a title for her child that says, "I am here!"

My legal name is Claudia Mariela Hinojosa Torres, a long name for a long life infused with change and growth. The name everyone called me as a child was Mariela. When I was five years old, my name was music to my ears, like a word begetting magic. That's how my life began.

Mariela was a wonderful little girl who dreamed of love, who wished to be accepted, and who longed to explore the world. Hers—and mine—was a journey that ended in love, of myself and the body I inhabit, one I had to learn to take ownership of.

Cold Walls Warming the Heart
My first home in Mexico City is a house that holds my heart. Concrete walls, cold to the touch in winter. They reflected thunderstorms lighting up the sky. Our kitchen window was so high up only my daring brother could climb out during the day, when Mom was away. A stone patio so tall and strong it seemed unbreakable, like me.

Some wonder how a place so cold to the skin could warm my heart so well. It represented, at one time, my identity, my fight for freedom, and my innocence as a child who dared to dream.

Our family was early to rise. My mother raced around, making sure my brother and I were ready. We went to different schools, so in the mornings Mom had no time to spare.

My school had huge wooden gated doors. When they opened, I imagined I was entering a castle. The quad area was spacious, and we had a pool to use for physical education. My school fostered love for learning and for play. It was here that my first crush chased me around the courtyard and gave me my first kiss. The pressure, guilt, and enjoyment brewed a storm within me.

I needed clarity for this new feeling. Joyously, I told my mother while she brushed my hair. She disapproved and told me this behavior was inappropriate.

I shut down. How did she know how I felt? Who was she to tell me I could not kiss a boy, as she kissed my father all the time? I was confused about touch, and this touch was different from anyone else's.

The Man
As the days carried on, there were times when I had no school. I was left home alone often, and I'd nap the day away, dreaming of my life.

While she worked, my mother had someone check on us, who I will refer to here as The Man. He played with us while our mother worked. He enjoyed playing with me on his lap while I glided back and forth on him. It felt gross, and I began avoiding him, instead opting to spend time with my brother and the older girls in our neighboring apartment.

One day when I was five, I went over to spend time with the neighbor girls, only to find them cuddled up. She invited me to join them, but something didn't feel right, so I left.

I began my sexual journey at a young age, unsure of what my body was, how to use it, and how to protect it. I had breasts by the fourth grade. I came from a home with a working mother and, at times, resented our situation. I recall memories that made me wonder why it felt so good to be hugged and held by my father. I learned why later.

A Giant Change

It was another wonderful morning of rushing around to get ready for the day, but something was different. We were going to visit relatives—my *tias* and *primos*! I couldn't wait; finally, a real family trip, not spending the day locked up waiting for my mother to return home or to see my dad so I could safely land in his arms and feel worthy.

I packed my clothes as my mother said goodbye to our neighbors; I recall asking for my father and wondering when he would be joining us. There was a slight pause as my mother took a deep breath and said, "Are you ready?" I nodded and continued to pack as her real answer was he was not coming with us. As usual, it was just us without him.

The night was dark and my tia was having a party—our farewell party. I had assumed it was a welcoming party since everyone was there. It was and continues to be one of my most confusing moments in life. Eventually, I felt so tired I fell asleep. As I slept, I was carried to a car. I woke up in a room with white walls and a midnight blue comforter wrapped around me in a warm bed. I looked around and noticed all the toys on the shelves and my brother sitting in the middle of the room playing. I was excited to know where we were. I said, "Hey, where's Ma?" My brother looked down and kept playing with the toys and said, "We need to wait here for her." Of course this was not the answer that I wanted, so I began crying for her. I bypassed him and walked out the door to find myself staring at the first Americans I had ever seen.

I was scared. Life didn't feel safe and my brother took me back to the room. Finally, a lady arrived and said, "Please calm down. Your mother is in the car. If you look downstairs you can see her." I looked down into her car from the second-floor window and saw what I thought was my mother's hair.

Upon arriving at the station wagon, I realized that the woman was not my mother and I stepped back just to be pushed into the car by my brother. Inside, there was a Doberman pinscher and the lady driving said, "You need to behave or I will feed you to the dog."

It was thirty days before we would see my mother again.

When I finally saw my mother again, she was there with my *tio*. My mother had arrived from across the border—she'd been returned a few times, but she did not explain to me what happened until I became an adult. We drove to my grandparents' home where we settled into a garage, which became our home for a few months until my mother could secure a better living space. I never knew the family who helped my mother nor did I ever see them again.

"Welcome to America" was the first thing I heard everyone say, but I didn't understand them and I felt angry and defeated. At a restaurant where I had my first American hamburger, it was so big I could only bite the bun. Yet, something was missing; my spirit wasn't happy. I didn't want to be an American nor Mexican. I simply wanted my dad, where life felt safe and I felt loved. I began to make promises to myself that I would not allow Mariela to disappear, as in America the preferred name was Claudia.

Claudia is the name used to address me when I was enrolled into my first public school. Claudia rang of discipline and authority when spoken with such respect. In English, my name brought a sense of responsibility and expectations of excellence, as I was now Claudia the Americana, not Mariela the immigrant Mexicana. My teachers would rave how special and unique I was, my name pronounced with an American accent, but I would just smile and nod. I wanted to be Mariela. I wanted to go home, although I was unsure now of where my home was.

My soul yearned to be elsewhere and the light in my eyes dimmed. My body and I became one. I spent so much time by myself that I found every inch of my skin faultless, smooth to the touch. This is how I learned home is where the heart is and sometimes the heart can become a dark place, depending on whether you truly understand the value of love and self-worth.

My elementary school years were full of confusion. Who did I want to be? Who was I supposed to be? When we moved, my mother reminded me not to speak to strangers, not to share anything personal, that I needed to fit in and not bring any attention to myself until our immigration documents were in order, or the authorities would come and take me away.

It was the first time I felt helpless and defeated by a system I had no influence over. I tried to learn, to be part of this new world, but this world didn't know who Mariela was. Mariela's light faded as Claudia became the protector. Mariela the dreamer fell asleep.

By sixth grade I was speaking English well enough that I no longer qualified for English as a second language (ESL) classes with the rest of the kids who came from Mexico, including my brother. The school decided that since I'd arrived young, I would develop English-speaking skills better without ESL classes. In some ways, I did, but I was disconnected from the world, always in my head, planning my exit.

Over time there seemed to be some relief as we settled in. I was with my uncles and grandparents and the sexual abuse I'd suffered from The Man had ended. A new experience began with my mother's physical abuse, and at times, it felt as if I reflected all her hardship and her fear that led to unreasonable punishments of physical assaults. I learned to endure pain.

I replayed the moment I'd see my dad again. I was so focused on not forgetting Mexico that I would slip into a nonverbal state. Eventually, the only power I had was over the pain my body could handle. Still, Mariela lived within me. She was always there, deep in my mind, when I needed a loving place to go. She disappeared as I got older and grew angrier.

It was then, in sixth grade, my anger evolved. I stopped caring about everything and let apathy take control. I cut myself. It was the only release I could find. It made me feel free and in control. I turned to abusing my own body due to the lack of love and hope in my life. The adults in my life didn't see me as a child. They either saw me as a burden or a sex toy with which they could live out their fantasies.

Taking Flight
God sends angels in the form of friends. He sent me my first angel when I was fourteen. She was a white girl who didn't act like the other families around me. She was different, a fighter. She saw me as a person, not a possession, and she told me my mother was abusing me, that I had rights. I laughed at her. More like the right to die.

Her words stayed with me. When I was ready to fight for me, I broke out of our home and ran away. I didn't bother putting shoes on and it was the first time I ran with all my might.

Barefoot and crying, I ran up her porch. I walked in the living room, with its wooden floors and the stilted stench of cigarette smoke in the air, and there she was: Grama Dela, my friend's grandma who took in every broken spirit. Grama Dela became one of the first women to come into my life and calmly explain to me my next steps, but first she hugged me and she created hope and planted a seed of taking the lead in my life. She said, "You can call Child Protective Services (CPS). I can house you here until things are resolved." It was that simple to her and yet I felt a sense of shame through it all as I reported my own mother to CPS, who then allowed me to stay with Grama Dela.

My first moment of resilience. I had to stand up and show up for me—all of me. I stopped cutting myself and hitting walls. I stopped destroying things because Grama Dela gave me Mariela back. Mariela thrived in this fight, ready to overcome fear and to dream freely again.

Eventually, CPS created a safety plan allowing me back into my mother's custody. The first day back I was in complete shock at the approach to return me to my mother. The police had to walk me into the social worker's car in case I ran; apparently, I'd become known as a runner. Grama Dela's hugs were priceless, but I had to learn to self-regulate without them. There was a lot of work involved, but with outreach and a caring group of teachers, the healing process had begun for me and my mother. Through therapy I learned how to reflect more and more on my own path.

This sounds so simple and yet, it was so difficult to find the right direction to go, given my past and my struggles with the language. I had to learn so much in such a short amount of time that sometimes, simply surviving was a major challenge.

The Price of Freedom
Although my friends helped me find freedom, I was not sure what that really looked or felt like. It took time making mistakes of being around the right kids who helped me in the neighborhood. It felt right, but the real issue was I began to avoid my life and disrespect myself. I would go out with friends drinking and hanging out with older students, and eventually, I

met my daughter's father. He was not a student but a fella from the neighborhood.

    Somehow, I believed I could manage this relationship and found myself overwhelmed with his life choices—I was barely learning how to manage mine. He was older and had already lived some, whereas I was just getting started. I became a mother at seventeen. My ex-partner and I were young and our choices led us down difficult roads. I lost him to prison for a while and when he was released, he finally met our five-month-old daughter.

    Work was challenging for him and he began to sell drugs to help out with our family's needs. I watched him go from someone who thrived for his family to someone battling addiction. I was too young to understand what and how this addiction would change him and our family. I stopped being around the circle of friends and family I had associated myself with and moved to another county. I began to make plans with my old high school teachers who made time to walk me through a separation and prepared me for my future. These teachers, Joann and Ms. Snapp, will never know how their stories and guidance helped me make a new life for me and my daughter.

    With my family now broken, I decided to make a plan for my life—one I could respect and stand for. My daughter deserved a successful mother, healed and ready to take on the world.

    I graduated from high school at nineteen, had some work training, and began to change my thought process on how I made money. I began to actually want to work a legal job and make legal money, an often humbling but respectful course. I secured a home for me and my daughter while I enrolled in school and started to really enjoy my life again.

Years later, I met my second love, who gave me two sons. I thought I'd broken the cycle. Abuse comes in unimaginable ways. Outwardly, we had the perfect family. It was an illusion. After he began cheating, he morphed into something unrecognizable. His kind words and affection dissolved into isolation, rejection, and emotionless sex. He became my new nightmare.

Six months after our first son was born, my partner graciously gave me an STD. Fortunately, I had stopped nursing a few months prior. I stayed and endured the pain for the sake of my children. Mariela and Claudia were both slipping away. Claudia had no fight left in her. I'd lost myself to a man who loved only himself and was careless with our family, money, and future.

After I underwent oral surgery, he abandoned me. He went to work, ignoring my health needs. The doctor reminded me I needed to have someone drive me home. I lied and said my fiancé was downstairs and drove by myself.

I made it home and heard from some concerned friends, including a male friend on the East Coast who returned my call that day, as I'd told him I was going to the surgery alone. I had fallen asleep and was woken by my sons' father dragging me off the bed by my feet, demanding to know who'd called his home. The surgery I'd had prevented me from speaking.

The emotional abuse escalated into physical abuse and led to financial abuse over time. I had no family, no support, and three children to protect. My savings went into a house he was legally protected in. I was naive and angry at myself for trusting a man who let me down time and time again, and yet I still showed up for the relationship until I could no longer thrive. My criminal justice degree was put on hold, and it was time for me to become a whole new version of myself—someone I never thought I'd be.

The Beginning of a Happy Ending
At thirty years old, my spirit broken, I left my sons' father, rendering myself homeless. I'd lost everything and was awake enough to feel it all. Starting over was surreal. I made one mistake after another, trapped in an emotional tornado trying to fix my life, unable to see beyond the storm.

In the beginning I was emotionally unmanageable, with anger and sadness all in one. I made poor, impulsive choices to regain some type of control. I spiraled and the monster I'd married enjoyed every moment of the crash as he kept me in family court slowly destroying my self-worth with each push. It was up to me to end this childish behavior and distance myself from such a heartless man. June 2017 was the last time I spoke to him in person.

"Be still," my spiritual mother said. These words live in me now; I had to learn to slow down to go fast and give myself a chance at becoming a mother who loved herself.

I rebuilt my foundation, secured an apartment, and met my third son's father. He wasn't an angel, but a friend who understood me. He was safe. My older boys' father no longer bothered me because of him; I was free to dream again.

Abusive behavior doesn't change until the lens through which you see your worth changes, and sadly, my self-worth lens hadn't changed—only the man had changed. Although this man helped me see I was heading to addiction and that my self-worth mattered, after our son was born he got lost in his old life and we no longer saw eye to eye on how to live.

When he died in 2021, I realized no one could keep me safe but me. I made a stronger plan and completed my bachelor's in criminal justice, although I no longer felt safe in the courts. My passion for right and wrong remained, so I decided not to stop there and finished my master's degree in psychology, which led me into a MFT/LCC track.

Today, I embrace and have decided to be **all of me**: Ms. Claudia Mariela Hinojosa Torres *la mas chingona*! Mariela gets to dream and be free while Claudia oversees our obligations. I am in sync with every piece of me.

What is in my name is fire, humility, and happiness. I cry sometimes, never losing sight of the work I must do to move forward. It is a daily effort. I am a survivor of domestic violence and sexual assault, and the list could go on and on, but now I own all of it, my body what I now call my temple home. Home is where the heart is and where my faith thrives.

I am a survivor of life and all its moments within my temple. I no longer shy away from who I am, nor do I allow any parts of me to be less than necessary on any given day.

When you're done reading this, remember that time stands still for no one. Let your soul shine. It's only the beginning.

*****

About Claudia Hinojosa-Torres:
I enjoy people and the science of the mind. I have worked in human resources for twenty-five years, supporting and educating others on legal policies. I then moved into direct patient care, leading me into the nonprofit world. My focus is on creating change in the front line and raising awareness of levels of care from a trauma-informed-care lens. My diverse skillsets

allow me to provide a holistic approach to care with impact on the individuals.

Chapter 5

Choosing Hope

Anika Samone

Dedicated to my mother Diane Manning. For teaching me my faith and for all the love and support you gave while you were here on earth! Thank you for believing in me and thinking I was the most talented and beautiful girl in the world.

24 Chapters

Everything you ever wanted is on the other side of fear!
—George Addair

Shattered pieces of a life forgotten on the floor of the world. Everything once good now exists no more. Can you run out of tears? The answer, I've found, is no, but it sure as hell can feel like it.

During the summer of 2015, I was living a life I felt I deserved. I had, as they say, finally arrived! I was comfortable financially, physically, and spiritually. I was in a fourteen-year marriage with a healthy five-year-old daughter, despite being told I would never have children. We lived in a beautiful three-story brownstone in a gorgeous neighborhood. We had two paid-off cars. I had a wonderful career with a prominent agency, and I was seeing success in my side gigs in acting and filmmaking.

I had started focusing on my health and was crushing my goals. I became vegetarian and worked out in the gym for three and a half hours a day, six days a week. My regimen involved weight training, a forty-five-minute cardio cooldown, fifteen minutes on the StairMaster, and thirty minutes on the elliptical. I prayed regularly and avidly studied the Bible. I had my two-translation Bible and my Greek and Hebrew lexicon, along with a fancy notebook containing my Biblical motivations at the top of every page. Thousands of dollars in available credit, a near-perfect credit score, and thousands of dollars in multiple accounts with no debt but my mortgage. The American dream was firmly in my grasp, and I was smoothly sailing through life.

Then we met him.

Him.

Mr. White, we'll call him. In August 2015 my then-husband and I were invited to a graduation celebration. My husband could not attend, so he asked me to go on our family's behalf. I agreed.

As I entered the party, the graduate was giving a speech, thanking everyone for coming. Toward the end, she said she was going to give her friend an opportunity to speak but made sure to say she did not care one way or another whether we endorsed him. In other words, "Deal with him at your own risk." Red flag #1.

Mr. White got up and explained that he was selling an item, which happened to be something my spouse was interested in. I called to let my husband know about the product and asked if he wanted me to purchase it for him, to which he said yes. I solicited Mr. White's services at the party, and he provided the item and his business card.

A week later, we were having problems. Red flag #2. Mr. White tried walking my spouse through the process of getting the item working over the phone, to no avail. He offered to swing by the house and look at the item, at no additional charge.

When he arrived, he was full of compliments and accolades about how well we were doing as a young couple. My spouse ate it up while I gave Mr. White the side-eye. He shared stories of adventure, his life endeavors, and bragged about his elaborate living quarters.

I didn't have time to listen to his nonsense. I needed to get to the gym. I grabbed my belongings and skedaddled down the stairs, saying pleasantries and goodbyes.

Three and a half hours later, I pulled up to my driveway and guess whose car is still there? You guessed it—Mr. White! Annoying. Why was he still at my house?

I entered my home to find Mr. White still sharing stories. My husband beckoned me over to partake in the conversation. My husband asked, "How can one make real money outside of working a nine-to-five?"

Mr. White shared his secrets. He mentioned several streams of revenue, along with a business venture between him and his brother, henceforth known as Mr. Pink. He and Mr. Pink were working on a new business, and they were looking for serious investors with the opportunity to become partners. I walked out of the room, fed up with his tales and this ridiculous proposal. It was absurd and far-fetched.

The following morning, my husband informed me of a business meeting he had scheduled with Mr. White and Mr. Pink at "the shop." I was caught off guard. Why was he even entertaining this guy? He'd driven up in a busted old Jaguar wearing sweatpants and a holey T-shirt. Nothing about him matched up to his talk, but I wanted to be a good wife, so I attended the meeting. It was, after all, just a meeting.

We pulled up and immediately I saw that nothing about "the shop" said "straight and narrow."

Mr. White introduced us to Mr. Pink and their business partner, Mr. Orange. We sat down and talked logistics. Mr. Pink went over the details: type of business, percentages, money-making potential, and where we would fit into the scheme of things. They could tell I wasn't satisfied. Mr. Orange tried convincing me of how lucrative this could be, but he failed to impress me. "If this works so well, why do you need us?" I asked.

They tried to explain but all I heard was unsubstantiated nonsense. No real answer to my question.

My husband was frustrated with me after the meeting. He got on my case about how unfriendly I was and how I could be messing up an opportunity to make some real money. I politely reminded him they needed us, we didn't need them, so why should I be nice?

The next day, we had another heated discussion. It escalated into an all-out yelling match. I was done. I could not take it anymore. I caved. He told me to retrieve $2,000 in cash and to go with him to start the paperwork.

There was no paperwork.

There was a lot of driving and putting things in our names. Offices, business credit cards, business licenses, company vehicles, insurances, parts and systems—if they needed it, we supplied it under our names.

"Why isn't anything going under the business name? Don't you think this is strange?" I asked.

My husband gave me a bogus spiel about how business credit must stand on your personal credit, and while I understood the concept, I felt it should go under the business name to protect us. But who am I?

The next few weeks were stressful, albeit kind of fun. We were part of something new. It was my baby. I worked tirelessly day and night. I'd gotten a promotion in my job, so I was working and training during the day and working at the shop at night. It was exhausting, but I thought I was fulfilling a purpose. I even thought I wanted to quit my job and work full-time on this endeavor.

*****

Three months into this venture, Mr. Pink and Mr. Orange were making personal purchases and seemingly turning profits, but nothing was coming back to us. I started receiving phone calls about late and unpaid bills. My husband tried to assuage my worries. "This is just part of business," he said.

How would he know?

I called our business partners, and they told me everything they thought I wanted to hear. Meanwhile, Mr. White was trying to break away from the other two men and do business independently.

We were funding three businesses and had more money going out than coming in, and a lot of it was coming out of my and my husband's pockets. Very little assistance came from our business partners. Mr. White kept making promises he couldn't keep while taking money that my spouse and I didn't know anything about, all without making good on any of the contractual terms. Worse, he gave my phone number out as a contact for questions, leading me to receive phone calls from people who thought they worked for me.

Finally, I sat my spouse down and told him we needed to talk. I expressed that I felt stressed and needed answers. He was oblivious to how bad things were. He thought it was just one big misunderstanding, that it could be resolved with a team meeting. He said, "This will either be the best decision I have ever made or the worst. Only time will tell."

Unbeknownst to us, Mr. White had stolen from Mr. Pink, burning that bridge and leading the latter to threaten to leave us high and dry in our other businesses if we continued working with Mr. White. Mr. Pink promised to get things back on track, claiming things were "slow" and he needed to "beef up the clientele." We agreed to sever ties with Mr. White, and soon after he went to jail. This should've been the straw that broke the camel's back, but it wasn't. I had fallen victim to the sunk cost fallacy—I didn't want to throw away what we'd already invested, so I had to keep going.

Six months in, nothing was getting paid on time. We heard excuse after excuse. No money found its way back into our hands. We were drowning in debt. I was so stressed I became ill. One by one, everything fell apart. Our so-called business partners pretended to take care of business, but crazy things were happening.

One day, I went to the shop and the fire department was there. Someone had set one of the company cars on fire. Another week I went in and someone had thrown a brick through the window. Over the next few weeks, two men kept coming by, asking for Mr. Pink or Mr. Orange.

Unfortunately, they were never there when the two men came by. They grew more aggressive over time until finally, Mr. Pink told me we'd no longer be taking walk-ins. For my safety, we'd be keeping the door locked, and he no longer wanted me to come in during the weekends.

The following day, someone shot up the shop.

I took a few days off to process, only to return to find Mr. Pink packing everything up. He looked surprised to see me. I asked him why it looked like we were moving.

He said, "We are."

"When were you going to tell us?"

"Once I got settled at home," he said.

Repo people came to my home looking for vehicles I didn't know I owned. My phone rang nonstop, bill collectors and creditors demanding their dues. Mr. Orange called me and asked me to sign off on a part. I thought nothing of it until I arrived at the destination. It was a motorcycle shop.

"What's in the box?" I asked the guy behind the counter.

"Handlebars."

I was furious. I signed the papers for them and delivered them to Mr. Orange.

"Why am I signing paperwork for motorcycle handlebars?" I asked.

He didn't know. Told me to ask Mr. Pink. So, I did. He had no answer either.

I looked through the transaction histories on all our credit cards, rifled through our files, and saw nothing but personal purchases unrelated to our businesses on cards that were in my and my husband's names.

Once again, we moved office spaces, this time to a rental house belonging to one of Mr. Pink's friends. I couldn't take it anymore. I wanted out of this situation. I wanted my peace of mind back. My husband and I weren't getting along. It was straining our marriage. I was crying all the time. It was difficult to get in touch with Mr. Pink, and Mr. Orange was nowhere to be found.

Soon, Mr. Pink disappeared.

It was evident by then that we had been taken advantage of. Scammed. I was getting sicker while trying to manage everything going on in our lives. I used acting as an escape from the madness of my life. I questioned everything. How could one bad decision shatter my perfect little world?

*****

One year into the situation, my husband and I looked for help to recover our property. We sought assistance from the police. We filed reports and opened investigations. It was hard. It took time, and the stress landed me in the hospital. The doctors thought I had torn my carotid arteries, but the stress awakened a dormant disease that caused rapid deterioration of my arteries. They went from straight to accordion shaped. I began having horrible migraine headaches. Our situation wasn't looking brighter.

Two years later, we slowly started recovering some of the lost properties. We tried taking care of things, but more and more problems popped up on our credit reports, including cards we didn't open and so much more. We had no choice but to file for bankruptcy. There was no way we could get this under control on our own. We consulted with a referral, who unfortunately messed up our paperwork, took our money, and stopped taking our calls. We had to hire a law firm to fight our case.

During this process, one of our creditors wasn't accepting our bankruptcy without a fight. They requested to be exempt from the bankruptcy declaration and wanted to file criminal charges against me personally. I was facing prison time. I was sick. How could this be happening?

I started having seizures. My home was in turmoil, my job promotion wasn't what it was cracked up to be, and my body was failing me. I had lost all hope. I had no refuge, and I turned away from the only thing I knew could get me through: my faith.

Throughout all this, I got pregnant. I felt so irresponsible. I found out because I was scheduled for a procedure, but they required a pregnancy test be done beforehand. The nurse came into the room and said, "Get dressed. There's no longer a need for the procedure. Congratulations on your pregnancy."

I looked away, laughed, and then looked back at her. She was serious. She smiled at first, but my devastated expression quickly changed that. I broke down and cried. Why was this happening? I couldn't possibly bring a child into this hell I called life. A baby didn't deserve this version of us as parents. My world was flipped upside down again. What was I going to do?

I went home and told my husband. He tried to be happy, but there was too much going on.

I got an ultrasound the following week. I heard the baby's heartbeat. It was faint, but unmistakable. The doctor said my uterus was filled with fibroid cysts and we'd have to keep a close eye on the baby. It was going to be a very high-risk pregnancy.

Two weeks later, I started spotting. The doctors referred me to an ob-gyn specialist, who coincidentally had delivered my first child. She drew my blood and ran some tests. Then she said the number she was hoping for wasn't high enough to consider me pregnant. She told me to go home and that within a few days, my body may start the process of termination.

I couldn't understand how she could sit there and say that so coldly, so matter-of-factly, as if informing me that the hospital was out of maxi pads.

I am a person with feelings and love for the life growing inside me. I had no words for her. I was angry. She may have dealt with this every day, but I did not. She may have had to break this news to multiple patients every day, but I had never lost a child before. I heard the heartbeat of my child, no matter how small or faint. That was my baby.

Screw your test and your messed-up statement.

Later that day, I began bleeding; before the night was over, I'd gone through the traumatic process of my body purging my baby. I had never experienced that kind of pain. I curled up on the floor, inconsolable, devastated, and broken.

In November 2019 I had a partial hysterectomy that left me feeling inadequate and less of a woman.

In December 2019 we were granted our bankruptcy with the condition that we pay one specific company $50,000, and they would agree to drop all charges against me upon final payment. We paid in full. We pulled from our retirement accounts to pay them off.

We thought we could at last put everything behind us. Little did we know, this one bad decision would haunt us for years to come.

*****

Our lives were never the same. It was overwhelming. We couldn't get back to where we were. My husband and I divorced in 2021 after a twenty-three-year relationship. We sold our home, split custody of our daughter, and peacefully went our separate ways.

That one decision to go into business with Mr. White was the catalyst of my life's downward spiral.

Shortly after my divorce, my mother was diagnosed with bone cancer. I moved in with my parents to help take care of her. I started working from home so I could assist my father with her day-to-day needs. The doctors said that four to five months of treatment would put her on the road to recovery.

My mother passed away on May 11, 2022. That day I lost one of the most important influences in my life.

I was lost. I felt misplaced and hopeless. I couldn't breathe. I was drowning, fighting, gasping for air. I fell into a deep depression. I no longer wanted to be on this planet. My life was overwhelming, and I didn't want to do it anymore.

I lay on my bed, staring up at the ceiling, angry that I'd woken up. I was grieving so many losses at once. So many things had happened so close together that I didn't have time to deal with each one individually. I was surrounded by people but all alone.

My two amazing brothers, my cousin, and three of my longtime friends were there for me. They were incredibly helpful, but I still felt alone. I had a great personal trainer at the time. I tried to "gym away" the pain, and when that didn't help, I tried to "drink away" the pain, and then I tried "counseling away" the pain.

Nothing worked. I cried daily. I was a zombie, walking through my life but not actually living. I had lost sight of any purpose or goal I'd been working toward.

My stepfather used to get up every morning and blast gospel music throughout the house. I'd become numb to it, but for some reason, one morning I actively listened.

The words were so vivid, I could feel them tugging at me. The song that grabbed me was called "Worth," by Anthony Brown and group therAPy. The lyrics talk about how Jesus saw the worth in all of us, and sacrificed His life so that we could be free.

This wasn't the first time I'd heard that song, but that day it hit differently. The words washed over me like a beautiful wave, and instantly, I felt hopeful. I hold on to that feeling today. I could feel again. I was reawakened, activated, and I embraced that feeling and ran with it.

I'd always been strong, but life had taken its toll. I felt beaten down by my circumstances and my grief. Worthlessness had bound me. But thankfully, I was born with an innate ability to never give up.

That song reminded me of my ability, and it put freedom back within my reach. It rejuvenated my faith. I was reassured that I could have a hopeful mindset, that greatness would be manifested into my life again.

I had to learn that my trials came not to break me but to make me, to give me the testimony of an overcomer. I will be like a tree planted beside flowing streams who bears its fruit and whose leaves do not wither. Whatever I do, I will prosper.

*****

No two seasons will look alike, but you can go through each season with the same frame of mind. Everything you ever need is already inside you. We can dig deep to hold on to hope. Life will get hard; you may feel overwhelmed, like giving up is the only option, but look within and know that every day you've been given another chance to choose life.

During the difficult times, I cried more than I ever had. Back then, I loathed crying. I referred to it as bleeding from my face. I thought it was a weak, pointless emotion, a waste of bodily fluid. But my experiences guided me to a different perspective, and I now know it's a necessary part of the cleansing and healing process.

Hope is a funny thing. It can be relative, like happiness. Regardless of the situation, we can choose our state of being and actively function in a specific frame of mind. Hope is a noun and a verb. A noun functions as an object or set of objects, a state of existence or ideas; a verb is an action word that describes what the subject is doing. Therefore, hope can not only be the work that you put toward manifesting your endeavors but also your state of being. This concept was difficult for me to grasp when I was lost. It was a concept I needed proven to me through trial by fire. A series of unfortunate events led me to this conclusion. I call it my Lemony Snicket phase.

I have been told that faith is the assurance of what we hope for and the certainty of what we do not see (Hebrews 11:1, Berean Standard Bible). I felt devoid of faith and surely hopeless. In 2016 I had no idea my life would take a turn for the worse, and that the eight years following would be loaded with the most devastating events of my existence. Some have said I went through the trials of Job and then some. I agree.

But the worst thing is that I had lost sight of what was important and turned away from what I knew to be true. I now keep these words at the forefront of my mind: "The Lord is my shepherd; I shall not want. He maketh me to lie down in green pastures, He leadeth me beside the still waters. He restoreth my soul, He leadeth me in the paths of righteousness for His name's sake. Yea, though I walk through the valley of the shadow of death, I will fear no evil, for thou art with me; thy rod and thy staff, they comfort me. Thou preparest a table before me in the presence of mine enemies. Thou anoints my head with oil, my cup runneth over. Surely goodness and mercy shall follow me all the days of my life, and I will dwell in the house of the Lord forever." Psalms 23.

Live it to the fullest. Know that what you go through isn't just for you; it's for you to help someone else.

*****

About Anika Samone:
Anika Samone is a poet, an award-winning filmmaker, and an artist in the truest sense of the word. Born and raised in Las Vegas Nevada as the oldest of three, Anika had been using her writing and drawing as an outlet for years. Anika loved reading, creating, and daydreaming in high school. Unsure of her path, she went to school for computer technology, but realized in the second semester of her freshman year she wanted to be an artist. Unfortunately, that was not what life had in store for her.

Wanting to try something new, Anika embarked upon an adventure and picked up acting and filmmaking. She won best debut film for her first film project, "That's Her," and performed on the Las Vegas Strip in, "Can a Woman Raise a Man." Her IMDB filmography speaks for itself. Anika's journey has come full circle and she has returned to her first love, writing.

Chapter 6
Making Every Move a Step Forward

Crystal Perras

To my family who gave me my Southern roots.

Hello, and welcome to my life story. My name is Crystal, and well ... my squirrels get loose a lot, so please try to stay with me for this chapter. It's going to be a real roller coaster.

I'm originally from a small town in North Carolina. When I say small town, it's exactly what you're envisioning. My entire family—parents, siblings, aunts, uncles, and cousins—all in the same town and almost all of us living on the same block and sharing family meals. My grandparents were the patriarchs who kept us all together. Since they have passed, things have changed, and we are all navigating what life is now in their absence.

While I had my extended family in the town around me, I lived with and was raised by a single mom who tried to make sure my siblings and I had everything we could possibly need, even if we had less than other families. I grew up living with my brother and sister (same mom, different dad). I was also around my dad's ex-wife's daughter, my sister, when I was younger. After my dad and that girlfriend had a falling-out, they broke up and I never saw that sister again. This was so hard for me to understand; I was young and I missed my sister.

I tried a few times to reach out to her mom just to say hello but was never able to reach her. This was especially hurtful because I later discovered that my missing sister had brain cancer and passed away. It was devastating. She was so young, and it broke my heart. Also knowing how scared she had to be, and all I wanted to do was to let her know that she had a sister who loved her so very much.

After my sister's death, I found out that this woman and my dad had a son as well—which meant I had a brother I'd never met. Parents really need to remember that the choices they make will affect the mental health and security of their children. It is crummy, cruel, and unfair for the children caught in the middle of these situations. Not being able to say goodbye stays with you for life.

My mom worked making furniture, starting when I was younger until she was injured on the job. After she injured her knee, I stayed home from high school some days to take care of her. At the time, she often needed shots in her knees. On the days she got those, she couldn't do the day-to-day things like cooking or cleaning, so I would step in.

Eventually, I was caring for her full time and ended up dropping out before I graduated. I liked the academic part of school, but the people made it hard. I was often bullied. Kids were meaner than they needed to be. They liked to judge people for the way they dressed or talked (even though we were all from the South). Even when you tried to be nice to them, nothing was ever enough.

I had always been a tomboy and was mainly brought up around boys. My big brother was and is one of my best friends. We would go fishing and work on cars and hang out with the family. I knew I was safe at home and with my brother, and I felt that my time was better spent there than being mistreated at school. My cousin had a mechanic shop, and I loved spending all my free time there working on cars and learning how to get older cars running. My brother and I have spent countless hours talking about our dream cars we'll have one day and who's going to win the drag race.

My sister was fun to hang out with, and even though she was more of a girly girl, we still had fun together. She also had her challenges being diagnosed as bipolar, but she always did her best to show she loved and cared about us and to be there for our mom.

After leaving school, I didn't have a clear direction in life. I spent my time drinking and partying. Eventually, in my early twenties, I got sick of my own shit. So I sat with myself and made a plan. I didn't want to, but I knew I HAD to move out of my small town. Living near my family was good, but for me to grow and reach my goals, I needed to be in a place that had more opportunities. It was time to spread my wings, and I was terrified.

I moved to Las Vegas where there was a lot of work opportunity and I met a few friends, which made it not seem like such a hard move. After I settled in, I worked a few different jobs, trying to figure out what I wanted to do and what made me happy. Back home, everyone either worked at the furniture factory, got a check from the state, or worked on cars. I thought I wanted to be a mechanic, but once I posted my résumé and saw all the different types of jobs that reached out to me, I was excited to try new things.

While interviewing, I discovered that everyone asked about education. Explaining that I dropped out of high school was not how I wanted to keep replying to potential employers—or even what I wanted to hear from myself. I decided to get my GED and signed up for my first GED class.

It was a weirdly accomplished feeling, but I was excited to finally have a high school diploma. I also was surprised to learn how many successful people only had their GEDs. I really didn't have a great background in structured or focused studying, so I would read a little through my books, then take the GED test and, to my surprise, passed with high scores. It felt really good to achieve this goal.

When you don't have an education, it is easy to feel intimidated or like you're less than people who do. Armed with my new confidence, I applied for better jobs and soon learned I didn't like being stuck in an office, and for sure, I didn't like working nights. I had a job as an IT tech for a bit, and then I heard about what defense contractors do and found out I needed a college degree for this career.

I applied for college and shortly after started classes. I quickly learned brick-and-mortar school was not for me. I love to learn, and I really love new challenges, but being in a structured classroom wasn't working. As I mentioned before, I didn't have great study habits and work kept calling me during my classes to come in for a shift, so by the end of my third semester, I was failing almost all my classes. I cried for a minute, called my parents like any Southerner would do, and figured out a new plan.

For a second, I wanted to run home to be in the comfort of my routine where I knew everyone and knew what to expect. But I knew that would not help me reach my goals and I would be going backward. If I were to go home, I wanted to do so with enough money to open a business and buy homes for my parents, which, as all children of divorced parents know, means buying two homes. As such, I still had some work to do.

After realizing that college wasn't for me, I went back out into the work field and started applying for any and all jobs. I tried doing almost everything, including DoorDash, working as a promo model, doing odd IT tech jobs, a job in marketing, and then finally trying my hand at sales.

While working in the sales departments for several different companies, I felt a natural draw to this field and knew I could excel. I loved being in the bustle of the city while meeting with clients. My clients, who were store owners, were my mentors and I learned a lot about business by watching and asking them questions.

In the past, I've disagreed with how some of the companies I worked with ran their business, so I would learn all I could and then move on to the next job. Also while still doing promo modeling on the side, I realized I could be making more money by working directly with my clients rather than for an agency. Taking all my past and current experiences and mixing in a dose of courage and a "can do" attitude, I settled in with my laptop, called all my friends, and learned how to open an LLC.

I opened my first LLC by starting a modeling agency. It was extremely challenging, but I learned so much, I wouldn't change it. Your mindset and level of accountability really do shift when you look at the same exact situation as a business owner instead of as an employee. Nobody calls asking where you are or gives you a time to clock in and out or a schedule of what is expected from you each day. Except for yourself.

Although I was at an unfamiliar level of organized chaos, I loved it. Very young, I learned if it's something I am passionate about, I can really focus in and reach my goals. I had my agency for about a year, then realized I could make more money in sales as a broker and distributor.

Now I easily hit my financial goals—goals that once I thought I could never reach. Growing up, I always glorified business owners. It was a big deal to me, and I felt them to be very accomplished humans. They seemed to be on a whole different level that I felt I could never reach. Now, these same humans I once glorified are calling me for products and advice on what to buy. I love it, and I feel accomplished and coming into my own.

*****

Each move I've made since I began this journey has been a step forward, maybe in a roundabout manner some days, but nonetheless, it was a step forward. Every failure has been a step forward, with the ability to regroup and come back with enthusiasm, humility, and a new plan of action. This will be my formula for success and how I intend to overcome every future obstacle.

Today, my life is even fuller with the addition of another little sister, thanks to my dad. My new little sister is so beautiful, and her mom is so kind and sweet. Thankfully, when the relationship between my dad and his girlfriend ended, my sister and I stayed in touch. Her mom also makes sure I'm involved in my little sister's life, and I don't miss anything. Getting older, you realize how much you want to stay involved with the family you have.

I fly home as often as I can and have daily FaceTime calls with all my family. It feels good to be able to provide for them when they need something now. There is still so much more to accomplish, but each day I get closer to my goals.

It's important to remember, though, as you go through the ups and downs that you remember to enjoy moments and all that life offers, both the good and the bad. Try not to take things too seriously, since we do not have much control over situations, but we do have control of ourselves. Roll with the punches, but KEEP GOING. Believe in and surround yourself with people doing more than you. Never be the smartest person in the room—instead, make sure you're in rooms filled with people you can learn from.

*****

About Crystal Perras:
Crystal, an up-and-coming entrepreneur from a small town in North Carolina, invites readers into her challenging but inspiring journey through life.

Growing up in a close-knit southern family, she learned the values of resilience and love amidst challenges, including the struggles of being raised by a single mother and the heartache of loss.

Crystal shares her experiences of overcoming bullying, navigating complex family dynamics, and ultimately finding her way to independence and success.

After moving to the city, she embraced new opportunities, pursued education, and discovered her passion for sales and entrepreneurship. Crystal's journey from a small-town girl to a thriving business owner is filled with moments of self-discovery, hard-earned wisdom, and the importance of family connection.

Through her writing, she encourages readers to embrace their own rollercoaster lives, reminding them that every setback can lead to a new beginning. In her spare time, Crystal enjoys being with her family and friends, fishing with her brother and dad, exploring new ventures, and cherishing the bonds that have shaped her journey.

Chapter 7

Breaking the Silence: A Path to Inner Peace and Wholeness

Dani G.B.

*To every soul who has endured the unspoken,
to those who have walked through shadows in search of light.
May this journey remind you of your resilience,
your capacity to heal, and your infinite worth.*

With Love, Dany G.B

"The wound is the place where the light enters you." – Rumi

At the age of five, I was abused by a close family member, and at sixteen by my best friend's stepfather.

I didn't speak about it for years. Not to anyone, not even my closest friends. I lived for many years with shame, guilt, and remorse, as if I were the one who provoked their abuse. To this day, I cannot even broach the subject with members of my own family. Even now, I cannot say who this "close family member" was. When someone presents themselves so impeccably to everyone around them—portraying themselves as a person of "great morale," hardworking, altruistic, adept at writing and reciting poetry, someone who forges incredible connections with everyone they meet—it becomes incredibly difficult to expose their transgressions. Who would believe me?

The reality is, there was a moment during my childhood when I simply blocked it out. Deep down, I knew the impact these events would have on my life and that of my family. So, my brain decided to suppress it, and I continued on until I was abused at sixteen by another man. That's when I remembered the earlier abuse, and the immense anger and sadness buried deep inside me resurfaced.

The Beginning
The family member who abused me had always been good to me. I don't remember experiencing any psychological abuse or mistreatment from him. However, I do remember moments when he would tell me stories: as he spoke, he would caress me, and like any child seeking love and affection, I never saw it as negative—until he began touching my private parts. At that age, I didn't understand the implications of his actions, but I did feel uncomfortable. I asked him to stop because I didn't like it, but it

fell on deaf ears. To be honest, I can't remember how many times it happened.

On one occasion, when I had a friend stay for a sleepover, I warned her to "be careful because he has a tendency to touch inappropriately." It wasn't until her mother confronted me, asking if what I'd told her daughter was true, that I started to grasp the gravity of the situation. It was shocking to realize that what I had perceived as innocent storytelling was, in fact, something unusual and "bad." Despite this revelation, I felt conflicted. I didn't want anything to happen to this person. I didn't want our family dynamics to change, nor did I want anyone to suffer. I just wanted everything to go back to how it was before, before I knew that what I thought was love was actually a crime and that it would shape the rest of my life.

I'd always considered myself very mature for my age. I tended to have older friends, and I often appeared more "developed" than most of my peers. Despite being a beautiful woman eager to explore my sexuality, my adolescence was marked by extreme self-repression. I never masturbated, and whenever my partners tried to advance to second or third base, I would panic. I couldn't understand why I felt this way.

Deepening Trauma
The circumstances were a bit different during my second experience of abuse. My parents divorced when I was fifteen. During that time, they were often absent, so I was usually away from home. I've always had many friends, but I tend to have one particular person who I'm closest with, as was the case during this experience. I spent a lot of time at my best friend's house. Her family was always very welcoming, and her stepfather was kind and affectionate. Over the course of a year, they made me

feel like part of their family, or at least I thought I was. It was comforting, especially since my own family was going through difficult times, and I often felt alone.

I vividly remember the evening of the nightmare, as if it were yesterday. We were packing because they were about to move. My friend, her sister, and I shared a room, but this time we only had mattresses on the floor due to the move. During our conversations, I felt her stepfather lying next to me. We continued talking until we fell asleep. At some point during the night, though I'm not sure how long I'd been asleep, I felt his hands caressing my hair, then moving down my back, exploring my body until they reached my private parts. I was in a state of shock, feeling extremely nervous. I tried to wake my friend by kicking her, but I couldn't find my voice. When I tried to make a sound, he covered my mouth, and I grabbed his hand to push it away, but he was stronger. It was then that I realized I was about to be raped. I managed to escape his grasp, pulled away as quickly as I could, ran to the door, flagged down a cab, and went home, never to return to that family again.

Seventeen and longing to escape everything that reminded me of past experiences—the shame, the remorse—I relocated with my mom to a new city. I yearned for a fresh start, and indeed, that's what I found. However, without addressing the emotional turmoil within, I soon realized that wherever I went, feelings of sadness, anger, and helplessness followed. Yet, I continued to navigate life as if the abuse were an unavoidable part of my existence.

I won't sugarcoat it—I went through a brief but intense phase with drugs. They provided fleeting moments of peace and happiness, offering a temporary escape from reality. However, this self-destructive cycle plunged me into deep depression and severe anxiety.

A Glimmer of Hope
Despite growing up with privilege—surrounded by mostly good people, attending private schools, enjoying travel and comforts—I still felt an overwhelming emptiness inside. I often grappled with feelings of ingratitude and nonconformity; my temperament was prone to sensitivity, my soul in constant turmoil.

During a period of residence in France, I promised myself never to use drugs again. The withdrawal was excruciating, exacerbating the overwhelming emotions I was already experiencing. From that point on, things couldn't have seemed any worse. Yet, amid my darkest moments, I found a glimmer of hope. An acquaintance visited me, serving as a beacon of faith, hope, compassion, and love. To me, she was an angel—a gift bestowed to inspire me to persevere, to refuse to give up. For that, I will forever be grateful.

When you hit rock bottom, the only direction left to go is up—to climb, to grow, to better yourself. Finally, I reached out for help. I began seeing a therapist, though I never felt satisfied with the feedback or my perceived lack of progress. In my journey toward healing, simply expressing my feelings in the moment felt like small steps, but they were movement forward, nonetheless. Unlike many, I didn't find therapy particularly helpful. While it was liberating in a way, I struggled with being vulnerable, sensing that something crucial was missing. Despite three years of therapy, I still felt the emptiness within.

That's when I turned to spiritual experiences. I explored various avenues, from hikuri ceremonies to numerology therapies, from courses on unblocking chakras and taking responsibility for my life, and even Diksha healing. Each endeavor felt purposeful—I was on a quest to find myself. As my teachers often advised, "I had to connect." At the time, I didn't fully grasp the depth of that concept.

From Anger to Opportunity
Several years later, I found myself caught in repetitive cycles. The discomfort returned, and I slipped back into self-destructive habits—though not with drugs. This time it was through my diet, smoking, alcohol, and neglecting exercise. Anxiety and depression resurfaced, and my body protested with various illnesses, signaling the need for change.

Then, when my first abuser passed away, I experienced a whirlwind of emotions and found myself grappling internally. The person who had inflicted so much harm upon me no longer occupied this plane of existence; it became unjustifiable for me to harbor continued anger toward him. But I couldn't help it.

I was consumed by anger and plagued with countless questions. Why hadn't I confronted him after all those years? Why had I never seized an opportunity to express the magnitude of the suffering he caused in my life? Now, I was using his death as a means to perpetuate harshness toward myself, repeatedly asking, "Why am I like this?" Being angry with someone who has ceased to exist only inflicted more harm upon me through the grudge I held. I came to realize it was a choice to continue suffering over a circumstance beyond my control.

Instead of perpetuating futile energy and thoughts, I began to view it as an opportunity—an opportunity for self-forgiveness, a chance to cease the facade of pretending that everything was OK. I needed something tangible to connect with, a pathway to rediscover myself. I deserved to find solace. I deserved a fresh start.

Driven to find techniques for calmness, anxiety relief, and connection with my body and mind, I dabbled in yoga sporadically but lacked regular discipline. Then, a close friend recommended meditation—not just any meditation, but a ten-day silent retreat to learn the Vipassana technique. I had nothing to lose. My life was in disarray—my relationship with my partner was faltering, my projects were failing, and my personal relationships were in shambles. On the contrary, I had everything to gain, so, I embarked on the journey.

For ten days, I observed silence, consumed vegan meals, adhered strictly to schedules, instructions, and discipline codes, and of course, practiced meditation—sitting for twelve hours each day. Initially, I resisted every aspect of the process; it was uncomfortable, and I endured moments of profound struggle. The dreams that visited me at night were intense, and I remained in a constant state of defensiveness.

However, as the days passed, I began to comprehend the essence of true self-connection. My mind gradually cleared, and a sense of serenity enveloped me. I started to perceive the beauty and wonder of life—the harmony in nature, the perfection in every creation tailored for our experience. I realized that every occurrence serves as a lesson, teaching us to learn, to empathize, to cultivate compassion, to forgive, to let go, and to trust. I understood that everything we seek *resides within us.*

Despite my limited exposure to metaphysics, I've come to believe that our reality is shaped by our beliefs—our beliefs give rise to our thoughts, and our thoughts, in turn, mold our existence.

I came to understand that my way of thinking was deeply unhealthy. My mind had taken control of my life, and to put it metaphorically, it was as if the computer's CPU had seized control of the screen, keyboard, and mouse, dictating and executing its own desires just by existing. I had crafted a persona of victimization, insecurity, and negativity, and it's so easy to fall into that trap, to believe in it. The mind doesn't want us to uncover its tricks, but breaking free from that state is a decision.

For me, the only way to take control back is by staying present, by observing my thoughts and emotions. When I truly become aware of this, I cloud the mind, and that's when I start to see the magnificence and perfection of life, filling me with gratitude. For me, there's no higher frequency than that of gratitude.

I leave the past where it belongs—in the past. If practical matters need addressing, I allow myself a brief visit. But if I don't want to inflict more pain on myself and others, if I don't want to stir up the remnants of past suffering that still lingered within me, I had to be in the present. It's all I have—making the now the primary focus of my life. I surrendered. I stopped resisting life, which is this very moment by saying YES to life.

Rebirth and Learning
Upon my return from the silent retreat, I felt compelled to share this transformative experience with all those dear to me. Witnessing so much suffering, I yearned for them to undergo the enriching journey I had just completed. To this day, it remains the most profound gift I've bestowed upon my soul. I continue doing it for myself, and I will continue to provide others with the same experience I went through.

From that point on, my life took a dramatic turn. It was akin to a rebirth—a recognition of boundless possibilities. Every preceding experience, no matter how arduous, had led me to that pivotal moment. I had traversed countless hells to discover my own piece of heaven.

I committed to disciplined meditation and cultivating healthier habits, which led me to a heightened state of awareness regarding my reactions, actions, and interactions with the world around me. This newfound clarity enabled me to identify what I truly desired in life. As my clarity increased, I initiated changes, removing people, projects, or situations from my life that no longer served me. However, my ego and fear often hindered my ability to let them go.

After a few months, I decided to relocate to Spain. I sold my belongings and embarked on a new adventure with my dog and two cats. I believed that Spain would provide a blank sheet and a fresh start.

Yet, despite my initial enthusiasm, I encountered unforeseen challenges. Firstly, obtaining residency in a foreign country proved to be difficult without a solid economic plan to substantiate my stay. Secondly, I was still in the process of detoxifying my life from certain individuals, which hindered my experience. And I stopped working on projects, thereby leading to a decline in my income. Most significantly, although I had gained clarity, I remained uncertain about my life's purpose. Upon my arrival, I realized that I had only a vague plan, and it was poorly organized and lacking direction.

Once again, I found myself immersed in learning experiences—though this time, I saw myself as an active individual, not just a bystander as events happened *to* me. It marked a phase of mourning, a process of releasing the traumatic experiences of my past. It represented the final leg of a journey through immense pain that I had carried with me for years. And this time was different—I had acquired tools to navigate through it. I constantly reminded myself: "Every challenge is an opportunity," "Let go," and "Trust."

I was overwhelmed with gratitude for the privilege of living these experiences, for encountering individuals who taught me invaluable lessons, for reconnecting with my family, for embracing vulnerability, and for learning to receive and prioritize self-love for the first time. I was, finally, not the passive audience of my own story but the active protagonist.

This newfound mindset led me to embark on incredible experiences. I rediscovered the joy of dancing, took up climbing, joined a Vipassana meditation group, enrolled in manifestation courses, and, above all, began to believe in myself. As I nurtured my desires and focused on overcoming obstacles, I witnessed the fruition of my efforts. I found myself embarking on new beginnings, engaging with wonderful people, and undertaking projects that resonated with my authentic self more and more.

Patience and time became my guiding principles. Eventually, I made the decision to move to Mexico. I had gleaned the lessons I needed to learn, always with the intention of returning to where I belonged.

Returning to my family, my friends, my people, was wonderful. Now, everything is a field of opportunities. I still feel like I'm on the right healing path. I'm filled with hope for life, for creativity. Having a healthy support network and unconditional love has been the greatest part of my growth and motivation.

Upon my return, I had a heartfelt conversation with my dad. He inquired about my aspirations, reminding me of our previous discussions about creating a project together. While we had brainstormed ideas in the past, this moment prompted introspection. I yearned to pursue something that resonated with my personal journey, something I was passionate about, and simultaneously, something that could aid both myself and others in understanding that the healing journey is a daily commitment—a journey guided by love, faith, and hope, capable of manifesting our intentions.

This is why my father, brother, and I decided to establish a sex education platform. Our personal journey prompted us to consider how we could contribute meaningfully to the world—by creating a space where love-driven experiences intertwine with personal, emotional, and spiritual growth for those seeking fulfillment and wellness in their lives.

It keeps me on my healing journey every day as I continue to discover sensations and situations in this area that I had blocked for a long time. I strive to overcome it by allowing myself to delve into the connection with myself.

What has surprised me most about this journey of healing is the sheer number of people who have endured similar unfortunate experiences. However, now more than ever, humans are committed to opening doors for connection, engaging in profound conversations, embracing and celebrating new perspectives on gender, and appreciating the diversity of cultures and viewpoints. Recognizing that it all begins from within, we share our most intimate experiences, hoping to resonate with others and inspire them to embark on their own inner explorations.

Sexuality is an integral aspect of the human experience—a fundamental need that, when approached with education and responsibility, has the potential to enrich our lives on physical, mental, and spiritual levels.

Throughout this journey, I've been reminded time and again that healing and transformation are attainable. I continually reaffirm to myself that <u>I am a survivor</u>, that I am worthy of love and respect, and that wholeness is within the grasp of everyone. I constantly reaffirm to myself that I deserve love and abundance in all its forms, that fulfillment is within everyone's reach.

Recovery is a daily choice, an introspective effort that isn't usually comfortable at first. It requires a lot of patience, a lot of trust. But I promise you that with perseverance and faith, everything is achievable. Everything is a realm of possibilities. We are creators, beings of light and love. I hold on to the hope that together, we can break through the silences, constructing bridges toward hope and wellness.

*****

About Dani G.B.:
I was born in Córdoba, Veracruz, Mexico, on August 26, 1991 and I hold a BA in marketing from the Anahuac University of Querétaro, Mexico.

My career has spanned various roles in marketing, where I've honed my skills in communication and storytelling. This professional background has been instrumental in shaping my approach to writing and sharing my personal experiences.

I always felt very alone in my process and was ashamed and guilty to share my story. When I started sharing it with close people, I realized how healing it is to talk about it and, unfortunately, how many people go through the same experience. The more I share, the more I heal, and I hope that reading my story and the stories of all the warriors in this group will help you in your personal growth and healing process.

Writing has become a therapeutic outlet, allowing me to connect with others and contribute to a community of resilience and strength. I enjoy meditating and connecting with my body and spirit, spending time with my partner, family, pets, and

friends. I also love traveling the world and observing different cultural perspectives.
Sphira platform: https://www.sphira.mx
Vipassana: https://www.dhamma.org/es/index
Breaking the habit of being yourself book - Joe Dispenza
Many Lives, Many Masters - Brian L. Weiss
The Power of Now - Eckhart Tolle
Social: htttps://www.instagram.com/sphira.mx/
Web page: https://sphira.mx/
Personal: https://www.instagram.com/daguzzi/

Chapter 8

Giving Yourself Your Love

Chantelle Pape

To Beverly: My gram, my rock. I will never stop carrying the torch you handed me for helping others. Until we meet again, I carry you in my heart.

When I was asked to contribute to this project, impostor syndrome set in. It's funny how often it rears its head when you have endured chronic trauma. The pendulum swings on an exaggerated angle—on one hand, you wear a mask to hide your trauma, playing a role to maintain stability. But on the other hand, you embrace everything you've attained, hoping that eventually you can integrate the core you with the masked you.

Living this way, I feel too inadequate to counsel others. The mask isn't me. All the wisdom gained through the lessons that brought me here isn't "me." I can't speak about this success because "I" didn't achieve it; the role I played made it possible. They say "Fake it till you make it," and while that's good in moderation, sometimes the result is simply feeling fake.

Under these circumstances, counseling others has a disingenuous aftertaste. You offer them advice that you don't even live, and the thought that you should take your own advice echoes through your mind constantly. Thoughts like, "Maybe I lived that way at one point, but I'm not qualified to help this person," are pervasive. You feel overwhelming guilt for trying to help others when you feel helpless. Sometimes, life becomes too hard, which hammers it all in further. Your mind says, "You're an unqualified impostor who happened to make it out alive."

That perfectly describes the last several months of my life. There isn't a day that goes by where the thoughts and feelings I described above don't weigh on my mind. I couldn't find the words to say "I feel like a fake," and who was I to encourage anyone else while drowning in the depths of my life?

The isolation was overwhelming. Our dear project leader for this book, Misti Harrelson, was the epitome of patience and understanding, even though she knew I was dodging her calls and messages as I sunk into this suffocating darkness. Misti, from the bottom of my heart, I am sorry. You are an angel on Earth.

While I was gathering my strength to endure the darkness, the incredible ladies involved in this project fearlessly told their stories for those who need to hear them most. They rallied together each morning in our group text chat. I lay in bed, watching my phone screen light up with their encouraging messages, but nothing could pierce the veil of numbness I hid beneath.

Why couldn't I get it together?

The physical pain and heaviness wracking my body was from lupus, an autoimmune disease. My mental health was deteriorating. My bipolar II disorder pumped precious little dopamine into my brain, gripping me in a deep depressive state. I prayed for a manic episode to feel normal again.

I was hyperaware of how trauma had changed both my physical body and my mental state. While everyone else was pouring out love, having triumphed in their personal lives, I realized I was more broken than I'd thought. For months, the impostor syndrome won, providing me with something more akin to a writer's quicksand than writer's block.

When I finally submitted my initial draft for this chapter, stories of my cult upbringing, my abusive husband, then my drug addict husband, and my miscarriage made it 3,000 words over the limit, even after leaving out key parts of my story.

Regurgitating my memories into text form laid me bare. It was the most exposed I'd ever felt. I couldn't read it back, let alone trim it down to the word limit.

I ghosted everyone. Sorry again, Misti.

Standing back and taking inventory of my life, I found it still up in flames.

Who am I to speak to another person's life when mine is in such a deficit? These thoughts plagued me daily.

I spent last year alone, addressing my wounds and practicing celibacy after divorcing the man I thought I would grow old with. He disintegrated before my eyes and unraveled the life we'd built with each weft of yarn weaving us together, one by one.

The week our first son together was born in 2018, my now-ex relapsed on heavy pain medication. He never quite recovered. I have spent the last several years watching my life deteriorate in unimaginable ways, from losing multiple homes and jobs to selling everything I owned and spending nearly six months living in a hotel room with my three children.

When this book project kicked off, I was undoing the damage my ex caused. I got a new job, bought a home in my name, and became the sole provider for my kids. Their father was too unstable to care for himself, let alone our children. I grieved for our marriage and life as I knew it.

I was building a new life while remaining somewhat responsible for my ex's mental health. When I filed for divorce, his addiction took a turn for the worse. He became suicidal. He had heart failure due to overconsumption of pills. He'd go on days-long benders, holed up in a hotel room, pushing his body to the edge, hoping he wouldn't wake up the following morning.

Since we were still married on paper, his mental health became my responsibility. I was forced to commit him to mental hospitals while he was deep in the throes of addiction, setting off a chain reaction. He lashed out at me for keeping him alive against his wishes.

This cycle went on for months. Every day I woke up shaking, waiting for the call that would ruin my kids' lives. I imagined telling them, "Daddy is dead."

I couldn't handle it. I was overwhelmed with images of my littlest boys, now five and six years old, respectively, running up to their father's casket and trying to wake him up. I couldn't escape the haunted visions of how it would play out.

It's impossible to function this way, with impending doom hanging over your head. Indiscriminately, it paralyzes you, but you know the show must go on. You must show up to that work meeting, cook that dinner, and play with your children, knowing you will eventually devastate them with life-altering news.

There was no escaping the darkness that consumed me. I tried frequency music to heal the broken neural patterns in my brain, numbing the pain with a couple glasses of wine each night as I cried on my porch, I prayed and journaled for hours on end, but nothing worked. All that effort to wake up the next day, stand strong like a smiling stone in the face of work, responsibilities, and familial obligations, while inside I crumbled.

It was unsustainable. I couldn't live a life where I woke every morning with full-body tremors. Fear controlled every move I made. I fell behind at work and lost touch with friends and family as I sank deeper into a depression that overwhelmed me with waves of panic, sucking the air from my chest every waking moment.

I examined the events that led me to those circumstances. I used to be confident, able to overcome even the bleakest situations. If I knew anything about myself, it was that I never stayed down for long.

But I'd lost my spark. I couldn't white-knuckle it through this fear that found its home in my chest, pressurizing my lungs, weighing down every square inch of my body with each task I took on.

I had to get to the bottom of this fear. There had to be a root that I wasn't self-aware enough to address. So, I did what any self-respecting woman would do in the face of this black hole eating its way through her: I started online dating. Isn't that such a human response? Let's look outside of ourselves for the answer we know is hidden within. "Great way to demonstrate years of healing practices, Chay! Good job."

Nevertheless, that was the path I chose. I have an unquenchable thirst for learning lessons the hard way. Can you relate? God, I hope so. Otherwise, why am I writing this? My impostor syndrome is peeking out again. It says hello.

The silver lining is that I am wired to observe the lesson that situations—or situationships, in this case—present. I was still on a freight train headed for disaster, and I was making record time.

I'd spent over two decades with the wrong man. To ensure this didn't happen again while I dated online, I communicated my boundaries and carefully weaved through conversations with multiple men who seemed like feasible options for healthy, long-term connections.

Everyone I spoke to was rowing the same boat. "I would rather be alone than trust another person enough to invite them into my life." Though valid, I needed someone to fill this emptiness within me by any means necessary. Yet, despite twenty years of being alone, imprisoned in broken and abusive marriages, I was attracted to men who were projects. It didn't matter what packaging they came in. Many of them were self-aware and financially established, but they were broken enough to "need" me—or so I thought.

Why couldn't I choose a man who wanted a real connection? Each failed attempt at connection was a reminder that I was drifting farther away from the answers that I needed to steer my life toward stability.

My anxious attachment and fear of abandonment consumed me as I met these people. I couldn't understand why I was simultaneously exhausted by "helping" men who were emotional projects yet still seeking them out. Why did I feel like I had to fulfill someone else's needs to be valid? What about their rejection made me fight harder? Why was I stuck in this loop after spending years undoing it? It took several acts of God for me to find the wherewithal to leave my marriages and start over from scratch, so why was I leading myself straight back to the situations that nearly ended me?

Eventually, after losing parts of myself in these futile attempts to fulfill myself with somebody else, I realized it wasn't helping. Thank God for ah-ha moments. You would think the special treatment, the kind words, and the physical touch would have made me feel better, but all those things had the opposite effect. So many days went by where I was unable to put an outfit together or apply my makeup for work.

Although my weeks were sprinkled with dates, the days in between grew bleaker. I knew what I was looking for. I knew what would quell the pain, yet it was nowhere to be found.

I grew bitter and despondent. How did I know the type of love I wanted in my life existed? Because it was the love I poured out for others. **I was physical proof of its existence.** That revelation was pivotal to digging out of this pit I'd placed myself in. I realized that the love I give may exist outside of me, but it was also readily available within me.

My bitterness and refusal to look at my dysfunctional patterns kept me from healing. After all, why should I heal something that I didn't break? I think we all reach this level of resentment at some point. You endure so much trauma at the hands of those you love that the natural result is the insatiable desire to have the person who hurt you *fix* you. And when they don't, we still don't want to claim the responsibility for pain we didn't inflict upon ourselves, right?

Hell no! Someone, anyone, come into my life and fix this shit for me!

But this mindset only perpetuates our patterns of dysfunction by replaying the past through a new experience with a new face. What a mindfuck. With this new revelation, I uninstalled the dating apps, feeling a small sliver of shame at how I came to learn this particular lesson. But I did say I had an unquenchable thirst for learning things the hard way. And for a good month, your girl was extra thirsty. Take that as you will. I digress.

It became obvious that the only answer to my problem was *me* choosing *me*, no matter how bitter I was about wounds I didn't cause. The love I needed in my life was my own.

Moving Forward with Self-Love
They say "Ignorance is bliss," but it's a twisted bliss caused by trauma. It creates a pair of rose-colored glasses uniquely altered by the experiences of the wearer, forever warping their vision of reality. Most of us spend our lives unaware of these contorted perceptions overshadowed in that ever-familiar sunset hue. We fight back with the resilience of a warrior disproportionately paired with the mental fortitude of our child-selves who are trapped in a state of arrested development.

The echoes of our inner children screaming the stories of their tragedies reverberate throughout our lives with fortuitous persistence. We numb ourselves to the sound with anything we can—we throw ourselves into work, drink, smoke, sex, and pursue broken people we can help in place of helping ourselves.

Why have we been hardwired to ignore the cries of the most innocent parts of us? We reflect on our childhoods with a knowing laugh, masking heartache that haunts us for a lifetime. And then we wonder why we make the decisions we do.

Our inner child handcrafted the unique prescription of rose-colored glasses through which we see life. Until we take the time to acknowledge that we're keeping ourselves from seeing reality for what it is, we remain the same helpless, naive children repeating the same trauma under different circumstances until we breathe our last.

I come to you in this chapter not as a woman who has overcome, but as a student of my own life trying to alter the predisposed prescription of my reality. If this chapter speaks to you in any way, I want to make sure you hear this: The love you need to heal is within you. You don't have to overcome your trauma to see that giving your love to *yourself* will change everything.

Sometimes, struggling while still finding the strength to move forward is more inspiring than the final triumph itself. Why? Because we're all flowing in and out of seasons of difficulty and triumph at any given moment. The seasons change and bring us to the brink, physically and psychologically, yet we stand ten toes down, refusing to quit. Your value doesn't diminish during hardship—quite the opposite. You are not worthless while facing a trial. You are being purified by fire. Don't confuse pain with failure. Embrace the presence of pain and learn its purpose.

While you face the pain, reflect on how you've romanticized poor treatment and accepted insecurities that created a convoluted view through your rose-colored glasses.

Those glasses block out your inner voice, the voice that values you and loves you, regardless of circumstances. That's true authenticity.

The rose-colored overlay on my life has never done me any good, and I doubt it's served you either. As you stand in this season, here are my suggestions to help you propel forward:

1. Recognize that you are wearing a pair of rose-colored glasses.

    Your perception of life is constantly influenced by the trauma you endured. You will repeat these lessons until you understand that there's a neural pattern, a mental construct, that developed in your formative years. It imprisons you and encourages those repetitive patterns because they are familiar. Healing cannot occur without acknowledgment. It is painful, but necessary. Loving yourself and living authentically requires removing the manipulated lenses we view life through.

2. The way you love others is a direct reflection of the love you're missing.

    The love I sought did not exist outside of me. I harbored it in my heart. I didn't realize I could turn that love inward. I poured myself into others, hoping for reciprocation, but others do not love the way I do. Your love is as unique as your genetic makeup. If you ever wonder why people don't love the way you do, try picturing a life where you received the love you give. Then, realize that you alone hold the ability to give that to yourself.

3. You have nothing to offer yourself or anyone else if you don't recognize what you possess.

    Your love is the rarest entity in existence. It's singular. No one loves the way you do because no one else has your exact experiences. To understand the love you share with others, you must pour it upon yourself. Approach yourself with the same empathy you extend to others. The most inward parts of you are aching for this unique love.

This isn't to say that someone else can't love you in a fulfilling way. They can. But they cannot repair the parts of you that have been shattered. It may motivate you to explore healing on your own. Often, we use others' love to keep us afloat instead of doing the deep work we know awaits us. Perhaps that goes back to the anger of having to fix something we weren't responsible for breaking. But no matter how you cut it, no one is coming to save you. The beauty is that you can save yourself, and you possess all the love you've been searching for.

My beautiful lost friend, turn inward. The most life-changing journey is the one where we turn within. The presence of difficulty in one area of life does not mean that you are a failure of some kind. At any given moment, you can experience impossible circumstances while flourishing in another area of your life. We are not the collective sum of the difficulties we face. We are an intricately designed kaleidoscope, capable of recognizing hope even in complete darkness. It is what we do with that glimmer of life, the emergence of hope, that determines who we are.

Inwardly illuminated by this newfound hope, the burning question is no longer, "Can I endure this darkness?" The question then becomes, "Can I hold on to my light?"

May we all find our inner strength, hold on to our light, and love ourselves without restraint, even in the moments we are consumed by darkness.

*****

About Chantelle Pape:
As an advocate for every woman who finds herself in struggle, Chantelle Pape has spent the last several years using her own story to inspire, uplift, and provide hope to those who are still searching for answers.

Chantelle is not only an author but a singer-songwriter who creates music based on the things she has overcome in her personal life to encourage others.

You can follow her page on tiktok @o_hey_its_chay for healing support.

Chapter 9
Letting Nothing Stop Me

Damire Major

This chapter is dedicated to my beautiful girls, Yays, Nani, and Goobie.

I remember when I fell in love with American music. I was eight years old, riding around in my mom's red Ford Mustang 5.0 convertible in Oakland, California. The sun was shining and I was new to America. Although I was born in Baltimore, Maryland, I only spent eight short months there before my mom left for her seven-year term in the navy. During those years, I lived in Carolina, Puerto Rico where my grandparents raised me. When my mom was done with her service, off to the States we went.

I'd always loved music. Both my grandfathers were musically inclined. My father's father had the voice of an angel, and my mother's father also sang and played instruments, like the congas, guitar, bass, and percussions. But it wasn't until I heard R & B that I was hooked. I believe it was Keith Sweat's "Nobody" that really had me in my feelings. It conveyed every emotion (except the sexual connotation), and it wasn't until years after that I realized what I once sang as a child was not for a child.

Nonetheless, I was invested. Give me some Fugees, Sade, Jon B, Donell Jones, 112, D'Angelo, Maxwell, Musiq Soulchild, Boyz II Men, Joe, Sisqó, Toni Braxton—the list goes on and on. I always knew I could sing when I was a kid, but it was in the R & B runs where I discovered I had a voice!

It took me a long time to buckle up and really believe in myself enough to take my music seriously. Twelve years, to be exact, during which I worked as a server and a bartender in the food industry. I wrote my first project going from table to table, in between breaks, and while doing my side and opening work. I watched the Jim Carrey documentary on Netflix, and his closing argument really touched home—he looked right into the camera and said something along the lines of "Just do it. What are you waiting for?" It really resonated with me.

So, I jumped up and said, "I'm gonna do it, that's it. I'm going for it." Nothing or no one was gonna stop me! I just had to figure out how to take this leap of faith. It wasn't an instant thing—like I said, I wrote some of my best work at my day jobs. But the universe has a funny way of forcing you to make a turn in the road. I got fired over the pettiest thing during COVID. If I'm honest, who knows when I would have put in my two weeks' notice and followed my dreams. After I was let go, I had no choice but to buck up—and oh boy.

Everything felt so foreign. I was so used to the workday clock that now being free to do whatever I wanted meant I didn't know *what* I wanted to do. It seems silly, really, but I think I was having one of those *Is the grass really greener on the other side* moments. I found out that in this case, for this girl, yes, it was.

It would take time to get my finances in order and figure out an income without a regular job while also having the luxury of making and distributing my music. I was thirty years old and I had to learn the process of *how* to make music, which was a lot different from how I'd always thought. Everyone just thinks you record a song and that's it, but there's actually a lot more that goes into it.

First, you have to find a dope beat you like and then you have to find a topic and then melodies and harmonies to complement the lyrics. Then you record it in the studio, have it mixed and mastered, and, of course, you have to find an album cover (two covers if you're dropping a double project—like, if you're pre-releasing a single from your album). You have to decide whether you are going to shoot a music video for your single. Following the distribution process and marketing, you have to perform and do it all over again and again, with no guarantee of returns.

Once I put my mind to something, I go full force. And even though it took me a second to catch on, soon enough, I was throwing my own events. I invited some of my fave artists onstage with me, including Jerome Dillard, Prynce Ink, and Jtruthpa.

I threw a show called Elements back in 2020 for my birthday bash and also joined in a fundraiser for the dance team I was working with at the time. The sponsors and I raised $4,000 for the team to rent their own gym. I am a firm believer that even if it's one person at a time, changing someone's life for the better is just as important as impacting hundreds.

Just like if an audience has ten people or 10,000, I'll always give my best performance because I don't know who is in the crowd who might need my positive energy. I can be making someone's day with my music and my words; I could save someone's life and never know it, and that's the beauty in it—the unspoken things that speak for themselves.

I have so many people tell me daily that I make their shitty days better and what greater gift could I ask for than knowing that my music is reaching its purpose and that I'm on the right path?

The first year consisted of a lot of learning and discipline, applying what I was grasping along the way to my day-to-day life and figuring out what type of artist I wanted to be. When I first started to focus, I listened to Ed Sheeran's "Thinking Out Loud." After a good friend gifted me a guitar for my birthday, I learned Sheeran's song and then started composing my own music. It's really amazing to make music from scratch. I like to think of it as the equivalent of making bread at home, baking it, then eating it hot and fresh, knowing you rolled that dough with your own two hands. Nothing is more satisfying than creating something beautiful for others to enjoy.

Music has the power to heal the mind, body, and soul. It's the universal language that breaks all barriers. It can lift you up as high as the sky, or it can bring you down to the ground. Music speaks and conveys all emotions, and that's why it's one of the most powerful gifts we've been given by God.

I headed out on a journey of self-discovery. With Negra, my guitar, by my side, I took my first trip as an artist to El Paso, Texas. I went to my first recording studio and recorded my first album. After doing the weekly talent shows at the Sam Ash music store in town, I gained some confidence onstage and behind the mic. I didn't end up doing country music, but I took home with me an experience of a lifetime.

Back home in Vegas, I decided to make Spanish music. What better way to represent my roots and where I am from than to make music that speaks to my hips? I started with Spanish reggaeton with hip-hop vibes, hitting them with the Spanish hooks and the English verses. Needless to say, it quickly turned heads and ears.

All of a sudden, I was wined and dined by businesspeople and really felt like my dreams were coming true. Little did I know, though, I had a long road ahead of me.

I had just wrapped up the summer of 2021 when I began a very short and drama-filled relationship with a young lady who was, sadly, using drugs. Before long, the stork paid us an unexpected visit. Shortly after giving birth, the woman I was seeing took off—and left me with her baby! It was definitely a defining time in my life having this new baby, Goobie, to care for and attempting to find the balance between managing a singing career and mothering an infant. Worse, Goobie's mother—and her drug addiction—were in and out of our lives. One day she would be present, then she would go to the store to get milk or diapers and we wouldn't see or hear from her for weeks. So, I had to live like a single mother, while still keeping space for her to potentially come back—and bring whatever drama with her. Luckily, Goobie's gam-gam has been in her life since day one so I had someone I could rely on, aside from my own family.

We sacrifice parts of ourselves and our lives for the people we love, and not once did I ever second-guess my love for Goobie, even though her birth interrupted my career—which was just starting to take shape. I was a bit stagnant for the first year with Goobie because she was so little and I was a single parent. If it weren't for my sisters, I don't know how I would have done it. I missed events and a lot of networking opportunities, but never once did I regret my decision to keep her.

Despite driving long hours to drop my daughter off with her grandmother and my sisters, I was still able to spend a lot of late nights in the studio. More zombie than a person, I made it work. I also learned that good parents don't make excuses—we figure out a way to make it work, and that's what I did.

Finally, on October 21, 2021—my birthday—I released my first official twelve-song album, *Oye Mala,* and I was well on my way to elevating myself as an artist. But I couldn't make the time to keep up the momentum, because I needed to take care of Goobie. While many of my peers advised me not to keep the baby since it probably wasn't the best career choice, when I look back on it now, one thing I know about parenthood is you never regret the sacrifices you make for your child's well-being. Just because I didn't birth my daughter doesn't mean I felt any less of a parent. I would be lying if I said that it wasn't a huge challenge, but I've always been very determined, and I go for and achieve whatever I put my mind to.

As I was adjusting to motherhood, I also had to spend months living out of hospitals watching my little sister fight for her life. Her battle with lupus was terrifying, and it was ripping away chance at living a normal life.

Shortly after my sister was released from the hospital, I brought my grandfather from Puerto Rico to care for him, since he had recently been diagnosed with dementia. There was a lot on my plate, but one thing I have learned is God will never walk you to something he can't walk you through, so with a lot of planning, time management and dedication I was able to juggle all these responsibilities. At times, I felt as if everything I did was for nothing since I didn't see results right away, but I'd simply remind myself that patience is a virtue and all good things take time and hard work. I also knew that everything I was going through would make me stronger and build the character for the person I would become. After a while until the storm settled and things moved smoother.

Almost three years later, I was lucky enough to have entangled myself with a lady friend who I'd known for a decade. Thanks to God and all His mysterious planning, Goobie and I found ourselves a mommy in Carmen. It was a perfect fit. The baby bonded with her new mommy, and this momma's heart was finally complete.

They do say "Home is where the heart is," and only God seemed to know His plans for us. But once His secret was revealed, it was time for me to get back on the Damire Major horse. It was like a great big welcome home, returning to the scene and the local community that I dearly love. My daughter was almost three, so she spent many days at dance practices and band rehearsals and running around music video sets. Thankfully, everyone loved her energy, she was definitely a bright light in this dark world.

In returning to music, I didn't skip a beat. It felt like everyone was happy to have me back, and I started releasing music again. Good thing about me is I love collab'ing with other amazing artists. During the time off with the baby, my music was still being heard. The features I'd done were released by the main artist on the track, so while my face wasn't seen and another voice was singing my songs, people were still bumping to Damire Major.

I went through a lot—uncertainty, doubt, depression. Even though it was tough, it taught me so much about myself. I learned that if I can do something once, I can do it again. More and more scouts took notice of me, more companies got in touch about sponsorships and collaborations, and more studios wanted me to record at their establishments. Restaurants, clothing companies—you name it—it felt like things were becoming more accessible, and it was great to know that the hard work was paying off.

Consistency is key to building a future, and I felt like I was taking all the right steps. I soon opened for R & B sensation Tootsie, and then Prynce Ink invited me to perform our song "Selfish" during his set when he had the chance to open for Tootsie at Ikon Presents. Later, I got the incredible opportunity to perform at Planet Perreo for Altura Presents (if you're Latino in Vegas, no explanation needed), thanks to Yoel el Nene. I also had the honor of opening for Immortal Technique at the NY Cannabis Festival, where I met and connected with the legendary Redman, who was hosting.

I then had the kickass opportunity to open for The Future Kingz during a night filled with incredible energy. After that, I accomplished something that might seem small to some but was huge for me—I had the pleasure of opening for Las Vegas' very own Dizzy Wright. Now, if you're not from the West Coast, you might not know who Dizzy is, but he's arguably the most successful mainstream artist Nevada has seen in the last decade. That show was a beautiful metaphor for my career—it felt like a turning point.

It felt like the baton was being passed to me, and the feeling was euphoric. The band absolutely crushed it, and I had the honor of Xiara2x as the backup vocalist. She led us in a beautiful prayer to open the set, and God was present—alive. Everyone in the room could feel His love through my music, and the adrenaline running through me was like nothing I'd ever experienced before. Every person had their phone out, every fan was fully invested in my craft. The praise I received afterward was beautiful, and in that moment, something was finally solidified: I, Damire Major, was next up.

Despite all the tribulations, self-doubt, and roadblocks, I made it through to the light at the end of the tunnel. Now, more than ever, the grind begins. I've got one foot inside the door, and I'm determined to do everything in my power to get the other in too—working hard, being good to people, paying it forward, and accepting my blessings with grace. I have big plans, not just for myself but for those around me and the world. Even if I'm changing one life at a time, I'm still making a positive impact. I truly believe that's what this industry needs again—role models, artists like Bob Marley, who stood for something and didn't stop until the world remembered that love is what helps us heal and prevail.

I think more than the man himself, it's the message that resonates with our reality—the understanding that we're all in this together. Sometimes, the bigger picture is more important than our own selfish beliefs. Some of us are lucky enough never to hear the sound of a bomb or worry about having running water to drink or shower with, or food to eat, while millions are starving around the world.

Where we go wrong is in praising material things. Yes, they make life more comfortable, but it's the little things that truly make it go round—like giving someone a smile as you pass by or helping someone in need. That's why people say it's the thought that counts—the gesture means more than the gift itself. If we could all see that the important thing is waking up every day, being able to tell the ones we love how we feel and being true and loyal to those who respect us in return, we'd see a different world.

Some believe that one person can't make a difference, but it's never that easy. Nothing changes overnight. However, if my music can be the tool that gives me the platform to do what I'm meant to do, then I want to help plant the seeds. It's your job to help me water and nourish them, so they grow into a beautiful plant called love.

I make music for myself, but I know it's bigger than me, and it's bigger than you. The message it leaves is one of perseverance and strength—overcoming obstacles and pain on the road to finding the peace we all desire. Leaving hate behind so love can conquer in our hearts. My promise to the world is to take accountability by helping others feel the empathy I feel for people. The only thing that can bring us together is letting go of everything that's been keeping us apart.

Whoever is reading my story—thank you from the bottom of my heart for supporting my journey. I hope to meet you one day and exchange a smile as we pass by. As Tigger always said, TTFN ("Ta-ta for now!").

*****

About Damire Major:

Brought from Puerto Rico to the state of California at the young age of eight, Damire Major faced a major culture shock. Yet, in moving from the island to the mainland, she learned how to adapt to her surroundings and to speak English. Today, she is a successful entertainment entrepreneur in Las Vegas Nevada.

Chapter 10

One Chapter

H. Kress

Everything in its time.

It was always the most difficult question.

"Why didn't you say anything about the abuse?" the detective asked coldly.

All at once, several thoughts tumbled through her already exhausted mind. Fragmented, the thoughts collided with the constant loop of overwhelm.

I didn't want this to define me.
It already does define you.
How did it come to this?
What's wrong with me—am I crazy?
Why do they always ask that?
I am here now.
You did something wrong.
You won't be believed.
I did tell someone.
You deserved it.
You let it happen.
Because it's suffocating.
It's awful.
I don't want to go there … again.
Hide.
He will always find a way to control you.
You aren't worth it.
You are weak.
Keep fighting.
You will never be free of this.
Why me?
Why us?
Why did I choose to be with him?
What do they want to hear?
Think about your girls. Protect them.

It hurts.
I'm so tired.
You're alone.

Sluggishly, one thought surfaces over the others that are rooted in the noise of self doubt. "If they are asking you that, they already don't believe you. They can't be trusted."

Truth.

She sorted through the noise in her head, trying to find a response as the question echoed, *"Why didn't you say anything about the abuse?"*

More fragments from the past crept in like she was used to. Always on edge, waiting for it to take over. A glance, a statement, a smell, a change in the lighting—sometimes just suddenly for no obvious reason at all—then it hits, she's in it. In the abuse, a lost sense of self.

She remembered the morning after he came to her home during their separation. She had threatened to leave him if he didn't take the deployment. When he did, in the stillness between, she filed for a divorce. The moment he left the house, it became her refuge. They had agreed to discuss the divorce papers while he was in the States on leave. Before he crossed what was once his and her threshold, she firmly reminded him, "Sex is off the table." Looking up with a crooked smile, he nodded.

The night is no blur, and the circumstances are revolting. The girls are sleeping peacefully in their beds. In the stillness. In the protection of their innocence.

As the sun peered in, she lay there, waiting for her daughters to jump into bed with her, like they had done each morning for years. One of her favorite parts of the day. It brought renewal, connection, and excitement for the day's waiting adventures. Now, robbed of that joy and frozen with fear, she contemplated, would they know? Would they feel it? Would they sense that their mother has been violated? Would they feel that something is different? That something is not whole?

She paused at the thought, and wondered why is this so familiar?

Deep in her knowing, a faint whisper told her, "He has been taking pieces of you from the moment he met you."

Truth.

Then relief.

(*Relief?*)

Yes, relief. Today would be no different. You've got this. Your Mormon upbringing prepared you for this. Rooted in blind faith, surrounded by misogyny, and no stranger to suffering. A system carefully designed to push one's strength to live outside of oneself. This is no different. Bury it. They won't know. She made a promise to herself, sealed in the quietest part of her knowing—they will *never* know.

Again, relief.

Relief was better than suppression. A welcome distraction from the confusion of her reality. She felt completely grounded in her ability to hide it. She waited for the shame and guilt to come, but it didn't. She waited for the pain to settle in, but it didn't come either. In that moment, she took refuge in the silent corner of her soul as she cemented her commitment to hide the ugly from her daughters so they would never feel the pain of betrayal. So they would never question who they came from. It provided some respite as she grasped to feel her body, a false sense of control. She had something to manage—the responsibility of doing whatever it would take to protect them from this evil.

Their little laughter grew closer. So pure. Carefree.

He gloated, "You know you were amazing last night, right? That was the best night of my life. You didn't fight me."

Still hazy, with her head pounding (which she now recognizes as a hangover), she thought to herself, she couldn't fight him? Amazing? Amazing for who? For him? The best night of his life? Why was this familiar? Did this really happen? What was wrong with him? What was wrong with her? That it was … that it was …

Timidly, she replied, "I—uh—you—uh—that was the worst night of my life?" He rolled over and stole a kiss as if it were just another morning.

The four girls jumped into bed, crawled straight to their mother for morning hugs and connection. A heaping pile of comfort.

She vowed to herself that he had invaded her home for the last time.

*****

Now, she looks at the male detective, his hand on his chin, emotionless. She wants to believe he can help. She has already lost her composure several times. Though she prepared as best she could, knowing she must answer each question from a place of strength, her truth was silenced from the moment she arrived. There isn't a way to completely explain the ever-morphing complex and layered world of psychological, sexual, and emotional abuse.

Fighting the tears, she looks at the stout female officer who keenly sneaks a sideways glance back at her male counterpart. Though she isn't sure if the female officer is there to support her or if it's protocol, she is sure that crying only weakens her testimony. She was once proficient in her ability to control her expressions, move through her emotions, and choose when they were released. However, in recent years, trapped in the legal system and with the repetitive strain of trauma, there is no longer a mechanism to hold back tears. She clings to the deep truth that just because she is emotive does not mean she is not creditable. Truth is truth, regardless of the emotion surrounding it. She knows she is the only one in the room that believes that.

 She's alone.

*****

They told her in the introduction phone call that she would be supported by the presence of a female officer. That offering came directly after the detective shared that he was glad to have finally been in contact with her because he had been trying for so long to connect. In that initial call, he shared that after leaving several messages and making multiple attempts to contact her, this was his last effort to do so. He was engaging and expressed interest in helping her, as if eager to aid in her pursuit of justice. She outlined that she only wanted a sense of safety for her and her daughters, and he swiftly agreed. Safety has always been the only thing she has hunted for.

 As he continued to speak to her on the phone, she took it all in hopefully, while also quietly wondering what she had done wrong as to not have heard from him sooner nor received a single message. She secretly blamed herself for being so flighty and so unorganized that she couldn't even keep track of important messages, despite the records showing no incoming calls from the officer.

*****

As she sits face-to-face with him now, she reflects on the first time she provided a statement to law enforcement, nearly three years prior, when she felt hopeful and powerful. Then, while vulnerably sharing her lived experience, naive, she did not recognize the jaded look of apathy on the officer's face.

Now, sitting across from the fifth officer to take her statement, she keeps her head low but glances up at him, wondering what she must have done wrong because he has changed his demeanor. He is no longer supportive. His eagerness reflects disdain. Time has made her all too familiar with insensitivity, or at best, judgment. She knows it well. Still, she wonders about what conclusions he has already made about her. Perhaps it is because he does not believe her, or because he knows there is nothing he can really do about it, or, like many she has encountered, he will always protect his own. In any case, another toxic blow from the system that claims to protect one from abuse.

*****

Why didn't you say anything about the abuse?

Why didn't she say anything when they were dating, and the abuser guilted her into sexual acts that were far beyond her named comfort level? Why didn't she say anything when he shamed her, convincing her she was naive to the ways of the world and could never survive without his safe and guiding wisdom? Why didn't she stand up for herself after he repeatedly marked her innocence as childish, and her boundaries as rigid?

She grasps for it. Searching, she finds it; principle is power, innocence has dignity, and boundaries are born from being deeply self-aware.

Truth.

Why didn't you say anything about the abuse?

Why didn't she say anything on their wedding day when he dismissed her on the altar as she desperately looked through his eyes, wishing this would be the moment he changed? Or during the weeks and days leading up to it that were filled with invasion of her privacy and claim on her body? When she had tried to tell him that she was playing a role to soothe his desires and threatened to leave him? Or when he reminded her that she must stay with him because of how intimate they had been together and then sealed the shame with a warning about how unhappy it would make everyone who had supported their union with love and generosity? Why not leave when he repeatedly wrapped his arms around her and reminded her how grateful she should be that he knew how to protect her from herself?

Increasingly more difficult to find it in the overwhelm of the moment, weighted by memories, she frantically chases it. Scarcely present, it floats up just below the surface. She listens; transparency is honesty to one's self and authenticity is honesty to one another.

Truth.

Why didn't you say anything about the abuse?

Why didn't she say anything when he invaded her creativity, the one thing that individuated her from it all? Why not just leave when he began prostituting her success so he could play the part of the supportive—managing—husband. Or when he inserted himself as the source of her genius? When he was always standing in the wings ready to twist information and keep her in her place—by his side. Why not say something when he demanded she monetize her gifts to support him not working? Why didn't she say anything when she knew the constant control and manipulation was poisoning pure inspiration?

Once the richest source of her knowing, her ideas became a reminder that she may never have the space to create again.

Unwilling to let go of her vision, she clings to it. She blinks slowly. The heart of creativity pulses in the stillness between.

Truth.

Why didn't you say anything about the abuse?

Why didn't she say anything as the children came? When she watched him grow jealous with rage and desperate for her undivided attention? At the same time that she was becoming, he was losing his grasp on her. Motherhood became her compass, rooted in the strength of thousands of women before her. It was motherhood that woke her spirit. It was motherhood that unlocked her knowledge. Motherhood introduced unconditional love.

He resorted to the aid of substances to undermine her wisdom, dull her spirit, and abduct her changing body. She discovered that if she could take it, he would then have the room he needed to respond to their daughters with a morsel of humanity. It was the same shred of humanity that she had inflated when she met him in order to justify her choice to stay with him. Why not speak out when she began to realize that her beautiful daughters would see the truth—because she proudly raised them to see people unconditionally and for who they deeply are?

This is when her silence became their survival.

*****

She considers telling the detectives that before she became a mother, she didn't understand abuse. She wants to say that once she became a mother, she recognized it but didn't want her daughters to feel its rancor. She is desperate to tell them that when he first started abusing her daughters, she knew it was wrong, but she was still too wounded and too new to its clarity to fully stand up against it all from a position of power.

It becomes too hard for her to find her truth; she sinks into codependency. Codependent with the abuse because at least this momentarily soothes the pain that comes with the shame of it all.

Longing to find it, too faint to distinguish in the moment.
Why didn't you say anything about the abuse?
Why didn't she say anything when she filed for divorce? When it took every bit of courage she had to leave him? When, for the first time, she thought she was in control? When she knew she couldn't embarrass him, or he would double down and sink her? When she finally tasted real freedom and couldn't risk it all falling apart around her? When she fooled herself into believing she would be free and he would behave.

She did not foresee that he would prey on the girls. She knew in time he would retaliate to hurt her because hurt people hurt people; but it never occurred to her that he would use her daughters to do it. Though his time spent with them was minimal, it was destructive. She knew she was legally helpless as her daughters desperately tried to make sense of it all. Though the law shielded her from the abuser, it did not protect them, and she began to doubt her own liberation.

The interview has only just begun, and already, only fatigue remains.

Still looking at the officer, worried about every word, fighting back tears, knowing they will use anything she says to attempt to break her, she almost stutters a word.

Silenced by the overlapping everything.

Defeated, disconnect consumes her. She is expected to come forward about abuse in a way that is calculated—carefully anticipated as to soothe everyone but the abused. Don't trust them. They will react just like all the others who winced as she told them. The noise settles in; they look at you differently now. You are wounded, damaged, tainted, and forgettable. They all do it. A family member, an acquaintance, a boss, a trusted friend. Once they know, any and every other thought, idea, or word that leaves your mouth is splintered with the emotional remains of abuse. Abuse nearly defines her. She is projecting, but not completely.

Spent, bare, she clings to her dignity.

Nothing.

Why didn't you say anything about the abuse?

She had been asking herself this question from the moment she encountered the bizarre yet familiar behavior from the abuser. Feelings that are familiar are supposed to feel safe. For a moment, she caught wind of her power. They have not earned the right to hear why she didn't say anything before. They were not in the trenches with her. They are nothing to her but a cog in his machine, powered by the legal system and weighted with paperwork they won't want to fill out. This whole charade is a formality to protect him instead of shielding her. Worse, to protect themselves.

No one with power to stop him wants to hear the truth about the impact on her soul. They don't want to hear that with a dulled spirit, she is resigned to suffering. They don't want the burden of having to quantify the inhumanity. The system doesn't know how to reckon with the grotesque, intangible, and unmeasurable damage that accompanies abuse. They reduce it to the violation of the physical body—a secondary casualty of the overall devastation. A task to complete, every motion should have exposed him, but instead, it emboldened him by providing him with subject matter to keep attacking. Just another system for the abuser to control his target.

Anyone who has felt the sting of repeated abuse shares an understanding—it is not about leaving, setting boundaries, standing up, or speaking out. It is only about what will appease the abuser.

This is a debilitating reality while also being a gross and dangerous deception.

Truth.

*****

Why didn't I say anything about the abuse?

Because I am embarrassed. I am ashamed that I let it happen. I'm humiliated that I stayed with him. I was disappointed that I couldn't change it. I am sad I couldn't save our family. I am confused why I let him take me, again and again, and again, and then again. I am mortified that I allowed it to go on for so long. I am disgusted that it felt safe and familiar to me. I didn't say anything because of disgrace.

To lose one's sense of self is to lose everything.

I wanted to tell the story about how I was raped. How I was repeatedly smothered by sexual abuse. Minimized to the whims and desires of the abuser. How I was defined by his ego. How I was played, used, and taken advantage of. How he claimed stake on my success by demanding that he be the source of my creativity. How I was conditioned to hustle for my worth. How I was coerced into trusting no one. How he convinced me I would fail without the protection of the man that he was. How I was beaten down by self-doubt.

Why didn't you say anything about the abuse?

The truth.

I am simply too tired to sort it all. I don't want to admit that I am stuck in the cancer that is abuse. I am afraid I won't be believed. It's easier to keep hiding. I'm continually grappling with the urge to question myself and silence my divine knowing. I push away the people who show up to help me. I am wasted, always feeling out of place in the world around me, a world that once provided inspiration and joy. Never knowing security. Always worried that my daughters will carry the burden that they helped inspire my strength to leave. Wondering if I can ever untether from something anchored so deep in my being.

I didn't say anything because saying it makes it real. Because naming his behavior still feels like it's giving him power. Even as the time passes and his behavior is reduced to simple terms such as, gaslighting, undermining, threatening, shaming, manipulating, controlling, mean, it doesn't name the malevolence. It's not enough to affirm the agony.

In the end, it was the system that defined it so succinctly, naming it abusive use of conflict.

*****

In a matter of seconds, she had relieved countless moments of pain.

"Why didn't you say anything about the abuse?" the detective coaxed.

Out of the whirlwind of thoughts, she impulsively replied with the first thing that moved from her head to her mouth, "Because I didn't want them to know." she said.

"Who? You didn't want who to know?" he clapped back.

"My daughters. I didn't want my daughters to know," she said.

Without hesitation, the detective shot another round, "If he's the abuser you say he is, wouldn't you have wanted to protect them?"

As quickly as the words left his mouth, she immediately landed in the space between. The space where she could rest in her knowing.

She is broken and she is weary, but she's familiar with abuse of power.

She remained silent. Comforted from within. She did not need to verbally share her knowing—it is her own.

*****

I did protect them. I am still protecting them. I will always protect the space they need to live in their own strength.

Truth.

I am devoted to unconditional love; it fuels me but doesn't define me. I am grateful for the souls that have seen me beyond the abuse and have carried me in my darkest moments. It inspires me but doesn't define me. I am awake in my body that has kept breathing even after I have taken her to death's door. It motivates me but doesn't define me.

As I move toward becoming—I practice living in my strength. Moments of clarity spark as I begin to rebuild my legacy. Stronger now, discerning, I keep moving forward. I choose who gets to see me. I will be defined by the art and the innovations born from my lived experiences.

Truth.

Landing in the moment, moving through their motions, all too familiar, I wait for the next question.

24 Chapters

*****

Chapter 11

Motherhood by Fire

DeAnna Thieme

God has made me fruitful in the land of my affliction.
Genesis 41;52(b) NASB

I was never like the many women who factor motherhood into their life's plans. By age twenty, I was raising my youngest brother and caring for my mom. That experience was enough motherhood for me. To be a mother is the most incredible privilege on earth. A mother is to be a mentor, a teacher, a guard, a guide, an encourager, a regulator, a parent, and a caretaker. She will be called to soothe, shelter, love, and listen. Being a mother means we are our child's safe harbor and protector, the one who makes sense out of the world when the world is not making sense to our child. A mom must be an automatic advocate for their child and the one who raises the alarm. Motherhood will ask you to pivot and yield while requiring you to be a willing learner for the lifelong journey you are destined to embark on. I cannot be the mother my children need with the limitations of my human nature. I cannot be a mother without addressing the existing wounds that scarred my soul.

Despite fully understanding those truths, when I was finally called to be a mother, I had no idea what that would fully require.

Dreams
I began to have dreams for my firstborn's future once I felt prepared to meet him. I was excited for him to have an unmarred childhood, free of harm, full of love and adventure. I dreamed that for both boys while they stirred in my womb. Yet, when my firstborn came, it was mere months before he was referred to his initial specialist, leading to the earliest of many surgeries.

By the time my oldest was six, he had three eye surgeries under his belt, including dodging blindness from a staph infection caught by my newly trained eagle eye. It seemed for me that motherhood was a baptism-by-fire reality, not shaping into the unbothered experience other moms seemed to be having. As my oldest was recovering from surgery number four related to a new issue, another eye surgery loomed for him, but at least we had some time. Our slight reprieve was a calm, gifted to us before a life-changing storm, and my attention was soon turned to my youngest son.

Ready or Not
My youngest son had just turned four and began to have problems descending the stairs or walking down a street. His walking issues worsened quickly when he could not walk more than ten feet without falling, making even the slightest travel challenging. Some family members accused him of being slow or clumsy, assigning blame to an innocent child for something he had no control. This hurt me as a mom, and it pinpointed another duty I was called to fulfill.

It became clear I was responsible for my child's environment; an assigned watchman, responsible for who was safe to participate in it. This required being intentional, cautious, and aware, vetting everyone no matter who they were. While I applied this approach to everyday life, I learned to be extra vigilant during hardship and affliction.

No one asks for pain and suffering, and especially for those things to befall their children. Likewise, none other than the person afflicted knows what they are experiencing. It does no good to tell people we understand what they are going through when we do not. We can empathize, and we can become available as support, but we do not understand how another person feels. Words can be extraordinarily harmful, yet they quickly come out of people's mouths. A mother must be watchful of the words coming their way in times of hardship to protect herself and the little ones in her charge.

Aside from my four-year-old falling more frequently, he complained about his stomach. Tests eventually revealed the cause of the stomachache, and that was the real gut punch. Every week, this child was poked and prodded as staff did their due diligence in their quest for a diagnosis. The doctors were disciplined to keep opinions vague and reactions casual. A specialist discussed creatine kinase levels and their rising numbers in my son's bloodwork. His little body was breaking down too much protein, and his liver could not handle it, causing a "stomachache."

It turned out that the average level of creatine kinase in a child his age was in the low hundreds, up to 250. However, my son's levels were several thousand, and I knew that was terrible news.

We went from one specialist to the next, and when I say "we," I mean my two sons and myself. No matter what errand or appointment needed tackling, it was always the three of us. I'd sacrificed everything to stay home with my children—my career, vacations, new clothes, dining out, unnecessary purchases, even a cup of coffee. We lived paycheck to paycheck. We could not afford furniture or cable television and could not pay for a heater to be installed in our drafty, 100-year-old house.

After choosing to stay home, which I believe is an incredible privilege, I dared not bother anyone to help with my children. On top of that, my husband worked long hours and commuted five to six days a week, so I was used to being on my own and handling what came my way.

The Monster

By age seven, my oldest son could read and comprehend anything, including things at very advanced levels. He would read the charts and diagnoses posted on the neurology department's walls and processed that information during his little brother's exams.

The neurology department at Children's Hospital is not an easy place to be for any child. My boys and I sat among children with severe disabilities and issues, children consigned to wheelchairs or with mouths that gaped open and drooled. At the time, I did not consider the toll this would take on two young children, especially when one of them was putting the pieces together in his tiny world.

As we exited our car for another Children's Hospital visit, my oldest son gagged, as if he was going to throw up, something he did when nervous. I asked him what was wrong, and he replied, "Mama, I'm so afraid of what they are going to say is wrong with Brother." I hugged him, validated his feelings, and encouraged him with what I knew was getting me through. This situation was beyond what I could handle on my own. My heart hurt for my boys.

I did not dream of this reality for my children. I'd worked hard to protect and provide their world with everything that would bless and benefit their little souls. To know I could not shield my children from these afflictions cut deep. I felt like I'd failed them, and somehow, all their health issues were my fault.

The day arrived to receive my youngest's diagnosis, and I'd been asked not to bring my children. My husband would never take time off work for these appointments, so I knew I would have to go alone. My husband's unwillingness to be there for me was more than a disappointment—it felt like a betrayal. We were supposed to be a team, and I was supposed to have a partner. So, there I was again, handling things alone and suffering in silence, something I'd gotten used to.

The neurologist delivered the diagnosis in a sad, apologetic tone. My youngest was diagnosed with Duchenne muscular dystrophy (MD). She described the awful course of the incurable muscle-wasting disease, the shortened life span, and all the loss the diagnosis promised to deliver. Both Duchenne MD and its slower version, Becker's MD, were monstrous afflictions that stole young men after it ravaged their muscles and robbed them of most basic abilities. The prognosis for Duchenne MD was any parent's nightmare.

On the night of my son's diagnosis, while everyone slept, I went to the farthest room in our little house and released a primal cry. It seemed that every dream I had for my child, my children, was a waste of time, a fanciful indulgence meant only for other people. I then grieved for my son's future, the losses, and the lack should the prognosis deliver as promised. I was powerless. Neither mankind nor money could change his diagnosis. The pain in that moment felt unbearable, and my deep cry was not deep enough to capture it.

The diagnosis was shocking, and upon considering who I could share this news with, I remembered one friend. She was a mom who shared a challenging road with her children, a mom who was authentic, sincere, and full of a unique love few people knew. I called my good friend, a mother of three, one of whom was diagnosed with autism and the other who had Down syndrome. I knew when my heart was tender and raw, I could trust her with it.

As I shared my son's diagnosis, she listened, chose few words, and said something I will never forget: "There is a scripture I am reminded of, and it says, 'Should we accept the good things from God and not the bad?'" I knew my friend well, and there had never been a time when she had spoken in haste. She pointed me upward, toward the God who knew me best and had never failed His children. I was extended a divine invitation to look at my situation from Heaven's lens and consider there was more happening than what was at hand. Her advice was the wisdom I needed at the moment because nothing the world offered could suffice as a balm for my heart's pain.

Facing It
After, I reflected on the scripture my friend had spoken of: "'Shall we indeed accept [only] good from God and not [also] accept adversity and disaster?' In [spite of] all this, Job did not sin with [words from] his lips." (Job 2:10 AMP). What did that mean?

Once in a relationship with someone, you talk to them regularly, spend time with them, resulting in a better understanding of who they are. At that point in a relationship, you can better understand what they mean when they say things and anticipate how they will move. This is how it works in a relationship with God.

By then, I had learned (and continue to understand) what God's love is. That was a process for me. My only reference for love was that of human love, which, in my experience, was very warped. Christ's love was unconditional, unchanging, and abundant. The love of God is divine, supernatural, and from a pure and perfect holy source. Therefore, I had to understand that God's love was not human love. The pages of scripture told me of a sacrificial love, a long-suffering love, and an intentional love.

It is true, as verified in the Bible, that God *allows* things to happen, even bad things. But a person cannot appreciate what that means unless you know the living God's character. I have experienced many bad things, awful things, unjust things. Bad things happen because evil people indulge their wicked desires in our fallen, sinful world. Yet, there is hope when grappling with why heinous things happen to humans, especially when we consider how some use their "bad" experiences for the good of others.

"You intended to harm me, but God intended it for good to accomplish what is now being done, the saving of many lives." (Genesis 50:20 NIV).

This scripture references the story of Joseph, a story of incredible injustices many are certain to identify with. The passage my friend shared was from the Book of Job, and it is the end of Job's story where we can witness God's love and ultimate purpose. Because I understood God's divine love, I knew God was in our moment; He had a purpose for it, and if He had a purpose for it, I could trust Him and face it. Indeed, I would not know the purpose right away, and often, we may never know God's purpose for things. I chose to trust His character and clung to His promises to get me through the pain and the unknown. Adversity and hardship were an invitation from God to learn more of His loving character, and see our faith proven and fortified.

Trusting God took time; those times were built with every affliction, hardship, and heart cry. When the time came for my trust to be genuinely tested, I was convinced that nothing we go through is in vain.

Hospital Pain
Time passed, and so did many more hospital visits. The healthcare realm opened my eyes to people and their difficult

journeys, many who were experiencing much more challenging things than I was. Seeing another parent in pain is always difficult, and my heart became heightened to the plight of others. Despite a mother's pain, our children need us to be champions of hope and sources of reliable comfort. It seemed such a tall order for a mother already commissioned for so much.

    Years before, I took my children for an outing at a beach near our home. The beach had been bustling with cars in the lot, people walking, kites flying, and school kids visiting. Within an hour of the bustle, my oldest son said, "Look, Mom, we are all alone." I looked and saw he was right; we were all alone, and a caution rose inside. It seemed that as fast as everyone had arrived, they had also left, except for one man. I had noticed him watching us for some time but did not believe we were the target of his interest. We were in a lower part of the beach, down an embankment, cut off from the view of anyone, if anyone had been around. I watched the man rise from the bench and slowly approach us. He stopped above us and looked to his left and then to his right. I knew this man had something terrible in mind. Though he had the advantage of position and could move down on us quickly, I wanted him to know I would not make it easy for him. My eyes locked on his as I shoved my youngest one's shoes on his feet, knowing we would have to run toward him before he came to us. I wanted this man to know I would not be intimidated by his presence, and I promise there would be a fight.

    In the same way I faced this man down, we mothers must respond to hardship when it meets our children. We are called to confront the pain, look it in the eye, and tell it we will fight. This will not be easy and is something I could not do alone. While people are necessary and helpful in many ways, human help alone does not provide this power. God's grace, His presence, allowed me to face what had come our way and be everything my children needed.

Grace
God's grace is not easy to grasp and an attribute only understood through experience. Grace is a demonstration of divine power, an indwelling that equips. I am human; therefore, I am limited in every way. There are limits to my strength, my thinking power, how I respond to stress, my love for myself and others, my abilities, and so on. As someone conditioned to "be strong," or lead and care for others, it was hard to acknowledge my weaknesses or limits. Survivors do not yield or ask for help; they have learned the nuances they need to get by.

Yet, when affliction came for my children, everything changed. I had no power in my hands to help my kids. There were no resources I could find or apply. In my frailty, I saw my weakness and humbled myself. I decided to trust God for the more I did not possess. And when I did, that humility opened the door for grace to enter.

God's grace is His presence in our lives as it intersects whatever natural limitation you may have and surpasses that limitation with a supernatural capability. I had ministered and taught young mothers at non-Christian residential recovery centers for several years. I was often mistreated, made fun of, ignored, challenged, and accused, yet it never stopped me from returning. One girl despised being in my class, and even though she openly mistreated me, I loved her like the rest.

Once she graduated from the recovery program, just like the other graduates, I helped her with a job and things for her new baby. My natural love for her would have stopped long before, but God's grace allowed His love for her to surpass mine and go a supernatural distance. I'll never forget the day when she told me she loved me. That is what grace can do.

My children were hurting and afraid. Their lives were consumed with doctor visits, physical ailments, and limitations. They were living in a way I never had to live as a child and unjustly required to carry weighty medical burdens. God's presence through scripture filled my soul with strength, hope, joy, encouragement, peace, and love. Grace gave me strength when I was weary or tempted to give up on hope's promises. Grace steadied me when I felt I would fall and gave me joy while my heart was shrouded in sorrow. Grace allowed me to laugh with my children and create a world for them that was balanced and still filled with good things.

God's grace was an authentic presence and something I relied on to get through every day. When death dared to approach, my children needed me to speak life to them, and God's grace allowed me to do exactly that.

Meanwhile, my youngest was in middle school, and the PE teacher required the class to run sprints. At that point, though he had struggles, no significant losses had occurred to his body. But as he was mid-run for his PE class, his legs "stopped working," and he could not move. He said he was terrified and began to pray, a response we were accustomed to in our dark valleys. Since that day, he could no longer run or walk long distances without adverse consequences, and the reality of these losses crushed him.

What must be noted is gratitude for my youngest son's body not fulfilling the Duchenne MD prognosis. After several years of him maintaining strength and no longer experiencing the initial symptoms, they re-diagnosed him with the "milder" version of Duchenne, Becker's MD. Unfortunately, this prognosis included congestive heart failure, which required more monitoring and caution, but it was clear that the miraculous *was* taking place in his body, though it was not quite like I'd prayed.

I was unhappy with his medical team at Stanford, so I advocated for a new one. I always asked questions and asked more if we weren't given enough. The medical world is an intimidating place, and if you do not push back and inform yourself, you will only receive what another person determines is sufficient. In most cases, those results would be satisfactory, but dealing with some of my children's afflictions, I found many responses unacceptable.

As my children grew and their needs became more complicated, I returned to college to learn about genetics, our bodies, and physiology. I diligently researched, and my newfound knowledge helped me ask better questions and find better help. While that improved some things, my youngest was hurting badly, broken under the burden of his diagnosis, which he, too, had been researching. All I could do was work hard to advocate for him, listen to him, be present, and pray for him. God's grace kept me. His love kept me. His words kept me. I felt I could not take it anymore, and yet, it kept coming.

During this time, I developed health issues. I was sick and debilitated by either gastrointestinal infections or kidney stone issues. I had a surgical procedure for kidney stones, which I hoped was the end of invasive procedures. However, my GI issues persisted, and after two years of continual affliction, I was scheduled for colon surgery. However, there was no time for me to be "down" as my oldest son had an awful new condition the doctors could not figure out. Regardless of what I wanted, I underwent major surgery, and despite the rest required for what was an excruciating recovery, my sons needed help with their dire medical issues.

I continued to pray for my oldest, and one day, after five weeks of misery, this mysterious affliction the specialists could not figure out left him and never returned. He would have two surgeries after that, and I thought he was in the clear until a freak accident came his way.

Living with Heartbreak

I wanted to see my kids run and play with other children, do their chosen sports and activities, and have a carefree life. I loved watching them happy or excited and delighted in their laughter. Our day-to-day, however, did not look at all like the dreams I had for them.

As basketball did not work out with my older son's depth perception issues, I encouraged him to try football. Part of the prep for football was team weight training at the school gym. As he was lifting a bar with 175 lbs., his "spotter" dropped the bar on my son's neck. My son's world, our world, faced an entirely new tragedy.

The accident did extensive damage. Aside from spinal stenosis and a fractured back, a nerve root was crushed, which brought unbearable pain. He was in the hospital for a while, constantly poked and tested, passed from one doctor to another. Though we had insurance, all our finances were sunk into efforts to alleviate his pain. Our sweet pastor paid for cryotherapy out of his pocket in hopes the pain could be minimized—as our desperation led us to alternative methods to help ease the immense pain and alarming symptoms our son faced.

My son's life seemed to stop. Sitting hurt. Standing hurt. Walking hurt. Nothing gave him relief. No one lived with us and saw my child's physical torment. I watched my teen son suffer, and it was unbearable to behold. I cannot describe how helpless I felt, and I hid my tears well.

To see my oldest endure what he has (and continues to deal with) in the way he does can only be described as God's presence in his life. God's intentional love gave my son the grace to persevere in hope instead of succumbing to hopelessness. Jesus brought the light in the darkness and the relief when it became intolerable. He was there with us, in it, navigating our way and protecting us from everything, even ourselves. My son eventually managed to enjoy life in the way he could, and then, as things began to improve slightly, he seized life and conquered.

Though I wish I could say my children's afflictions stopped, they did not. In the last few years, my youngest received a disappointing report about his heart that shook us all. However, by God's grace, he remains hopeful and says with genuine pride, "I never lost faith in God, Mom, no matter what." He still believes and trusts God regardless of what he faces. To see him overcome the mental hit of carrying his diagnosis and thrive in his world can only be credited to the grace of this loving God.

My hope and faith have been sound, and my messages to my children are consistent. Our family was hit with other hardships woven within this time of continuous medical complication. My motherhood journey has not been easy. I've had my issues and struggles, both physically and mentally, but I accepted motherhood by fire. I was called to possess a strength beyond training and an arsenal of words fueled by conviction. None of this was within my human capacity to decisively and soundly influence a soul. My children's souls needed a supernatural shield and a divine voice; only heavenly expression could rise to the challenge.

My children only thrive because of Christ. I put my faith in Christ and believed Him for what I did not know I could ask. This was no "blind" faith, as some refer. My eyes were open to His truth from scripture. His words in those "stories" and letters revealed that He could be trusted for the miraculous, the unimaginable, and the incomprehensible. And in my world, nothing less would do. He spoke to my heart too many times through scripture, which healed my wounds and squelched my worries. When it seemed I was helpless and had nothing, Jesus became my everything.

My life and the lives of my children are advancing. They are loving, laughing, learning, and excelling at their interests, which is proof of His abilities working in and for them. The living God, Jesus Christ, is my hiding place, and He alone has made my way secure. Though I have not lived a faultless life nor have always kept the best witness, His faithfulness has endured and reminded me that through His love and long-suffering nature, I have the potential to do more and be more through Him.

Our Charge

Children are precious and counting on us to be all we can for them. Being called to motherhood is the most incredible privilege, even if many of us feel unprepared for the role. Know that nothing disqualifies you from the call, as the mission of motherhood has been gifted to you by the Creator of heaven and earth.

I was a very broken woman, enslaved by fear, shame, and regret. I was filled with self-loathing and convinced myself I was every lousy thing people spoke about me. The abuses in my life labeled and led me by their constraints. I felt worthless, unlovable, and stupid on every level. I never experienced affection or affirmation. I was not told I was beautiful or had great value and purpose. No one told me I was "wonderfully made" and had a destiny written for me before I came to be.

"For You created my innermost parts; You wove me in my mother's womb. I will give thanks to You, because I am fearfully and wonderfully made; Wonderful are Your works, And my soul knows it very well. My frame was not hidden from You When I was made in secret, And skillfully formed in the depths of the earth; Your eyes have seen my formless substance; And in Your book were written All the days that were ordained for me, When as yet there was not one of them" (Psalm 139:14-16).

I shifted into a work-mode mindset when I was expecting my eldest son. I had experienced significant trauma, most of which is unknown to family members, all of it hidden away. I knew I needed serious help to manage motherhood. So, I devoured every book, joined a mom group, and watched television shows in search of how to be a "good" mom. I thought I was prepared for motherhood, and I knew if I relied on my "push through" mindset, I could handle it. I was a survivor, the oldest sibling who navigated a dysfunctional upbringing and learned quickly how to adapt.

As victimization pursued me into early adulthood, so did my unhealthy coping responses. I had gotten used to the various harms done against me and was comfortable following their dictates. I learned to "be strong," while shame taught me to be silent. I knew the dance well, and it seemed I could handle anything and hide everything, all while keeping step and moving gracefully for the audience who watched.

But when affliction came upon my children, that was something different. There was nowhere to run, and it was not something I could hide. I was a mom now, a trustworthy caretaker of children who needed me to be more than what I was. It would not take long after affliction came when I realized that relying on myself would no longer suffice.

I could not have been anything helpful to my children had I not encountered the healing power of Christ. He found me where I was, broken, dirty, and discouraged, and spoke to me tenderly of His goodness and love. He healed me and set me on the right path, the good path I was destined to walk. He has never left my side and continues to lead me if I am willing to follow. I possess the Truth, and it rings with freedom in my soul. I am more than a conqueror through Christ. I am the crown of His creation and called to be a mom.

*****

About DeAnna Thieme:
DeAnna is an accomplished author and overcomer. She has been a dedicated advocate for women and children for more than twenty years.

Mother to two sons, DeAnna has been married for twenty-seven years and brings a wealth of personal and professional insight to her work. Her journey and dedication have empowered countless individuals, inspired change, and forged hope in communities.

24 Chapters

Chapter 12

Finding Myself

Heather Marianna

Thank God.

During my childhood, my mom wasn't around. My grandparents raised me while my mother was off doing ... whatever. She was in and out of my life, and on the few occasions I saw her, she always made a point to tell me I was a mistake. Although I was fortunate to be raised by my wonderful grandparents, I often found myself in solitude, detached from other children.

My upbringing emphasized the importance of studying and learning, a path I embraced wholeheartedly, driven by the desire to avoid repeating the mistakes of my uneducated and sloppy mother. Little did I realize then that this relentless pursuit of perfection and self-reliance would only deepen the underlying wounds stemming from my unresolved childhood traumas.

As my life unfolded, I began to recognize the profound impact of my past experiences on my present being. The independence I had cultivated, while a source of pride, had also become a shield, protecting me from facing the abandonment issues that had plagued me. In my thirties, I embarked on a transformative journey of self-discovery, learning to make choices that would lead to healing, growth, and a fundamental shift on my perspective on life.

I had a deep desire to attend college, and my academic achievements certainly warranted it. However, at that juncture in my life, I faced a significant obstacle—I needed my mother's social security number, which she was unwilling to provide. Determined to pursue my education, I decided to take matters into my own hands. During one of my visits with my mother, I gained unauthorized access to her belongings, skillfully manipulating the lock on the small safe hidden beneath her bed. I retrieved the necessary information and went on to complete my college applications. Eventually, I secured a spot at the University of Indianapolis. I was brimming with pride, having accomplished this feat entirely on my own, no parental support or encouragement.

During my junior year, I had an unexpected opportunity come my way—an invitation from a modeling agency to work with them. At this turning point in my life, I embarked on a journey that eventually led me to establish my own million-dollar company, specializing in booking promotional models. With newfound success came all the trappings: a lavish office, lively nights at clubs, a gleaming Benz in the driveway, and even a string of attractive boyfriends. It seemed as though I had it all.

Yet, looking back on those years of my early twenties, I realize that there was a crucial aspect of my life that was sorely lacking—self-respect. I didn't truly care about the company I kept or the reasons behind my constant need for companionship. I just craved social interaction, wanting to be surrounded by people twenty-four seven. Now, with the wisdom of hindsight and better life choices, I understand that this behavior grew from unresolved childhood trauma related to abandonment.

As I entered my late twenties, I grew weary of the modeling world and the poor choices that often accompanied it. The days when I enjoyed jetting off to the Playboy Mansion for wild, alcohol-fueled parties in revealing attire felt like a distant memory. Eventually, I made the momentous decision to close down my modeling agency, ending that chapter of my life. While the circumstances surrounding the agency's closure didn't align with my initial aspirations, I wholeheartedly believed it was the right move for me at that point in my journey.

The next two years were tumultuous. I didn't really have a plan after closing the agency, so I was basically stagnant. I didn't work and I gained weight. Still, I was fortunate to have the unwavering support of my true friends—those cherished individuals to whom I still hold dear to this day. Together, we weathered the storm, and during those trying times, I sat in solitude and delved deep into my innermost desires.

A Leap of Faith
It was during this period that an unexpected call came my way, courtesy of a headhunter. Deciding to take a leap of faith, I went for the interview and was immediately offered the job at a company specializing in food and beverage profitability. Around the same time, I started dating someone who lived outside Indiana. Everything seemed to be falling into place, or so I thought.

About nine months into my new job (while still managing the boutique), I made the life-altering decision to relocate to Las Vegas, also known as Sin City—a city synonymous with wealth and endless opportunities. My goal was to pursue a higher position within the company I was working for. With the casino industry being a substantial percentage of our clientele, the allure of Las Vegas called to me.

However, this significant step didn't come without its fair share of challenges, particularly in my personal life. My partner was less than thrilled about my Sin City move. Who could blame him? In a desperate bid to make me stay, he offered everything from marriage to the prospect of a carefree life as a housewife, complete with endless shopping sprees—a dream come true for many, but that wasn't the path I wanted to follow. While we remain great friends today, I knew that I didn't need anyone to define my success. At the age of thirty-two, I was resolute in my choice to move, and no one could stand in my way.

I kept my decision a closely guarded secret until the day my friends came over and stumbled upon packing boxes stacked throughout my home. Within two weeks, I was ready to embark on my new adventure to Vegas. That's when the intrusive thoughts and nagging doubts began: What if it didn't work out? What if I wasn't good enough? These thoughts consumed my mind day and night, yet I took the chance, a leap of faith that I'll forever be grateful for.

Starting Over
Arriving in Las Vegas with two dogs—Baron, who remains my loyal companion to this day, and his beloved brother Coco, who has since crossed the rainbow bridge—was a journey unlike any I had undertaken before, especially on my own. With only six suitcases, I embarked on this foray into the unknown. Landing in a city renowned for its extravagance, excess, and dazzling lights, I was carving out a new stage in my life.

I initially settled in a high-end hotel, an oasis amid the chaos of the Las Vegas Strip. Those months felt like a chapter out of a novel—a modern-day *Eloise at the Plaza*. It was a time of both solitude and introspection as I contemplated the path I was forging.

Before long, I found myself calling a high-rise on the Strip my home. My neighbor happened to be a renowned artist with a gallery, and I soon became immersed in the vibrant art scene that the city had to offer. My career required frequent travel, and I became well-acquainted with the ins and outs of Vegas, from its glitzy entertainment to its hidden gems.

Around a year into my new job, I was at a crossroads once more. The demands of my career, coupled with a long-distance relationship that tethered me to two worlds, began taking their toll. The constant travel, both domestically and internationally, lost its luster. I juggled an increasingly draining job with a relationship that was growing more challenging to maintain.

One evening in 2012, as I reclined in the bathtub and gazed out the window, I couldn't help but ponder the path I was on. It had been a year and a half since my arrival in Las Vegas, and aside from brief interactions with sales associates at high-end boutiques, I had minimal social exchanges. The only thing filling this void was my unhealthy love for shopping, as evidenced by yet another extravagant $20,000 shopping spree in my transaction history.

As I sat there, surrounded by luxury but feeling a sense of emptiness, I asked myself a profound question: Is this truly my life? Is it fulfilling me in the way I had hoped? The flashing lights of the Strip suddenly felt like a stark contrast to the deeper contemplation I found myself sinking into.

This moment of reflection set the stage for a transformation in my life, one that led me down the next unexpected path.

Making That "Beauty Stuff"
It was during this period that a pivot took shape, one that would forever alter my life's trajectory. The morning after my contemplative bath, I resigned from my job. To my delight, my significant other wholeheartedly supported my decision. As we jetted off to Greece for a month-long getaway, it felt as though three distinct worlds were converging—the past, the present, and the uncertain future.

While we explored the enchanting landscapes of Greece, a whirlwind of changes was unfolding back home. I was preparing for a major shift, transitioning from the city's vibrant chaos to a tranquil haven by Lake Mead, nestled in the serene town of Boulder City. I needed to distance myself from the constant bustle of Las Vegas, seeking solitude to gather my sanity, my thoughts, and chart a new course.

My excitement was palpable. However, looming in the background was the daunting realization that, in just four weeks' time, I would be moving into a new home without a clear plan for my professional life. This uncertainty weighed on me, but I was resolute: I would not depend on anyone else to shape my destiny—a decision driven by the specter of my abandonment issues that had haunted me throughout my life.

I reached out to a friend I had known since childhood. She had witnessed my journey from my earliest days and had a unique perspective on my abilities. I asked her for guidance. She told me, "Make that beauty stuff." At first, her words seemed cryptic, but then it clicked.

YouTube was hitting its stride and taking the world by storm. My mind raced with possibilities. The idea of sharing beauty tips and skincare secrets through video tutorials bloomed. This revelation marked my entrance into the world of beauty and skincare.

I wanted to become the next beauty star. At that time, I had no idea how to achieve this lofty aspiration, let alone how to create a website, but one thing was crystal clear: I was going for it with unrelenting determination. My days stretched into nights, and I poured every ounce of my energy into this endeavor, often working up to fifteen hours a day.

I vividly remember the birth of my first website, though, looking back, I can't help but cringe at its amateurish design. I was so driven to share my passion for beauty and skincare that I hired a production company to handle the video aspect of my content. Those early videos, which you can still find on my channel, serve as a testament to my humble beginnings. I had no time to learn the intricacies of video editing; my focus was on becoming the most famous beauty guru, and I wouldn't be deterred.

It was during this phase that a unique phenomenon engulfed me—a passion unlike anything I had ever felt in any of my previous business ventures. This time, it wasn't about monetary gain; it was a burning desire to share my knowledge and love for beauty with the world. Remarkably, I received commissions from my previous job, providing me with a financial cushion that allowed me to fully immerse myself in this passion project.

In the realm of my professional journey, my tiny little YouTube channel from 2012 has blossomed into a thriving global beauty brand. Through perseverance and dedication, I have cultivated spin-off companies that empower women and men to build their skincare empires. In 2023, I took a bold step by taking a beauty brand public, ultimately exiting with 15,000,000 shares to begin a new venture where I retain full control.

Shifting the paradigm of my business, I initiated my own manufacturing, bidding farewell to the middleman and allowing myself to manufacture for over a thousand brands. I've graced the screens of countless television and news shows, achieving milestones that exceeded my initial goal of appearing as a beauty guru on the *Today Show*. Today, I find myself in the company of celebrities I once journaled about, rubbing elbows with those who once were distant. My life has transformed into the manifestation of my deepest desires, and as I stand here, I am reminded that this journey is only just beginning.

Manifesting Destiny

As I reflect upon the simple decisions I made in 2012, twelve years from where I sit now, I am struck by the significant transformations that have taken place. I can't help but marvel at the incredible journey that lay ahead, a life I could never have predicted. The turning point came when I delved deep into the practice of manifesting my dreams. At the age of thirty-four, I began journaling, pouring my heart and soul into documenting all the aspirations and goals I longed to achieve.

I wrote with conviction, "I want to be on a Bravo show." Check. Manifestation accomplished. "I want celebrities to use my products and creations." Check. I manifested that too. It was nothing short of miraculous—everything I had journaled and visualized was coming to fruition. Within the first year of this intensive practice and through the journey I am still on, I witnessed, and still do witness, real traction and a series of dreams turning into reality. The power of manifestation unveiled itself in my life in ways I had never imagined possible.

I want to encourage every reader to believe in themselves, to journal their thoughts, and to document their aspirations, then take tangible steps toward achieving those goals. As I sit here writing this, two green prosperity candles burn beside me, while a yellow candle for clarity illuminates my workspace. I needed that clarity to share my story, as I've never delved into my narrative at this depth before. Writing this feels liberating, and I hope it inspires you to pursue your own journey of self-discovery and manifestation.

The little girl within me who once carried the weight of past abandonment has found solace and healing through the supportive and nurturing relationship I now cherish, the one with myself. This connection helped me shed the remnants of insecurity and allowed me to fully embrace my worth and capabilities. I've learned the invaluable lesson that I deserve nothing less than the best life has to offer.

My evolution extends beyond this newfound emotional strength. While I have always possessed a fiercely independent spirit, I've also discovered the importance of vulnerability and seeking assistance when needed. Just as I am capable of conquering challenges on my own, I've come to realize that there's strength in embracing my softer side and reaching out for help when necessary. This lesson is not exclusive to me but applies to all of you who are reading these words.

Navigating the intricate web of relationships, I've encountered my fair share of dating mishaps along the way. However, I no longer hold myself responsible for these missteps. Instead, I view them as valuable lessons, orchestrated by the universe to teach me precisely what I needed to learn. It's essential to remember that we operate on the universe's timeline, not our own, and each experience contributes to our growth.

I never envisioned that my life would lead me to such unexpected places. From a tender age, I faced the harsh reality of abandonment, and little did I realize that these early experiences would shape the course of my life. Life, as I've come to understand, is a journey filled with countless choices, some of which may lead us astray. Yet, it's important not to harshly judge ourselves for these missteps, as they serve as opportunities for learning and personal growth. In every choice, no matter how challenging, there exists a lesson that, although often unwelcome at the time, is profoundly necessary.

At times, we may attempt to assign blame to others—our parents, our circumstances, or the absence of parental guidance. However, my story is one of genuine resilience, a journey marked by the transformation brought about by making positive life choices. Whether it's consistently going to the gym or managing my diet and maintaining my sleep hygiene, everything I do is focused on nurturing and caring for myself. But to make these adjustments, you have to really want to change and heal. You have to want it and take the steps to do it—and that starts with realizing you are worth it.

The most crucial lesson in life is recognizing that the relationship you cultivate with yourself is paramount. It serves as the foundation upon which all other relationships and life experiences are built. When I was that scared little abandoned girl, I settled for anything. At forty-five, I am just getting started.

*****

About Heather Marianna:
Heather Marianna, CEO of Heather Marianna LLC, is the driving force behind Beauty Kitchen, a luxury skincare brand renowned for its natural, cruelty-free products. With her start as a YouTube beauty expert, Heather launched Beauty Brand Coaching, offering personalized mentorship on brand development, media exposure, and white-label products.

Featured in Forbes, E! News, and over 100 TV segments, Heather also curates high-profile events, such as her Harvest and Enchant Celebrity Gifting Lounge during the Primetime Emmys and Oscars week, elevating the gifting experience for media, celebrities, and VIPs and offering major exposure for brands and companies.

- https://deluxeversionmagazine.com/heather-marianna-connects-brands-to-the-stars/
- https://indieentertainmentmedia.com/heather-marianna-makes-her-mark-in-the-bespoke-event-space-with-ignite-luxury-gifting-

- lounge/?fbclid=IwAR2SX4tvjI3sOZ83WwqnkL_6YK EFXUcyiSxMVuEtCK68SKhuJWcW89RV_ws
- https://finance.yahoo.com/news/blair-kaplan-communications-announces-innovative-070000634.html
- https://thelosangelesentrepreneur.com/2024/04/17/beauty-brand-coaching-elevating-brands-with-celebrity-collaborations-and-luxury-events-emmys-2024-on-the-horizon/

CEO, Beauty Kitchen - Good vibes and great skin, BeautyKitchen.Net
Cell 310.600.8280 txt only
Office 702.534.7550
Warehouse / Factories 702.778.9338

Join my mailing list here, to stay in touch: http://eepurl.com/dK5-Tw
Join my weekly beauty brand coaching motivational newsletter here: http://www.beautybrandcoaching.com/newsletter-sign-up
Follow me on social media:
Ig HeatherMarianna
   BeautyKitchenJunkie
   BeautyBrandCoaching
   AskHeatherMariannaBlog
Press links: https://beautykitchen.net/press/
View my news segments, interviews, and more:
https://www.youtube.com/user/HeatherMarianna
https://www.beautybrandcoaching.com/tv-appearances

Heather Marianna

24 Chapters

Chapter 13

A Dance with a Hellion

JoJo Rimmer

Bertha Ward (sunrise, 9-5-1954 to sunset, 10-14-2024). My Sister Queen, battle fought and won.

24 Chapters

I am the Hellion I set out to be, a fierce yet gentle reminder of the Warrior Queen I was born to be on October 3, 1962. Armor on, spirit intact, carrying not one single iota of shame, guilt, or regret. It is my hope that after you read this, you will realize that nothing is as it seems. Nothing is nor ever has been.

Not even in my wildest dreams did I imagine it possible to experience such mentally devastating, emotionally distressing, disrespectful, self-esteem-crushing, spirit-killing pain ... Yet I did. And yes, some of it even by my own hands. The exact same hands that write to you now, with the benefit of hindsight, will illustrate how the hell this magnificent journey got started.

I am a healed victim of domestic violence, a walking, talking former addict, hooked not just on drugs, but also on the accompanying self-destructive, toxic behaviors you find in these environments. I am pieced together by experiences endured while on the wrong paths to better designed ones with deeper purpose. Each path was exactly as I paved it, and I guarded each of them fiercely, as though my life depended on it.

It is vital that you keep an open mind to my words. At sixty-one, I am at the age where I spare no truths. My goal is to reach your very core. After all, it was I who walked the path and endured the pain you will never have to experience in your life journey, unless you take it purely by choice.

As you read my story, I ask that you take a walk into your own choices, process them meticulously, and choose whether the dance with the hellion within you is worth it. It's always BEEN your choice. It will never NOT be your choice.

With that said, you also must remember that no one deserves to inflict pain on you in any manner, shape, or form. I don't condone them doing so and definitely would not recommend it as a lifestyle choice. With all that out of the way, shall we begin?

Where'd She Go?
One minute I was playing with dolls, getting into mischief with friends, making mud pies, swimming in the front yard ditch on rainy days, and exploring my grandparents' farmland in Bellville, Texas. The next minute, it was my twelfth birthday and the woman who gave birth to me just up and disappeared without so much as a goodbye.

I'd had no idea that death was a part of living. My mother's death showed up, took a seat in my head, and made me dance uncontrollably.

No one explained the part about how her death would simultaneously affect my heart, my life choices, my responses to others, and so on. Since no one explained to me how to process death, I met it where it left me mentally and emotionally on any given day, night, or hour.

I can't remember how long it took me to get angry—or whether I actually did. I can't remember how long it took me to accept it, because with death, that choice is made for you. I can't remember how long it took me to even consider or embrace my siblings' responses to our loss or the various memories she left each of us. What I do remember is being born to a mother who birthed kings and queens, the fifth of seven children.

Between the ages of twelve and the peak of adulthood, I tore up as much stuff as I could. I would say this was my first unintentionally selfish act, because this caused a lot of problems for my father, whose needs weren't taken into consideration. Had I considered his needs, I might have thought about what it was like for him losing the love of his life. Or maybe I would have thought about how he needed his kids to stay in school and become better human beings. The last thing this twelve-year-old was thinking about at the time was anyone else or their feelings, including my father or siblings. Death does that.

Death is a sneaky little bastard, chock-full of control over your entire being—for good, bad, and everything in between. It commands respect and leaves us pondering the where, when, how, and whys surrounding it all. I don't know exactly where my mother went after her brief life ended, but I'm very much aware of where she is now for me: in my head, our hearts aligned and in respect of her final destination.

One thing I'm sure of is that she would not have chosen to leave us. She didn't give birth to us to leave us all in limbo. I firmly believe that she was never given the opportunity to see the lives of her husband, children, family, and friends play out to their fullest. I also firmly believe that she, her husband, children, friends, family, and the world were robbed of her light.

Beneath the Surface
In the beginning of this chapter, I said that nothing is ever as it seems. At first glance, my childhood seemed idyllic, up until my mother's death. Likewise, for the past twenty-three years I've enjoyed utter bliss. But my early years were, let's say ... less than stellar. I know now that this is how they were supposed to be, because I didn't yet understand choice or self-respect.

I was molested and raped frequently by an older sibling beginning at about age five, up until my mother passed away. It took me years to come to grips with this as an adult. Getting verification of the abuse from family was like pulling teeth, coming long after their "mass denial" of anything that would tarnish the sterling reputation of the older sibling, now deceased, or our family name. Later, I discovered I wasn't his only victim.

I mentioned that after my mother died, I tore things up. More specifically, I began drinking alcohol. I snuck beer and liquor out of my dad's stash. I resented my mother for abandoning me on my twelfth birthday. I saw this as an omen.

I attempted suicide for the first time in junior high. I wasn't a social butterfly and was failing miserably in school, although I was smart. I just didn't fit in. Worse, our small Texas town was unforgiving to the plights of a young female trying to find her footing. My father was raising a house full of girls, the oldest of whom was pregnant. I became a full-time babysitter and guardian to my two younger sisters. I also became a full-blown alcoholic at the age of fifteen and soon after dropped out of high school.

One night, while partying with some so-called friends, I was raped. I had passed out from drinking too much and when I woke days later, I was naked. I continued drinking and began smoking marijuana to ease the pain. The rapes were too much to handle. I added powdered cocaine and pills to my routine, eventually graduating to become an all-out crack cocaine monster in my early twenties.

Over time, I held various odd jobs, none with the desire to make any of them permanent careers. Just enough to keep my habits up—and that I did. My family wanted nothing to do with me, and eventually, I had no job, less than nothing, and "a nobody" was my title.

I tried to get clean. Got married. He was a real catch—fresh out of prison and looking for someone he could control. I signed up without a second thought. The relationship became physically abusive after six months. Both of us used drugs and drank heavily. Our move to California from Texas was supposed to be a fresh start, an opportunity to get our lives on track. Let's just say the crack-relocation thing didn't work. Before long, we were homeless.

I tried to get clean again and got a job at a thrift store in Sacramento, California. Rented a small apartment and bought a car. I was proud, but my relationship was still abusive. The last straw came when I left the rent money with my unemployed husband. Instead of paying the rent, he took the money and sold my car to a drug dealer in exchange for a twenty-dollar rock of cocaine.

He didn't tell me that, though, so I scoured the Oak Park neighborhood in Sacramento looking for the car. When I found it, I went to retrieve it. When I stood up from grabbing the spare key underneath the tire area, I heard a gun cock and felt cold metal against the side of my face. A hand moved around me, placing the title of the car on the hood. The man holding the gun to my head said, "Sign it or die." I signed the title quickly, crying the whole time. Before I left, the dealer vowed to blow my head off if I ever stepped foot on his property again.

With the rent money stolen and no car to get to work, I soon had no job, no money, no apartment—again. I began smoking more crack cocaine and drinking, picking up right where I left off. After taking off with the rent money, my husband cheated on me and supposedly impregnated another woman. I called one of his sisters back in Texas and told her, "You can get him back in one of two ways—on the Greyhound bus alive or in a casket. You choose." His sister paid for a Greyhound ticket, and I sent him back to Texas after eight and a half years of marital hell.

Meanwhile, I escalated my addiction so I could handle watching my life spiral out of control before my very eyes.

Un-Suppression Before Inspiration
Many of you reading this fall into one of two categories:

1. You are in a place you don't want to be and desire change.
2. You're exactly where you need to be but seek validation and inspiration.

Whichever space you're in, you've been challenged by the universe to fill a void—one that's stopping you from writing the next chapter in your life. But time is just an element that will remain unchanged, no matter how long it takes you to realize that your birthright is still at stake. Periods of suppression only last for seconds, not months or years. When we acknowledge that life is not what it seems, it means we also conclude that remaining stagnant is no longer an option.

Some of the good emotions that come with realizing you deserve more are anger, disbelief, disappointment, fear, depression, and/or a combination of them all. The objective is to flow with whatever emotion shows up, one at a time. For instance, processing anger means recognizing it for what it is. It does not necessarily mean acting on it. Many have gotten this one wrong. To be angry is to feel, so get as angry as you need until the emotions settle you snuggly into the next phase without causing harm to yourself or others.

I had to learn to be angry while using my best tool ever: silence. My anger was a force to be reckoned with, and that little rascal got me in more trouble than you can shake a stick at. I was running around like a one-woman terror squad on steroids. Even when things were going right, I was determined to send them into left field and over the fence.

It's written somewhere that individuals like me spend their adult lives where they left off in their childhoods: trauma struck, as if it's the result of not having the guidance necessary to become better-rounded young women nor do we possess the wherewithal to recognize our own emotions and feelings. I felt very little emotionally, and what I experienced certainly didn't come with a diagnosis or therapeutic remedy.

Rarely do our life experiences come with instantaneous clarity. The hidden feelings developing will return under different circumstances, unsuppressed and unleashed with a vengeance. Their release begets choice. This is a good thing, whenever and however it comes to fruition. Be on the lookout for a ray of sunshine in your darkest hour. It's there, shining brightly on the crown you deserve.

Just because you can't see or feel the crown upon your head and in your heart will not change that it is yours for the taking. Do not ignore its existence. This is not a fairy tale. You are real and so is your crown. It will fight to make its way into your life, one way or another. May that event take place for you sooner rather than later.

Done and Undone
Eventually, I remarried, entering my second emotionally and psychologically abusive marriage. While my husband was at work, I drank and used drugs. At some point, my father moved in with us. My siblings probably thought this was a grandiose way for me to get clean, but it was short-lived because soon after he moved in, my father fell ill and died. I was by his side with other relatives when he took his last breath, his organs shutting down one by one as he lay in my younger sister's home under hospice care.

When the light in his eyes went out, it took life out of mine simultaneously. Nothing mattered anymore. No one mattered. I became numb to everything, good or bad. Life became unbearable. I had lost my only friend.

My husband wanted me to be "fixed," so he dropped me off for a twenty-eight-day stay at a residential treatment program in French Camp, California. Soon after getting out, I enrolled in school to become an EMT.

Nope, that didn't work either. My addiction lured me back in with its sickeningly sweet song. I relapsed not two weeks after graduating. My husband alerted my drug counselor, and she showed up to my home to tell me she had a bed available in the treatment facility.

I went. To this day, I don't know why.

After treatment, I tried to be "normal" and got a full-time job and enrolled in a local community college. Once my financial aid was approved, it was smoked up faster than I could deposit it into my account. It didn't help that, during one of my moments of clarity, my husband admitted to having a pornography addiction.

By this point, my husband resented me and repeatedly tried "fixing" me. I refused to be "fixed." What once was love dissolved into hate almost overnight, ending in divorce after three and a half years. I left with my belongings stuffed in a garbage bag, piled into a raggedy little car on its last leg. In the back of my mind, I always thought the "genie in a bottle" with its mesmerizing swirling smoke would win and would have all the answers on how to survive, how not to feel.

Life on my own wasn't better. I attempted suicide for the last time and was raped again—in broad daylight—after leaving a mental health facility for trying to commit suicide.

I was arrested twice while under the influence of drugs, yet I continued using. With no permanent place to live and no friends, I managed to reach an all-time low by smoking enough crack cocaine to hit a weight of eighty-nine pounds.

I slept where I could, washed up when I could, and ate what I could. I stole, manipulated, and used my body and mind to traverse this path of self-destruction. Crack and alcohol turned against me, transforming me into a nobody full of hatred and resentment, living under the freeway in Stockton, California.

By my late thirties, I realized that I had experienced many traumatic events, none of which I'd ever forgiven. I hadn't forgiven my mother for leaving me alone at the difficult age of twelve; I hadn't forgiven my family for not validating the abuse I'd suffered by my older sibling; I hadn't forgiven the men who'd raped and abused me; and I hadn't forgiven my father for dying and leaving me alone. But most of all, I had not forgiven myself.

From Me to You
For some fortunate reason, I never blamed my mother for me being the promiscuous, self-centered, drug-addicted, toxic situationship–seeking person I became. I believe I had the capacity to change from living an unhealthy lifestyle and all that came with it. I simply chose not to.

Since then, I have worked hard and forgiven myself to live as a healthier wife and woman today. I earned the right to be on the battleground of life. I am no longer a soldier to the unhealthy lifestyle but a Warrior 4 Life.

The events described only comprise a fraction of who I am as a whole, healthy, strong woman. You will notice the events I wrote about have a beginning and an end. The end of unhealthy living for me began many years ago, but it was not a path devoid of doubt, pain, and mistakes. The road back is not nearly as long as the road taken.

This personal message is from me to you, and believe me when I say, "The eighty-nine-pound crack monster is dead and gone. I have walked the talk. I took ownership of my past to ensure I could live a better life. I found my footing and have never looked back."

But it's also important to remember that I am who I am now because I was not someone else back then. I chose less-than-stellar personal relationships before the twenty-three years of bliss I'm currently enjoying. But those past relationships were supposed to be miserable because the options of choice and self-respect hadn't yet appeared.

I remember having normal situationships and crushes in high school, but the love I thought I was experiencing was far from what it was cracked up to be. I had no idea what love was nor how to manage the sexual aspects, never mind the fact that men and women weren't exactly designed to be together perfectly under any given circumstances.

Every situation gives birth to a variety of relationships. I sucked at personal ones. I intentionally and unintentionally chose partners who had no clue what they were doing either, so the ultimate journey through immaturity, pain, and heartbreak made me a team player. As I think back, I learned that the actual team included ME, MYSELF, and I. Defining who I was depended on knowing myself and was crucial to this part of my journey.

Seems simple? Not at all. The recipe requires setting a criterion for what I bring to the table of any situationship and who all the players are. Each friendship, dating-ship, marriage, society-ship, community-ship, and career-ship must be defined with laser precision.

We can't classify ourselves as a part of the human species if we don't remember that we are allowed to choose: which *ship*, the size of it, and the crew operating it while plotting each destination. Rarely will we have the option to choose the life span of each. The morons I chose to remain in relationships with were brutal, both physically and mentally.

If you consciously choose a moron, please do not place high expectations or dreams of normalcy on them. Some people are not wired for normalcy, however you define it. We don't always prioritize our needs over our wants and can end up in a world of trouble. Entire communities believe the lives they are currently living are where they are supposed to be. It is not true. They just don't know it yet. Some may not live to see it change nor do they want to.

Heed your actions and responsibilities. How do you want others to respect you? How do you want your family to love and accept you? How are you doing on your career path and is it fulfilling or are you fulfilling some other purpose? The answers to these questions lie within you and must be considered.

At some point, I came to a few conclusions: I'm not OK being called a name that isn't on my legal birth certificate by anyone who thinks I'm a piece of damaged property, from total strangers to those I know personally. I'm not OK suffering from physical pain inflicted upon me for any reason whatsoever. I'm not OK with anyone who believes they can break me mentally, emotionally, physically, financially, or otherwise. I'm not going to be somewhere I haven't chosen intentionally to fulfill a positive part of my life, including with family or an employer.

Pop the ejector seat or escape hatch if you find you've chosen wrong. A person who believes they can control your every move will eventually slip up. Remove the fear—it was put there to challenge you for your birthright. Make it a point to safely find that window of freedom.

And you absolutely may not love someone else more than you love yourself. Period.

One last note: If you've chosen your partner while under the influence of drugs or alcohol or during a period of lust, your capacity to live independently of pain has been chosen. I am the Hellion. I speak from her directly to you. There are no words here that will harm you, and I've walked through the pain so you don't have to.

What Damned Crown? You're Kidding, Right?
I don't care how many times you've screamed about your situation to the mountaintops. It doesn't matter if your knees are blistered because you've gone down on them so many times, only to find your requests for relief continue to go unanswered time and time again. It does, however, matter if you take a deep breath right now so you can reconfigure your circumstances, process the past, and dust off the foundation upon which your crown resides.

Who am I, a total stranger to your plights, speaking to you as though I'm an authority on who you are and how you live? I am you and you are me. You cannot expect that you are destined to live a lifetime of misery. The situation you are in does NOT define what happens next. Is it not time that you remove the debris surrounding your crown? Is it not time that you stop removing it from your head and giving it away to any and everyone who asks for it?

Being selfish and in tune with what you need means never putting your crown at risk. It was not tarnished at the time of your amazing birth, and from here on out, you must protect and respect it at all costs. Your birth crown was designed out of love, even if your conception was not. It was placed upon your head when you took your first breath so that you, too, would one day honor yourself with the gifts that life will give you.

There are a few elements your crown does not include in its design: fear of being alone, fear of change, fear of leaving behind those who cannot see/feel their crowns, fear of the unknown, and fear itself. Your crown will allow you to see fear for what and/or who it is and decide for yourself if the battle is worth engaging in.

Be specific in your adventures. Be the one who can hold your head up high because the decisions you make are for *you*. You are the only one who can decide what situationship to be included in. Stop living in the shadows of doubt cast by not believing in the power you wield as a human being. There is nothing more powerful than being in a place of despair, knowing you have your crown, and using its power to leverage the goodness within you. The goodness associated with freedom will also bring love to everyone in your circle of support, including your family, friends, coworkers, and then some.

I am here to help you awaken the truth you have known all along. It is your truth to embrace. This is your opportunity to release all fears of something or someone who can no longer harm you. Our wounds heal when we give in to the freedom of recognizing our crown as the powerful part of ourselves that cannot be removed, despite the battles we often wage against it. Your internal battles must be identified to be conquered.

Life challenges us to become stronger, wiser, and more experienced as we age. Choice allows you to take a deep breath and embrace the power you have while fulfilling every obligation to honor your one life. Please do not use choice as an option to ignore your birth crown. It never has been and never will be your destination to leave this world without being true to yourself.

Every breath you take is important. Within those breaths you will find that life is simpler than the complexities we indulge in. Never allow someone to disrespect your crown because they cannot or refuse to see it.

Today I am one of the strongest sixty-one-year-old female warriors in existence. I know that may sound egotistical, but I tell you no lies. I chiseled certain truths into my crown long ago and am true to my mission. As for the dance with the Hellion within me, her grasp upon my inner twelve-year-old has been tamed. My sanity is no longer hers to toy with. I got to her just before she became the devil herself. There is nothing you can do to stop becoming the best version of yourself. It is in your DNA.

And there you have it. Welcome to our battleground. Our battleground is life.

Peace,
JoJo Rimmer

*****

A note from JoJo:
Hello there, world! I'm excited, terrified, and inspired all rolled up into one huge, magnificent mass of positivity-infused humanness! From an introverted, eighty-nine-pound, crack-induced, hot mess of a human being to a "Warrior4All Life," to an extrovert filled with compassion for humanity and the plights of a variety of life journeys. I am who I am because I'm not someone else. For this I am grateful.

While you figure that part out; here's a few highlights of what fuels my passion for humanity as a whole.

I've worked tirelessly within at-risk populations over twenty-four years by serving as a stealth-mode community advocate. This has included enhancing lives within my community with resources, donations, and referrals to assist in getting their lives back on track.

There has been a dire and ongoing need for food, shelter, and clothing for the homeless, as well as alternative life skills training and advocacy to assist those with substance use disorders and mental health issues. Providing these resources ensures that individuals affected by domestic violence and crimes have a voice and are able to become the healthiest members of our communities they can be, under any given set of circumstances.

I am the former director of family services for a nonprofit homeless shelter as well as the coauthor and birth mother of "Ownership Life Skills Training" taught by my best friend within a criminal rehabilitation setting for the past twenty years. I am a substance abuse counselor and California Consortium of Addiction Programs and Professionals (CCAPP) certified alcohol and drug counselor level I (CADC-I) and the current substance abuse program supervisor at San Joaquin County Behavioral Health Services. A public speaker for at-risk populations across the realm of humanity, I am spreading my Queen Wings within this magnificent work.

We are not broken and not all things broken remain so. Fix it, even if it means starting with self. This is who I am at my very core. I was born in "The Quarters" in Sugar Land, Texas and raised by the good, bad and the ugly of my life experiences. Who knows where the next chapter leads. There's always a next chapter.

signature

Chapter 14

From Survivor to Thriver

Jennifer Hass

To my fellow survivors. May my words inspire you to rise above your past and embrace the possibilities of a brighter future.

When asked to write about your life, you feel a rush of emotions—a thrill because you are finally able to share your story and find your voice and your power. But then, fear and doubt set in. The reality of having to face yourself and delve into your own mind, the place where scary childhood memories you hide from still loudly and painfully reside. You know, the really dark memories lurking in the shadows, behind locked doors and under beds.

To muster the courage and willingly go back to those dark and scary places, wiping away the cobwebs and shining your gifted light is what it takes for you to love yourself, heal your inner child, and break the generational curses that have plagued us for so long.

It's intimidating to be vulnerable. Growing up, I was taught that vulnerability was weakness. I quickly learned that if you tell someone that you have a cut, they will inevitably pour salt into it, and usually, it's those who are closest to you who pour the most. I always wanted everyone to view me as a strong, capable person. To admit my fears and my failures in writing—in a published book—is something nobody would want to do.

So, I did what any other person striving for growth and wanting to help those who are going through the same darkness would do: I wrote about my experiences. All of it—the good, the bad, and the ugly—intentionally, hoping these words might brighten your journey.

Longing for *Full House*
My parents were divorced when I was very young. The court granted my biological father, who is schizophrenic, every other weekend and alternating holidays. He really did try to be the best father he could. I grew up in a lower-income household, our

income mainly consisting of child support from my dad, the state help, and my mom's occasional housekeeping or babysitting jobs. I never felt poor, though.

Until the age of eleven, I was surrounded by extended family who made me feel loved. My aunts, uncles, and grandparents always made sure we were OK and had what we needed. My best friends and cousins became my brothers and sisters, and my grandparents became more mother and father figures than my real parents. My aunts and uncles were amazing role models who I was thankful to have. Those first eleven years were not perfect by any means, but they made me who I am today.

Being an only child taught me how to be independent and self-reliant. It also left me feeling pressured to work harder to be "perfect" to fit in and avoid being alone all the time. But as we all know, perfect is a fantasy. Nobody is perfect; life is never perfect. The greatest action we can take is to make the best of our situation with a positive attitude and strive to be better than we were yesterday by always moving forward.

My mom had a steady stream of boyfriends who acted as my stepfathers. Unfortunately, she didn't have the best taste in men, and aside from one, all my stepfathers were a bit of a nightmare. As a young child, I helplessly watched my mom be mentally and physically abused by them, to the point where one shot her through the foot while she sat next to me on the couch. Starting at age twelve, I was also physically, mentally, and sexually abused by my last stepfather. This abuse lasted for a few years, as my mom and this stepdad took me out of school and "homeschooled" me, an experience that consisted of being sexually abused, forced to smoke weed, and living in random hotels or in our van as we traveled from state to state to make sure nobody noticed what was actually happening.

During that time, my stepfather got me pregnant, and I had my daughter at a very young age. Not long after, my daughter and I both went into foster care. We were placed in a string of unfit foster homes that were much safer than being with my mom but still taught me how dysfunctional the world can be. I vividly remember being told by social workers, "We want you to see how a 'normal' family lives." I just kept thinking, "What is a 'normal' family?"

I remember watching *Full House* and wondering if anyone ever actually lived like that. I longed for the peace and joy that I saw within the families on that show. I fleetingly experienced happiness and safety around my grandparents, aunts, and uncles during visits, but it was just a small taste of familial heaven.

My daughter and I emancipated out of foster care when I was eighteen and she was two. Completely terrified yet excited, we went out into the world. Thinking back, the one thing I think the state really lacks and fails at is giving foster kids a mentor, someone to teach them what they can aspire to. As a foster child, you get branded as a problem. Not only is this unfair, it's also mentally harmful and does not do anything for your self-worth or confidence. Especially when your parents are the problem, and you end up having to carry the weight, stigma, and shame of their mistakes. Current and former foster children may act like it doesn't bother them, but it does. After all, becoming a human chameleon to fight for approval and fit in with all the different foster families becomes our norm.

The other thing they don't prepare you for while growing up in the foster system is that all your unhealed trauma can, and inevitably will, show up and reveal itself in your adult life, no matter how much you try to pretend like it doesn't exist, even after years of therapy. In my opinion, going to a therapist is like going to a trainer at the gym. They teach you the basics and how to do the work to reach your goals, but if you don't follow through in real life and do the work on your own, nothing changes. Also, just like in the gym, growing new muscles hurts and, coincidentally, growing emotionally hurts—but I promise it's worth the pain.

After emancipation, my daughter and I drove with my grandparents, uncle, cat, and a full U-Haul to our new life. It was the first time in a long time I didn't feel alone. Instead, I felt free. My daughter was and is one of the most amazing human beings I've ever met. Without knowing, she grounded and kept me focused by making me want to provide a loving, stable, and safe future for us. She is genuinely the best thing that ever happened to me. Through all the abuse, she gave me hope, a purpose, and meaning.

Starting Fresh
My daughter and I lived with my grandparents and my biological father. I was so thankful for the family environment and how it fulfilled my craving to be around people who knew and loved me. I honestly had no plan for my life or our future. I was taught in foster care and throughout my court trials I should get my GED, go to college, and get a job. Well, I finished my GED in foster care and started college, but being out on my own, I lost the structure I had in foster care—even if it wasn't perfect, it was structure. I was now trying to navigate finding a new job in a big city and making sure I was also maintaining being a good mom, daughter, granddaughter, and overall human.

To be honest, I was terrified. I wanted and needed a playbook. I was very thankful for God and my faith that helped me through dark times, but I was still young and learning how to find my place in the world. I went to church every Sunday and prayed for answers and guidance.

Trying to find a career was terrifying and discouraging, to say the least. My job history consisted of helping with oddball jobs on construction sites, cleaning houses, some retail work, and then, while in foster care, interning as an assistant at the courthouse. At one point, I also worked at a credit card company call center, and I discovered I was good at sales. This gave me the confidence to start on a string of interviews in that field. I got callbacks for work and was able to stay employed at each one for a bit, but none were a comfortable fit.

The first callback was for a salesperson at a call center, and I hated it. It was so much pressure and they literally bottle-fed us Red Bulls while we were stuck in cubicles with headsets connected to a computer. Then I took a job as an assistant for a stockbroker. It was a temp job, but it was something, and something was better than nothing. The gentleman I worked for was amazing, and he referred me to a temp program through the casinos. The first job I was offered through this temp service was in the event planning department as an assistant, which mainly consisted of me making copies and doing the grunt work. These were nice offices. I was learning a lot, and the woman in charge was amazing. She was always impeccably dressed, well spoken, and people would be so excited to meet with her. I learned a lot from working in that office, and it was refreshing to see such a strong female role model.

After that job ended, I was offered a full-time position in the casino as a cocktail waitress. Was this my dream job? No, but the money was good, and the environment was good, giving me the opportunity to meet and network with a variety of incredible people.

While cocktailing, I fell in love for the first time in my early twenties. He was incredibly talented and smart, and he taught me a lot about life and love. But this is also when I learned how guarded and broken I was when it came to intimacy and being loved. He knew a little about my childhood, but he could see me struggling. He was so thoughtful, he bought books about women who had been abused in their childhoods and had overcome it to lead successful lives and have successful marriages. I would find the books with notes he wrote in them, his way of trying to help me through my anxiety.

Eventually, he asked that we go to therapy. I agreed and tried therapy, but I wasn't comfortable talking about my insecurities and opening up about my childhood. We tried to overcome our past to create a better future. He was genuinely not just my boyfriend but my best friend.

We'd been together a few years when he passed away from a heart attack. I hadn't felt pain like that before, even with all the abuse as a child. My own heart was broken. Thankfully, I had my family and friends to love me through it. Without them, I don't know what I would have done. That was the first time in my life I'd experienced depression. I think as a child, when I went through the abuse, my anger kept me from feeling sadness, if that makes sense. But this was pure heartache.

As time passed, I returned to work and life went back to normal, as much as possible. But he will always be in my heart and never forgotten.

Creating a New Narrative
After my boyfriend's death, I continued cocktailing, but I wanted to branch out. Instead of taking a full leap to a new career, I began opening small side businesses with my friends

and family, trying to find something sustainable. I opened an online bookstore, I tried buying and selling storage units, restoring furniture, started a catering company, then a food truck company, and a tax appeal company after the 2008 real estate market crash. After that, I sold clothing on Amazon and also opened an eBay store.

Throughout each of these adventures, I learned a lot about myself and about managing finances, a company, and employees. I learned that you always want to be in business with someone who has experience, and you never want to be the smartest person in the room. None of my ventures turned out to be a great success, as in I did not make the Fortune 500, but they were extremely good learning experiences that honed my skills to what they are today. My mentor told me it's not a failure if you learn from it.

I started dating again, and boy, let me tell you—that was much harder than running a business. At this point in my life, I'd seen a lot of beauty, but I had also seen a lot of pain and ugliness in people. I knew I loved to work, which was all logical and not emotional, and I knew if I worked hard, the result would be great.

With relationships, it's so different. You can put in all you are and end up with nothing, and have to be OK with that. It's a risk we take when dating. Being a mother brought me the most happiness in my life. My daughter is this incredible ray of sunshine and lights up every room she enters. She's outgoing and confident and sees the beauty in everyone and everything, which has inspired me every day to have this same outlook.

Eventually, I went back to the drawing board and started fresh, trying to figure out what I wanted to do, not just for my career but overall in life. I needed to reset and create a routine. I am at my best when I have a plan. I reset, worked out, read, journaled, improved my diet, and spent more quality time being present. My family and I opened a new company, and thankfully, we are blessed and it's doing very well. I was also blessed enough to open a second company with two of my best friends.

Don't get me wrong—it's not all sunshine and rainbows, but it's good, and each day, I genuinely love what I do. I don't wake up to an alarm clock anymore, and I am able to not only work for myself but do a job that highlights my strengths alongside the people I love.

Every day is still a growing and learning experience, but I am showing up and doing the absolute best I can. The best advice I've ever received was, "Life is a journey. Remember to enjoy the ride." Life goes by so fast, and if you stay stuck in the past, you will have missed so much. My best advice for you is to follow your heart, don't quit when it gets hard, and surround yourself with people who love and support you. Do this, and you will become unstoppable.

Sending lots of love and wishes that all your dreams come true!

*****

About Jennifer Hass:
Born in California, Jennifer Hass is a survivor of an abusive upbringing. Today, she is a mother, an author, and an entrepreneur. Jennifer is deeply involved with her community through her church, business, and nonprofit, dedicating her time to encouraging her fellow survivors.

When she's not working or writing, she enjoys swimming, surfing, playing with her dogs, hiking, and spending quality time with family and friends. With the publication of her first book, she is riding a wave of speaking events and exploring new ways to support others.

https://everafter.foundation/

Chapter 15

Hopeful Roots, Humbled Growth

JoDee Castello

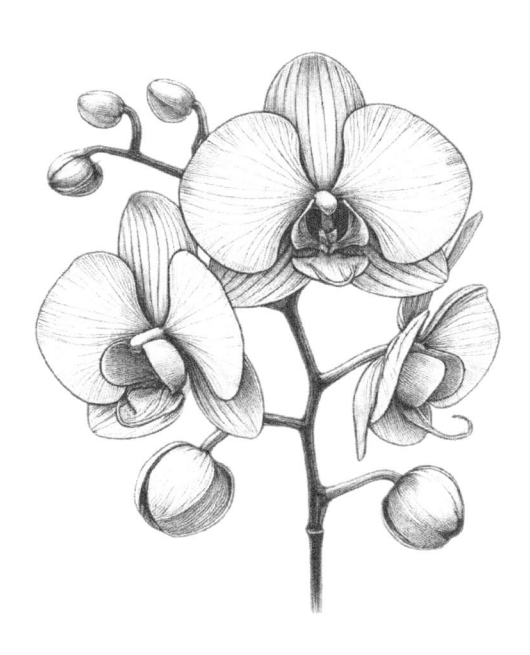

When the soul is ready, the teacher appears.

When I first volunteered to contribute to this book and tried to write about a specific memory, I was overwhelmed. In large part, this is because I know our lives are not defined by a single trial or triumph, but a popcorn string of experiences that we cultivate and wear as our identity. Even now as I write this, I feel the pressure building in my chest and apprehension tensing my fingertips with each keystroke. My mind is racing—attempting to grab concrete thoughts to convey the moments in my life that helped shape the human I am today.

While thinking of what to write, a mixture of positive and negative thoughts race to offer themselves up to those readers seeking solace and connection in this chapter. Attempting to be careful in my language and presentation of thoughts, I find myself asking, "How will the readers feel?" or "How will the readers respond when I recall my experiences?" An individual's perspective shapes and influences how they view and interact with the world, often creating its own version of reality. Trusting readers who've never met me to truly understand *my* perspective of reality feels overwhelming and daunting.

Ultimately, complex interactions and perspectives come together to weave the tapestry forming the backdrop of our individual worlds. To help show you what's been woven for me, I want to share some of my background.

In this chapter, I've written about significant moments in my life that shaped me much more than my achievements. While I am grateful for everything I have been able to achieve, in this essay, I wanted to examine and focus on moments that felt insignificant yet had a profound and lasting impact.

Somehow, my earliest memories of disappointment, coupled with my most recent unimaginable joys, create the filter forming my viewpoint. My internal monologue often sounds like a late-'90s daytime talk show. Like the guests on these overly dramatic programs, my emotions sit across from each other on my mind's stage, jockeying for dominance.

I developed a very strong personality as a child. Born of involuntary emotional martyrdom and exposure to the harsh elements of the world, the persona I present is tuned and adjusted daily to better serve its objective of providing me with mental and emotional security.

But in the background, insecurities and painful emotions linger like a chorus of demons. Then, when I seek inner strength or enjoy quiet moments before bed, they perform a private sermon, reminding me of who I think I am deep down.

The Making of Me
I don't want to negate the struggles I had growing up, but I want to begin by acknowledging that I was privileged during my childhood. I say this not only to identify the advantages that I have had but also to highlight the hardships I experienced despite my advantages. In the '90s movie *Clueless*, the main character, Cher, says of another person, "She's a full-on Monet. It's like a painting, see? From far away, it's OK, but up close, it's a big old mess." Similarly, my life was like a Monet. From far away, most things appeared fine. I had a plethora of opportunities and access to Girl Scouts and summer camps. Essentially, I enjoyed a relatively normal childhood—better than most of my extended family members and neighborhood kids. The last of three kids, I hadn't known the mac-and-cheese nights as well as my siblings had. My parents were in their thirties by the time I came along. Since they were more established and aware, I enjoyed the spoils of their labor. From the outside, it seemed I had a mostly peaceful experience.

My siblings were four and eight years older than me, so we did not have much in common. With them being older and my parents busy with their careers, I began to heavily relate to the *Home Alone* character, Kevin McCallister. At a very early age, I became aware that I was on my own in a variety of ways I was wildly unprepared for. I also understood that my parents had a full plate, and I felt obligated to be "good" because they were dealing with my teenage siblings.

By making this commitment to be self-reliant, I created a false sense of security within myself by deciding they weren't emotionally neglecting me, but rather I was choosing independence because they knew I could take care of myself. It was easier for my brain to comprehend my own conclusions, rather than face the facts that their best wasn't enough.

I had all the nice clothes, a great house, and generally everything tangible I asked for. The challenge was articulating the level of emotional support I genuinely needed. I knew something was missing, but I wasn't aware of what specifically I was lacking.

Being a '90s Kid
I was bullied pretty harshly by my siblings (we've found peace now), but my strongest memories surround the focus on my weight every single day of my life. When I was at home, I was monitored and reminded of my weight constantly. School offered even less mercy than my family did, so generally, it didn't feel like I had a safe space. It wasn't that I was not well liked; I just wasn't skinny enough to be "cool." The cute, popular girls never deemed me as a threat but saw me as a funny accessory that wouldn't challenge their conventional attractiveness.

I was always chubby and never really fit into regular clothes. Being a plus-size girl since birth, I was subjected to shopping at the lower-scale clothing stores whose athletic area consisted mostly of Oakland A mesh shorts and T-shirts. To add insult to injury, I was a Giants fan.

I guess we are all born a blank canvas, not yet scared of the outside world. For a while as a child, I genuinely felt like I had this nice bubble of protection, despite the bullying. I was a sweet blond-haired kid who was eager to explore and convinced I was going to be the next Spice Girl. But then, when I was in seventh grade, 9/11 happened.

I vividly remember the day and the call from my friend whose dad was a marine. I was aware that something terrible had happened, but I had no knowledge of the World Trade Center prior to this or what the world would become after that incident. My friend kept reiterating how serious this was, but I don't think I was capable of understanding just how much things would change. New York felt so far away—how could it impact me so profoundly when I didn't know it existed until a few minutes prior?

An interesting aspect of the school I attended was that most of my educators were from the Middle East and we had students from the Middle East as well, including a girl in my class who was from Pakistan. I remember when I saw her, I couldn't believe how pretty her hair was. She reminded me of Princess Jasmine—with my limited cultural exposure, this was my only reference point. I really enjoyed her company and I thought she was fascinating.

But 9/11 changed all that. I became someone who bullied her for trying to fit in. I was bullied all throughout school for my weight and not really fitting in with the other kids, so I made it impossible for her to fit in as well.

She contacted me years later and was gracious enough to allow me to apologize for how poorly I treated her. I missed out on so much, including the genuine opportunity to have a front-row seat to a new culture and experience. I squandered it to fit in, and it has remained one of my biggest regrets, a lesson I consistently refer back to when reciting the millions of things I would do differently now.

In the post-9/11 era during the "No Child Left Behind Act," America was in the height of its patriotism and propaganda, and I was a loyal patriot. I replaced critical thinking with every ounce of denial I could muster. One of my high school English teachers was the first to open my eyes to my own cognitive harshness. When she asked my opinion regarding the war and related issues, I boldly and ignorantly spouted regurgitated talking points and headlines of media I consumed, without having any actual knowledge in that field. She asked me to defend my opinion with sources and facts. Again, I confidently quoted the news channel and waited for her to retract her opinion while I took my victory lap.

I remember the class snickering as my teacher stated that I would need a scholarly reference to support my claims. I was so agitated, I spent the better part of the afternoon cursing her name to anyone who would hear me. I kept bringing up the soldiers sacrificing themselves for her to have the privilege to criticize the war, not truly understanding that she was, in fact, the one genuinely concerned for the soldiers' well-being.

By directly questioning the motives and purpose for these wars, she was showing concern for the soldiers' lives and sacrifice, while I was the one endangering them by not questioning the situation.

This teacher continued to encourage us to constantly question why things are happening, who they directly benefit, and who they directly impact. She remains one of my favorite teachers, despite her giving me my well-deserved C.

Much like analyzing a Monet, the closer I examined my life, the more I saw that everything was an absolute mess. It wasn't until I went to college and had teachers more like my high school English teacher that I understood how things had gotten so fucked up. Finally, I saw how my parents' neglect and bullying by my siblings and peers created conflicted emotions and the chorus of self-critical, internal demons. Yet, this awareness didn't save me from a failed marriage filled with toxicity and domestic abuse.

Always Healing, Never Healed
Today, I am healing—but I know I will never fully mend. Life has humbled me consistently in a variety of ways. When I was first drafting this chapter, I planned on focusing on how I have overcome the toxicity and abuse I suffered in the last few years. But as I wrote, I realized that it might be more meaningful to concentrate on that popcorn string of childhood experiences that shaped the adult I would become—the adult who would have so very much to overcome.

I have an interesting viewpoint when looking back on my childhood and adolescence. I imagine this is true for everyone who is lucky enough to reach adulthood and glance back at how far they have come and all that they have conquered. Examining my previous experiences—both traumatic and positive—through seasoned eyes and a more mature perspective is a bittersweet experience that my brain offers up at the most inconvenient times. Even now, as I write to you about my life, I feel hesitant and stiff. After all, my life may be far from perfect, but it's closer to perfect than most will experience.

One of my dearest friends (who really introduced me to the idea of unconditional love—the kind that comes with zero strings and no expectations) explained that people drown in various levels of water. It can be an amount the size of a teaspoon or the volume of a snarling ocean; both are able to bring about the same fate. I kept comparing my grief and anger and frustrations with those who had far less than me and much more to complain about, and I kept coming up short—not realizing I simply drowned in less water than them.

Hospitals must rank and triage external wounds by order of urgency and level of critical care. This is easier to do when the wounds are physical. Emotional wounds can appear as simple as paper cuts, yet they can seep into the depths of your soul and require a level of trauma care that you are underfunded and ill-equipped for.

The uncomfortable reality is that we can never truly understand what the individuals around us have endured. Ideally, we should remain in solidarity with other people as we are all at the mercy of the human experience. I try to keep this positive energy all the time, although I do sometimes find myself cussing in traffic.

Hope is often described as this beautiful and strong light—a peace that comes from within. But hope can also be a notion we create through despair and difficulty. Hope comes from the depths of despair and undignified moments that don't provide any other opportunity. It can be beautiful, but it often comes from the ugliest of times.

Much like hope, personal growth can come through positive experiences as well as trauma. I feel like I was told so often, "That'll toughen you up" whenever I expressed the challenges I faced. Which is sometimes necessary but not a one-size-fits-all approach to dealing with root sources of trauma. A humbling aspect of life has taught me that we are all equally susceptible to misfortune. Despite making all the right choices, sometimes life takes the reins and forces ordinary people to shape-shift for survival.

Life will continue to humble me as well as provide blessings. To get through, I know I must trust the balance and have faith that better days are on the horizon. Accepting this has forced me to learn to trust myself and become comfortable with understanding my triggers and traumas and having ways to safely express them. For me, retaining positivity is an arduous process that takes effort, but it always pays off—even if doing so means white-knuckling through parts of your existence. Days when your coffee tastes like magic and you happen to get all green lights on your way to work provide an amnesia of sorts for when other days feel like the universe has a vendetta against you and someone shit in your cereal.

*****

About JoDee Castello:
JoDee Castello, born and raised in Northern Nevada, holds a master's degree in criminal justice. As a dedicated parent of two, Jo skillfully balances family life with a successful career, ensuring that both personal and professional responsibilities are met with equal commitment.

With a solid background in sales, Jo has consistently demonstrated a commitment to excellence and customer satisfaction. Over the years, Jo has built a reputation for reliability and dedication in the sales industry. Just over a year ago, Jo took the entrepreneurial leap to open her first business, showcasing a drive for innovation and resilience in the face of challenges.

Jo's journey is marked by a blend of professional success and community involvement. Her path reflects a deep dedication to fostering strong connections and contributing positively to the community while continuously striving for personal and professional growth.

Chapter 16

Kintsugi—Fractured and Repaired with Precious Metals

Misti L. Harrelson

Be strong and of good courage…
Deut. 31;6

#DoGoodTodayThenBetterTomorrow
#IAmMyBrothersAndSistersKeeper
#YouAreToo

What is the difference between something that's broken and something that's ruined? For those who practice *kintsugi,* the Japanese art of repairing damaged pottery, it seems the only difference between the two is hope. Instead of throwing away vessels that have been broken, these artisans use kintsugi to mend the pieces back together, filling the cracks with precious metals, such as gold, silver, or platinum. Once complete, a piece repaired through kintsugi is again functional—just as it was before the trauma. Yet now, its unique imperfections are beautifully highlighted as a testament to its history and resilience. The pottery also gains more value because of the precious metals used to heal the brokenness.

My name is Misti Lynn Harrelson. Since August 2016, I have been free from bondage and an intensely controlling and abusive relationship. Much like the beautiful pottery repaired through kintsugi, I have experienced and lived through what should have killed me 100 times over.

During the decade I spent with an abuser, I

> … woke from sleep to chunks of my hair being cut out;
> … had boiling oil poured on me;
> … endured countless beatings and was choked unconscious so many times;
> … stared down the barrel of a shotgun as he pulled the trigger over and over;
> … was prostituted;
> … suffered continuous sleep deprivation, enduring his tirades and abuse for days on end;
> … felt the burn of many cigarettes, the scars from which can still be seen today; and

… spent almost two years locked in a room, held hostage behind a nailed-shut door. The only window was covered, so no sunlight came through and I had no access to a phone. I had to ask permission to use the restroom. If I was allowed, he would move the chair to the hallway to watch me or just give me a bucket to use in the room.

Even today, I still wake myself up fighting, crying, or trying to protect myself. The nightmares are as intense and as horrible as when the actual events took place. If my dreams are not violent, they involve me escaping his hunt. Sometimes the worst is when those dreams are of us at our absolute best. All of these scenarios haunt and pain me.

Yet, these experiences do not define me. Why? Because, just as the shattered pieces of pottery are restored through kintsugi, I have been mended, restored, and reborn. Today, I am mother to a brilliant, kind, and hilarious teenage daughter. I work with both sides of victims of crime and perpetrators of violence and am a full-time master's student, studying and working within my field of purpose and passion, championing for victims' rights and community safety as well as restoring empowerment, emotional connection and hope to those I work with.

Kintsugi discourages throwing away objects due to imperfections and fractures and, in fact, valuing each piece even more for what it's been through. It teaches us that breaks and fractures do not signify the end of a vessel's existence. Instead, it represents the acceptance of change and a new way of being.

A reassembled vessel possesses a richer narrative, exuding a greater sense of authenticity and reality. It symbolizes strength and resilience, versus a vessel that has remained intact without blemish. I think human beings should practice the same art internally. That's why I want to tell you my story—so you understand that no matter what you've been through, what you've endured—you are a survivor. You deserve to heal yourself and, with awareness and focused work, you *can!*

You are not alone and you will need support, guidance, real talk, and a lot of hugs on this path called healing. But if you have air in your lungs, you have the opportunity to make a difference in your life and in the lives of your loved ones.

The Beginning of the End
One of the last violent incidents with my former abuser took place August 18, 2016. I never knew the punch was coming. I was in the bathroom putting my hair in a ponytail when he came from behind and threw a haymaker with his fist. According to criminal forensics, either his thumb or index finger knuckle landed in my eye. When I woke up on the bathroom floor, I remember feeling around the floor and screaming, "Where is my eye?"

My right eye had completely ruptured, the cornea and retina instantly detached, and I passed out. Later, my surgeon explained that everything that had once been inside my eye orbits was now outside of it, and there was no chance to save my vision in that eye.

After the attack, as I fell in and out of consciousness, he dragged me down the stairs by my arm and hair. The wonderful elderly woman who lived downstairs tried to come upstairs with a hammer as she screamed, "I called the police!" He threw me in our van and when I next woke up, I was in a hotel room and he was sexually assaulting me. There was blood everywhere; the mattress was soaked with blood from my eye, head, and face. I begged him to take me to the hospital, not to let me die. I kept saying our daughter's name over and over.

The abuse in the hotel continued for almost two days until he finally decided to take me to the hospital. As he drove me there, I remember passing an area with so many trees it seemed like an orchard, which makes zero sense logistically in relation to the location of the hospital. Later, recalling these memories, I wondered if his first plan was to find a dump spot to leave my body. By the grace of God, he did take me to a hospital a few cities away. Every day of my nine-day hospital stay, he was there … bringing treats, fruits, and lunches to the nurses and other staff while I lay there with a broken back, fractured face plate, too many bruises and lumps to count (the hospital stopped counting after 100), and blindness in my right eye. This, by the way, was the fifth black eye of *that* month.

No one in the hospital, not a single doctor or nurse, asked me personally what had happened. The one place I thought I might be safe was just another place of torture. The hospital staff believed his story: that I tripped over my dog at the top of the staircase and tumbled down the stairs, landing face first on the furniture below, causing the blow to the eye and face. Naturally, all the other lumps, bumps, and bruises were caused by the violent tumbling down the stairs.

The attack I suffered wasn't new. This man's talons of manipulation started right from the gate. He was "too good to be true," which I now know is a red flag. Every night when I came home from work, he had cooked dinner, cleaned the house, and drawn a bath for me. He told me stories of tragedies and losses endured while he was growing up, encouraging my compassion and empathy to take over. From then on, it became my job to love and to fix this broken man.

Holy herd of squirrels—there I was, donning my codependency-colored Wonder Woman cape. I thought my adoration and my regal treatment of him would restore his faith and trust in humanity and love.

Now, as I think back, I realize *that was not my job*! I am not his creator—so who was I to dance with the devil and think I could repair his brokenness? Who was I to try to fix him? Yet, I made that near-fatal choice and put my everything into him. I sacrificed my time, effort, energy, family, friends, career, and almost my life on more than a few occasions.

*****

Domestic violence is everywhere, endured by people we would never expect to suffer it. I was a college athlete who'd received a basketball scholarship to the University of Hawaii. We won NCAA championships my freshman year. What happened? Why and how did I go from that successful, ambitious young adult to spending the next decade rationalizing, hiding, denying, lying, and normalizing his constant and intense abuse?

However it happened, those days of hiding and denial are over. It's time for action. It's time to regain my power and walk with audacity in the face of fear and uncertainty. It is time to give the world my gift of purpose, my heart of love, and my incredibly hilarious, dark, and corny sense of humor. With the guidance of my Heavenly Father, a strong support system, and a lot of hard work, I will make these horrific losses of love, time, self, and the devastating near loss of my life into a beacon of light and hope for others in their darkness.

Time for Justice
After I was released from the hospital, the abuse and violence did not stop. I really wanted to go home. I was exhausted, my entire body hurt, the light caused such horrible headaches due to only having one functioning eye. But he did not take me home. Instead, he took me to another motel, where the violence continued and escalated until I had to run to the police station with my broken back, eye still bleeding, and all my other injuries, because I knew with every single fiber of my essence that he was going to kill me.

I spent hours at the police station, trembling with fright because he had chased me in the van the entire way, until I was outside the doors of the building. The officers immediately went into action and showed a lot of compassion. They knew from looking at me that this was not the average domestic violence case. The judge approved an emergency warrant, and the officers went to the hotel. They kicked the door down only to find him in the room with another female, naked and doing drugs. That was how he was arrested, the pathetic, lowlife coward.

The officers and another agency got me into a hotel for the evening. In the morning, a different set of officers came, interviewed me, and then drove me over to our local Family Justice Center. I was scared, alone, ashamed, hungry, malnourished, extremely sore, and bruised. I wore only my abuser's sweatpants, a hospital gown, and his shoes. This was all I had besides the hospital band for identification. At the Family Justice Center, I was able to locate a shelter and begin my healing process, understanding his reign of terror was finally over.

During the court process, I was in therapy, both group and individual, but was not able to make much progress due to the emotional roller coaster of attending the trial. The court procedure was stagnating and such a lonely time in my life. Just because my abuser was physically gone from my side didn't mean the abuse stopped. On the contrary, as so often happens, I became my own abuser, with guilt, shame, and anger fueling me.

Now I realize that even in the center of a huge urban environment, people everywhere are alone. We are isolated, bruised, battered—but never ruined. Even then, I knew my light was still flickering! I knew I did not deserve his treatment, all the beatings, and the low-down, degrading names he called me. He tried with all his might to extinguish my light. Unbeknownst to him, that light was not given to him. That was *my* light. *My* birthright, given to me by our Father.

I was still healing physically and learning to navigate the world with one eye. I fell off many curbs and walked into countless street poles and doors due to the vision distortion and realigned depth perception from becoming a human with monocular vision. The rehabilitation process was super frustrating. There wasn't any place to go to relearn all of this. I was just released into the world, alone, and I had to learn new ways to do almost everything. Life is really different with only one eye. Now, almost eight years later, let's just say **I am able to see much clearer.**

The doctors gave me thirteen different psych meds to deal with anxiety, sleeplessness, PTSD, and nightmares. I took them for about two weeks and then refused to remain numb to my pain and deal with medication side effects. Pharma was not for me personally, so I walked, I talked, and I prayed to God—a lot—all day. I watched people during my days outside and knew, after still being able to see compassion, humanity, and love within the world, everything was going to be more than all right.

My abuser took a ten-year plea deal for this last incident. The court proceedings took a bit over a year and continued to emotionally and mentally traumatize me. Even though I had a compassionate, supportive, and strong victim advocate, DA, and inspector assigned to me, it was still a rough go. I was physically ill and mentally shaken before and after each court date. There were so many court dates, delays, and rescheduled hearings, which worsened the anxiety and hypervigilance.

Here I was, exposing and speaking of traumas and violence to an entire courtroom of strangers and my parents, when I'd never even allowed it to register within myself all these years. The courtroom experience was shameful, embarrassing, intimidating, and really hard to endure. He was there, not too far from me, and would make eye contact and other intimidating gestures. Internally, I was so confused—I knew I needed to say what happened to me, aloud, for me and everyone to understand who he was. I needed to regain my voice and power, but I ultimately felt as if I was betraying him.

You might read that and think, "WTF is she saying?!" I thought the same until I understood the psychological reasons behind trauma bonding or Stockholm syndrome. It was a hurtful experience to stand up for myself finally, because it also felt as if I was betraying him—the only human I spent time with for years, twenty-four hours a day, seven days a week, 365 days a year. No one else, no phone contact, with family or friends. He had 100 percent complete control and power over me.

Today, he is out of prison due to good ol' government sentence restructuring and, of course, he earned time off for good behavior. Since his release, I have made additional police reports and there is an active warrant issued for his arrest, due to his attempts to contact me, despite a restraining order, as if nothing ever happened. I pray for peace and compassion to be within his heart. I pray he stays close to Jesus and far from me. I pray he finds purpose and goodness and becomes a productive member of society. I pray, but also—I stay ready.

The Time for Healing

After court and sentencing were over, I was able to focus on healing and getting to know Misti again. What did I like to do? It had been years since I was allowed to have an opinion or thought or to make a choice of my own. I was very intimidated and extremely sad when I was asked what I liked to do. Shame and brokenness left me unable to answer that question, so I just cried. I cried with anger and fury behind each hot tear rolling down my face. I had been *THAT* fractured and oppressed *THAT* badly.

To heal is magical—and it is not an easy undertaking. **Healing takes courage**. Courage to acknowledge, to name the pain and trauma. Courage to take the steps needed to regain your power. Courage to smile with grace and love. **Healing takes strength.** Strength to love yourself and others fully and without hesitation. Strength to forgive yourself and others fully. Strength to continue to step forward each day and never give up. We may have to reroute the plans a few times, but we will not give up at all—period.

Healing also takes a dark sense of humor to get you through the toughest times and at least one friend who can take as much delight in the dark humor as you. I promise your life will be enhanced because of this friend(s). Healing takes a village of compassionate and strong warriors to guide, encourage, and love you as you embark on this path.

I continued attending therapy, both individual and group. I also studied codependency. I believe that every single human on this planet needs to become very familiar with codependency, as doing so will expose and resolve many mental and behavioral issues that start within and are transferred to others. Understanding codependency will make it much easier to navigate life and create healthy boundaries.

One very important first to-do after I was away from my abuser was to go buy a beautiful bra and panties set. I knew no one would ever see this, but I wanted and needed to feel like a woman again. As I wore my new beautiful and sexy bra and panties, I noticed I walked a little differently; I walked with playfulness and audacity. I often smile with this memory and can still feel the warm sun and cool breeze on my body as I wore this new set under my sundress, the sensation of being grateful to be alive and actually feel like a beautiful woman and human again.

I also dove into empowerment and leadership as hard and fast as I could. It became very clear early on in my path that my purpose was to help others. My dad once told me that if I saw a dog foaming at the mouth with rabies, I would still go help it, even though there was a 100 percent chance of getting injured. This could be both positive and negative.

So, as we all should with the gifts bestowed upon us, I refined my skills and learned how to use my gifts more discerningly and with focused intentions. This is how my life is lived now, with intention and purpose. I am not one to partake in fuckery and things that don't make sense. I calculate my steps and measure the value of the efforts being put forth and determine whether they are going to be impactful for the betterment of those around me, especially my family. Hypervigilance, of course, comes into play, as does safety planning. There is also a little room left for spontaneity, because life and adventure require this.

At some point during the court process, I applied to go back to college. Before I knew it, I was enrolled in my first semester at a junior college to earn my psychology degree. I was also connected with the Department of Rehabilitation, which assisted me with my educational path. I highly encourage those US residents who are serious about their education and career path enough to get connected to their state's Department of Rehabilitation.

As I started my college degree, I went all in. You have to remember—I am a little older. At that time, I was in my mid-forties and I needed to accelerate my education to achieve my career goals and retire with any type of money in my retirement account. I pushed and enrolled in at least 23.5 units during the semesters. I was interviewed by the deans of the school and a panel to ensure I was able to handle this workload. Ohhhhh, could I!

I graduated with my psychology degree within two and a half years versus the traditional four years, and I graduated with two honor societies and the dean's list for maintaining at least a 3.5 GPA throughout my academic career.

These were my rebuilding years. I rebuilt my life on all levels. I was reunited with my daughter and my family. I learned to walk this planet with one eye and to smile at others when they looked at me with pity and shock. I think this is why I always make it a point to maintain eye contact. I do not want or need pity. Although I will always take a hug, pity is not something I want anyone to feel when they walk away from me.

This may be the first reaction or thought, but I promise after our interaction, you will be inspired to do and be better. You will have a better understanding of our purpose as our brothers' and sisters' keepers. You will have a better understanding of how to be more intentional with our precious time. In the future, you will think of me with a smile and know that I love Jesus, will NEVER give up, will continue to keep my inner warrior focused on altruistic values toward others, and you will always have a solid-ass sister with me.

My Life, Reborn
My life has transformed, and now I get to

> ... talk to my family and my daughter each and every day;
> ... make my own decisions;
> ... smile again;
> ... be accountable for my actions;
> ... go to church; and
> ... release some of the rage caged inside of me by turning it into positivity, into fuel.

The pain and evil I endured mustn't be forgotten. The atrocities I survived can be used for good.

As unbelievable as this seems, it is my mission to have all this evil, torture, captivity, abuse, and hatred transformed into a beacon of light and power for others to flock to.

My beloved brother Jim, who passed away one year after I escaped, loved and lived by this quote from Ben Franklin: "Do well by doing good." I am now and will always walk this line representing Jim. I also feel there are two words we should use to measure ourselves and our company: *accountability* and *temperance*.

We must have both to strengthen our own being as well as our relationships and communities.

I personally feel we were put here on this earth to be helpful and kind to one another. We are our brothers' and sisters' keepers. Learn to be kind and altruistic every day. Learn to smile and be compassionate of others always. Wouldn't you want this also extended to you? Lead by example and be the light. We need to know and measure our own worth to honor the worth of another.

I am shining the brightest light I can, including by sharing this with you today. Use my light to strengthen and harness yours, so that you may share your light with someone else.

When folks find out what I do in my professional life, they are shocked and confused and then ask me why—why do I go back into the trenches to work with both victims and perpetrators of violence? I do this to show others that if I can do this, *YOU CAN TOO*. If I can survive and go through everything it took to get here, *SO CAN YOU*. Both victims and perpetrators need to be acknowledged and put their work in so they can heal.

I work closely with several probation departments teaching anger management and batterer intervention programs (BIPs) to male and female offenders. I also work with youth offenders, both in and out of incarceration. Helping to restore or make emotional connections with oneself and others is something that assists in impulse control and making better decisions to live a life free from mental, emotional, and physical violence, thus creating a more peaceful existence for them and those around them. By doing this work, we can stop the cycle that creates more victims of crime and trauma while also keeping offenders free from incarceration and the pipelines created to keep humans in them.

I work with victims of crime to help them navigate the criminal justice system. I assist them through different legal, family court, and parole issues, help with safety planning, and locating housing, educational, and employment resources. I assist in connecting them to group and individual therapists and work with them to feel empowerment and hope after enduring the traumas of being a victim of crime.

Another hat I proudly wear is sitting on a board CVAA, where we work and fight for victims' rights by drafting policy, laws, and measures. I am the executive director of Resources and Crisis Management for ICAN. Each year for the past five years, I have been asked to speak to the incoming law students at USF who are studying domestic violence. When I meet with this class, I tell them a little about my personal history with domestic violence, what it was like to go through the criminal justice system as a victim, what they will need to know, and how to best serve their clients while maintaining a healthy environment for themselves due to the secondhand trauma they will experience in their line of work.

I have also been part of the domestic violence fatality review team (DVFRT) for the past few years. I partner with California DA Association as a co-chair and assist in writing the restorative justice modules and manuals all DAs will use when considering restorative justice in their cases. I have also opened my own nonprofit and foundation, Healing Hurt Humans, where I do all of the above mentioned for those in need as well as work with clients on safety and life planning to rebuild and restore after trauma and violence. Hope and hugs can inspire change.

My passion and purpose in life was borne of my horrific personal experience with domestic violence. It forced me to learn how to navigate this world differently after escaping multiple attempts to extinguish my life and light. I know, one eye and all, this is where I am supposed to be.

It has been a lot of hard work, on every single level—and there is still work to be done. That is the beauty of this thing we call life. There is always work to do. Take to heart what you discover and learn along the way, the good and the bad. We are all vessels, and I know my vessel has been broken, shattered, and fractured multiple times. There have been blows in my life, as well as yours, that we will never completely heal from. But I promise you, loved one, it will be all right. It may not be what you want, but everything will be all right. Bob Marley said so ☺.

Find your higher power, pray, and make a plan of action. Decide what you want and determine what it will take to get there. Get involved with your church and do good in your community. Be gentle with yourself; your inner voice will attempt to creep in with cruelty and self-doubt, but remember, YOU ARE A WARRIOR! You are enough. You are capable and will be better than you've ever been. You are finding your purpose, Warrior. You have been fighting battles your entire life, and you are at war for your very survival and existence right now. We walk by faith, not by sight. Be strong and of good courage. You are incredible. God loves you and so do I. You've got this, and God has got you.

Take your brokenness and repair yourself with precious "metals," consisting of the hard work you invest into yourself, your healing, your accomplishments, your confidence, and the knowledge that you are doing your best each day. That is what makes the gold, silver, and platinum to mend those breaks and fractures we have in our vessels. The precious metals you make will mend you fully. Do not rely upon, want, need, or ask anyone to bring, make, or buy precious metals for you. God will put the angels on your path as you need them. Ask for help. You are not alone.

*****

Deuteronomy 31:6
"Be strong and of good courage, do not fear nor be afraid of them; for the Lord your God, He is the One who goes with you. He will not leave you nor forsake you."

Website:
Everafter.foundation
Healinghurthumans.com
24Chapters.com
Social Media:
TikTok: @misti.harrelson
Instagram: @harrelsonmisti
Facebook: Misti Harrelson
YouTube Empowerment:
Today I Rise - Philip Chircop
Be Great, Powerful Beyond Measure - Yuri Anischenko

Chapter 17

Phoenix

Shawna Rainwater Turner

My Dearest Tyrel,
For now, and for all of time, I will cherish the extraordinary love we shared. You are the light in my darkness. In the reflection of your eyes, I saw the most glorious version of myself. Thank you for saving my soul.

When I was six, while other kids played hopscotch and jumped rope around me, I sat in the middle of the playground, convincing myself that I was stronger than the man who'd spent the last year and a half stealing my innocence. This predator had purposely weaseled his way into my mother's world when she was vulnerable. We later learned he preyed on women with young daughters.

"I will never let one human be the reason I don't succeed in life," I told my six-year-old self.

Silence became my best friend for the next decade. Finally, after ten years, I told someone what this man had done to me. Every time he touched me, every time he made me watch him masturbate to completion, every time he forced me to sit in his lap so he could get an erection while he drove my mom, brother, and I down back roads, every time he threatened to kill my mother and brother if I ever told anyone what he was doing.

The day I finally broke down and said something, I was sixteen and my mom was driving me home to our small apartment in Northern California. As we turned onto our complex's street, I looked up and thought I saw my molester. I asked her multiple times if that was him, but she assured me it wasn't.

I unraveled. She knew something was seriously wrong and I knew I was about to shatter her heart with what I had to say, but it was time to free myself from the chains of his abuse, threats, and manipulation.

My mother immediately contacted the authorities in Wyoming and Colorado, the states where the molestations occurred, to begin the process of making him legally responsible for his actions. My dad went to Mexico on a manhunt. My mom and brother were left with a slew of emotions, mine and theirs. They felt they'd failed to protect me; my biggest fear, except for my molester taking their lives, was that they'd blame themselves.

I never want anyone else harmed due to his actions.

Two years later, authorities arrested my molester. Another of his victims, from before me, had come forward. During his arrest, authorities discovered he was married to a woman who had a teenage daughter. He had been raping, molesting, and selling her body to his friends for the last five years. She was finally safe.

It took three more years before we were able to go to trial. A district attorney in one county refused to pursue my case because they didn't feel like they could win it; they didn't even try. Thankfully, I had multiple detectives and attorneys determined to seek justice, and they did exactly that.

As the case proceeded, the judge allowed each victim to present a victim impact statement in front of the court. This was the first time I'd seen this man since I was six years old; I was twenty-one by this point.

I was terrified as I stood with my mom and brother outside that courtroom. We stood in a family huddle, our arms wrapped around one another. My brother kept reminding me that I was safe, and that my molester couldn't hurt me ever again. He wrapped his arms around Mom and I and reassured us that he was there to protect us.

When we entered the courtroom, I located my offender immediately. I looked into his eyes, so he knew I was no longer that fragile little girl he tried to destroy fifteen years ago.

I stood before the courtroom, face-to-face with this plagued man, telling the world how he stole my innocence to fulfill his uncontrollable desires. I said I would never let this man, or his actions, stop me from living my life to the fullest. I begged and pleaded with the judge to put that man behind bars before he destroyed more lives and corrupted more innocent children.

After my statement, the judge gave my offender the opportunity to respond to my statement. He sat before the court and gave his insincere apology, followed by, "Shawna seduced me."

Shocked by his blatant lie and refusal to take accountability for his actions, I sat there, speechless and horrified. I knew he was crazy. Nobody could possibly believe him. But the fear-driven part of my mind flooded me with guilt, as though maybe I *had* seduced him. For a moment I slipped back into the body of that child who was scared to death of this man, that child who had been convinced she was a sexual seductress at four years old, the child whose value rested in the filthy hands of a sexual predator, the child who shouldered the weight of her mother's and brother's safety in her silence.

As the day came to a close, I and two other victims had said all we could. It was up to the justice system to determine his fate.

He was sentenced to three consecutive seven-year sentences, one for each victim. Although he hadn't been an immediate threat in my life for many years, I felt an unbelievable sense of relief knowing he was going to prison.

Dealing with the Fallout

In the years that followed, I struggled with self-esteem. My lack of self-worth manifested itself in poor relationship choices. I mastered the art of overachieving in academics, sports, and my career. Romantic relationships, however, were a constant struggle. From alcoholics to control freaks, the men I consistently chose landed me in one toxic relationship after another. I even stayed in a job with a boss who had a Jekyll-and-Hyde personality for six years.

During the summer of 2007 I started a new job and had been single for nearly a year. I finally pursued my dream of competing in rodeos at a professional level. Eliminating the negativity in my work and love life created a wave of new beginnings.

I entered my first professional rodeo in Cody, Wyoming. That weekend, I met a man who'd turn my world into something I believed only existed in fairy tales.

Some friends and I went to a local bar after the rodeo, where I met the cowboy of my dreams: tall, muscular, extremely handsome with kind eyes and a gentle soul. We talked until the sun rose. Two weeks later, we went on our first official date.

After a month of dating, Tyrel asked me to marry him. Four months later, we committed our love to one another before God, family, and friends.

I never believed I'd meet a man like my husband. Deep down I wanted to believe I deserved a man of his caliber, but a little voice haunted my thoughts, created by the actions of the man who stole my innocence. That voice said I wasn't worthy. I'd been stuck for so long in a pattern of unhealthy relationships that I thought were the best life had to offer.

Tyrel changed everything. He scaled the walls I'd built around my heart and erased my self-limiting beliefs. He was my cowboy, the head of our household, and the man to whom I surrendered my heart and soul.

I never truly understood, nor was I open to, the idea of a woman surrendering to a man as the head of household. I had a few great examples of healthy marriages growing up but had witnessed many failed relationships too. Healthy relationships seemed unattainable until I married my cowboy. He was a humble but fierce leader. He was kind and respectful to me in every capacity. His devotion to God and our marriage became the driving force in everything he did.

When I decided to chase my dreams of becoming a doctor of chiropractic medicine, Tyrel was on board. We knew it would drastically change our lives. We'd have to move. We'd have to sacrifice time spent with each other. We'd be starting an entirely new chapter in our lives, without the safety net of family in proximity. We were young and brave, and we relied on each other.

A New Start
We'd been married for three years when, in 2010, we moved from Wyoming to Texas. The first several months were a whirlwind as we struggled to find housing for ourselves and our animals. A cross-country move with four horses, two dogs, and a cat proved challenging. Through stress, we found peace in each other and our faith. I loved being married to that man. I felt comfort in the knowledge that we could conquer anything if we had each other.

When I found my groove in chiropractic school, my husband worked various jobs until he found something stable and sustainable. My brutally honest but shy cowboy took a job as a retail salesman in a western store. I never envisioned my husband as a salesman, but he shocked us all. He was surprised too by his excitement around this line of work. That sales job brought Tyrel out of his shell. I told him how proud I was of the man he was becoming. He was finally figuring out who he was without living under the shadow of others. I was proud to be his wife from day one, but I fell deeper in love with him after we moved to Texas.

Overall, the transition to Texas was extraordinary. When we encountered roadblocks, we found a solution together. We didn't have a perfect marriage, but it was perfect to us. I felt an inexplicably profound love for him. He loved me for all that I was and all that I was not. For the first time in my life, I was loved by a man who accepted all of me. I was the queen of his world, and he was the king of mine. I never wasted a chance to remind him of how proud I was to be his wife.

While at his new job, Tyrel made rodeo connections leading him to find a place to practice steer wrestling. After we married, Tyrel had taken a hiatus from the rodeo for a few years. But Texas is known for its abundant rodeo opportunities, and they sparked his inner fire. He was ready to chase his long-term dream of making the National Finals Rodeo. My husband was in the best physical shape of his life, and he was perfecting his steer wrestling, prepared in every capacity to pursue his goals. I wanted nothing more than to support him.

Three weeks before his return to professional rodeo, an eighteen-wheeler T-boned Tyrel on the driver's side of his pickup truck. When I received the call that he had been in an accident, my heart fell to my feet. Before I heard the details, I knew it was bad.

I had no information about the location of his accident. I called 911, hoping they could help me locate him. Several calls later, one dispatcher told me of a reported accident ten miles from our home. I was about an hour away from the scene, but I made it there in a little over thirty minutes.

As I pulled closer to the emergency vehicles, I scanned the scene, searching for Tyrel. I spotted his truck. The driver's-side cab was caved in. As I frantically looked for him, a highway patrolman approached me.

"Ma'am, are you OK?" he asked.

"My husband. Where is my husband? How bad is it?" I cried.

"Was that your husband in the red truck?"

"Yes, that's his truck. Where is he? Is he OK?"

"Well, ma'am, your husband is one tough cowboy."

He was trying to comfort me, but I needed information, not comfort. He told me Tyrel's condition wasn't good, and that he'd been transported to a level one trauma unit in Fort Worth by helicopter. He didn't have any information about Tyrel's status.

A few dear friends of ours helped me locate him. They made it to the scene shortly after me. God knew I needed their love and support. We got my car back to the house, fed the animals, and they drove me to the hospital.

Every moment after leaving the crash scene was a blur. I couldn't escape the terror permeating my body. I considered every possible scenario as to the severity of Tyrel's condition. I was caught in the middle of the twilight zone. I needed one thing: Get to Tyrel.

Every minute of that hour drive I begged for God's grace. I was no stranger to the fear of losing someone. For ten years, I feared losing my family if I broke the silence of my molester's truth. In this moment, the fear of losing someone I loved was front and center. I didn't believe I could live life without him, and no part of me wanted to.

Upon arriving at the hospital and finding our way to the intensive care unit, my terror became nearly unbearable. When I told the receptionist my husband had been flown to this hospital, she said she had an unidentified John Doe brought in about two hours prior. She asked if I could identify my husband.

I thought she was asking me to identify his body. My heart raced, my stomach knotted, and my head spun. The chaplain appeared from the back, exchanged pleasantries, and asked if I was ready to see my husband.

As we walked toward Tyrel, the hallways of that hospital closed in on me like a vacuum-sealed bag.

When we finally arrived at his room, a nurse opened the door. There lay my husband, looking just as he had when I kissed his sleeping form goodbye before leaving for classes.

He looked so peaceful in the hospital bed. He didn't have a single broken bone, nor any visible bruises. He was unconscious with extensive brain damage.

I couldn't control my tears, but I knew I had to control my reactions. His nurse gave me what little information they could, but I'd know more when the doctors returned.

I wanted someone to walk through the door and tell me this was a nightmare. I wanted to wake him from his sleep so he could tell me everything would be OK. It was surreal. We all hear about tragedies like this, but we never expect to live them. My worst nightmare had become my reality.

I shed hundreds of thousands of tears, begging God to take me instead of Tyrel. It wasn't fair. I didn't understand how or why this happened to such a special man. If there were some way to give my life to save his, I would've moved mountains to make it happen.

Difficult Decisions

Tyrel spent three long weeks in the ICU. We almost lost him several times. His life hung in the balance of touch and go. I refused to leave his side. I convinced the nurses to let me sleep in his room at night. I observed every detail of his care, wrote notes on every component of his treatment, and educated myself to effectively advocate for him.

He woke from his coma after eight days. His eyes were open but empty. He was incoherent. Waking from the coma was a miracle, but it was the tip of the iceberg. Doctors warned me that his chances of survival were slim to none. They said if he survived, he'd never walk, talk, or eat on his own. I refused to settle for their grim outlook; they were experts in medicine, but I was an expert in my husband's will to live.

Traumatic brain injuries are unique. The brain is the most complex organ in the body, with many unknowns about the inner workings of its eighty-six billion neurons and their networks. Recovery looks different for each person. Doctors and therapists do their best to treat brain injuries based on what they know. Treatments are experimental, outcomes are surprises, and recovery is unpredictable. There are no manuals telling you what to expect or how to handle situations. You learn to be grateful for every little gain while warding off discouragement during the setbacks.

I had just started my second year in chiropractic school when the accident happened. Two years and four months of schooling lay ahead of me. I used my excused absences for the trimester to be with Tyrel in the ICU. My classmates became my lifeline to school, bringing study material to the hospital and doing everything they could to help me. The dean of students and a professor tried convincing me to quit. They said they didn't think I could handle the academic demand in addition to helping Tyrel.

Underestimating my tenacity and determination was a mistake of the highest degree on their part. When they said I couldn't do it, I made it my personal mission to succeed. I knew my time and attention would be divided between advocating for my husband and studying for my doctorate degree. Passing grades were nonnegotiable. Direct involvement in Tyrel's recovery was too. I had no idea *if* I would get through this, much less how, but those who doubted me fueled my fire.

Once Tyrel was stable enough to be released from the ICU, the road ahead was long and arduous. We moved him to a long-term acute care (LTAC) hospital for one month. He needed to gain strength to qualify for concentrated rehabilitation at a specialized facility. His first night in LTAC, he nearly died. Thank God I was there because when I heard him struggling to breathe through his tracheal tube, I jumped into action.

His lips were blue. I called for the nurse and started suctioning his tracheal tube. I paged a second time while continuing my efforts to clear his airway. Several minutes later, someone arrived and began treating him.

This marked the first of many sleepless nights for me. The harsh reality of healthcare is that some employees are there for a paycheck, not for the patients. For the next fourteen months I advocated for my husband to receive the care necessary to recover. It became my mission outside of school.

I questioned every move, every change, and every decision regarding his care. I watched him like a hawk, observing the smallest changes. I researched every medication he was given. I asked for explanations on every decision the doctors and therapists made. I refused to back down in the face of arrogance, ignorance, or laziness. If they didn't match his level of determination, I held their feet to the fire. When they refused to rise to Tyrel's level, I fired them.

Throughout his recovery, Tyrel gave his best effort every single day. I figured out how to assist him as best I could. We found creative ways to communicate because he couldn't speak.

Nearly five months into his recovery, I laminated an alphabet sheet. This let him point to letters and spell words. It was monumental in his recovery because it gave him a tool through which to communicate his needs. As his proficiency improved, he started sharing his thoughts. His doctors and therapists tailored his rehabilitation program accordingly.

It was eleven months before I heard his voice. He had to relearn talking, walking, and basic everyday activities. It was painful and frustrating for him. I fell apart many times, but never in his presence. It seemed unfair for me to break down in front of him because he suffered so much. Watching him fight so hard humbled me. His perseverance motivated me. As Tyrel pushed through his struggles, I matched his efforts.

No one could predict how much or how little he would remember. He recognized me but called me by different names. He couldn't connect all the dots for several months. My mind knew his brain injury caused confusion, but it shattered my heart nevertheless. The man to whom I'd devoted my life barely remembered me. I dug deeper into my soul, extracting every bit of strength buried in the depths.

I knew God had His arms around me every second of every day. My love for Tyrel knew no limits.

In total, Tyrel spent fifteen months in several facilities. When he returned home I was in my last year of chiropractic school, which was the clinical portion of my education. I made arrangements for Tyrel to come to the student clinic with me. My classmates came to the rescue again, offering to help care for Tyrel when I was treating patients. He was able to speak, but he was confined to a wheelchair, and he still required assistance transferring when he needed to use the restroom. In a school full of eager students, Tyrel had more assistance than either of us could've anticipated. My classmates orchestrated a therapy schedule based on their availability and individual focuses within their studies. From neurology to musculoskeletal rehabilitation, my classmates graciously poured their time and knowledge into Tyrel.

Chiropractic school gave me an outlet during Tyrel's recovery. Graduating was the only option. We didn't know if he'd ever fully recover, which meant I had to provide for our family. I could not fail.

I knew I would attain my degree and build a successful business. I also knew I would provide my husband with the best care. My certainty stemmed from my faith in God's presence in my life, especially this journey through tragedy. It was purely by God's grace that I balanced caring for Tyrel, graduating from chiropractic school, and maintaining our household.

In December 2013, I graduated as a Doctor of Chiropractic, right on time with my classmates. Tyrel stood in the front row, cheering me on as I received my diploma. From September 2011 to December 2013 I was Tyrel's biggest cheerleader. Now, seeing my cowboy rise from the constraints of his wheelchair, cheering for me as I walked the stage, filled my heart with profound gratitude and love.

My motto throughout Tyrel's recovery was that I'd be there for him as much or as little as he needed. His needs changed as he recovered. I was hands-on during every stage. When he asked for help standing or transferring, I assisted him with every step. When the canned food they fed him via his feeding tube left him emaciated, I began making more nutritional meals for him. When he wanted to ride a horse, I gathered the help I needed. When he set a goal to burn his wheelchair one day, I helped him regain strength and coordination to walk. Helping him in every possible way was my primary purpose. Life as my husband's caretaker wasn't easy, but I was fully vested in caring for him for the rest of our lives. Loving him was still my biggest blessing.

I never expected to experience this kind of tragedy. I don't think anyone anticipates life taking these turns. But we faced it, and despite the hardships, Tyrel and I mastered our new normal. Then, life threw another curveball.

There came a point in Tyrel's recovery that his behavior became unsafe for both of us. His brain injury caused many behavioral changes, and somewhere deep down I believe he struggled watching me take on so many responsibilities. Tyrel was a man's man and the head of our household. No matter how much I reassured him of his value in my life, I was his greatest trigger. He knew what his life used to be, and he also knew what his life may never be again.

I never imagined I'd have to step away as my husband's caretaker and wife. I vowed to love him and care for him in sickness and health, for better or worse, but after three and a half years, we decided it was best for him to live with his parents.

On Christmas Day 2014, I put my husband on a plane to fly him home to his parents. I thought the day of his accident was the worst I could ever experience. I was greatly mistaken, and I learned that the moment I put him on that plane.

Over the next six months, I hit rock bottom. I was empty inside. Tyrel, my purpose for moving forward, had left for his new home. I still managed to build my business, but I was falling apart inside. I entered a darkness I didn't know how to navigate. I felt like I was standing on the edge of the big black hole of depression, one foot in. I thought I was a failure as a wife and as a person. The only thing that kept me from stepping into the abyss was my work.

My chiropractic practice continued to grow, primarily for animals. I adjusted a few humans, but my passion was adjusting animals. I found peace and healing in every animal I treated. As much as I thought I was healing them, they were healing me. From the time I was young, I had a passion for and gift in dealing with animals. Becoming a chiropractor was my vessel for sharing my God-given gift. It later became my vessel for self-healing.

Feeling God's Presence
When we walk through tragedy or trauma, we are faced with difficult decisions. Somewhere, in what feels like the depths of hell, God is holding our hand as a father hold his child's hand to safely cross the street. It is easy to overlook His presence when life gets difficult, but He is omnipresent. In the darkness, He will show you the light. At rock bottom, He extends His reach further to wrap His arms around you.

God blessed me with the love of a lifetime when He gave me Tyrel. I was blessed to have loved a man with my whole heart and to have been loved wholeheartedly by a man.

In retrospect, I return to the question of how a six-year-old declares that no one would dictate the outcome of her life. Today, I realize that these inner thoughts were the purest form of God's presence. I didn't consciously know God at that age, but it was clear He knew me, and He protected me as I lived through the unimaginable. God gave me the courage to come forward when it was time, and He blessed me with the strength to carry the burden of that secret for over a decade to protect my family.

When it was time, God opened the doors for me to blaze a trail. He gave me a voice that would allow other young women to take their power back. The little girl whose innocence was stolen by a monster overcame trauma. I never lost sight of God's role in my life. I cautiously but trustingly opened my heart to a man who showed me the beauty of pure, unconditional love.

Like the phoenix in Greek mythology, I arose from the ashes of my predecessors and overcame adversity.

"The phoenix must burn to emerge." – Janet Fitch

*****

About Shawna Rainwater Turner:
Dr. Shawna Turner resides in north Texas where she owns and operates a successful chiropractic business. Animals are her primary focus and passion.

Growing up in a ranching family, Shawna fell in love with horses at a young age. Their majestic presence enamored Shawna and she felt a deep, safe connection when she was around them. She discovered their innate ability to bring peace and healing.

After being sworn to silence by her child molester, survival became her way of life. Later, when the love of her life sustained a traumatic brain injury in a motor vehicle accident, her resilience would once again be tested. It was her faith in God and love for animals that carried Shawna through trauma and tragedy. She is not just a survivor; she is a thriver.

TikTok - @docshawna
Instagram - @docshawnat
Facebook - Shawna Turner

Chapter 18
A Path Worth Walking

Katie Meadows

My life hasn't always been easy. Looking in from the outside, you never could have guessed that I struggled. It's not easy to talk about, but I hope my story helps someone else overcome seemingly insurmountable adversities. I am proof that anything is possible.

When I was a child, my family moved from Las Vegas, Nevada, to a small, quiet town in Mississippi—the storybook kind of town, where everyone knows everyone, gossip travels quickly, and where you feel like you're part of a big, crazy family, which is both a blessing and a curse.

It didn't take me long to realize, however, that in this town, your differences painted a target on your back. My insecurities erupted after we moved, egged on by trauma. I didn't fit in. My makeup and clothes were different, and that was unacceptable to my peers. I wasn't part of the popular crowd. I was voiceless and didn't feel pretty. My classmates bullied me, and my introversion made it harder to find my place.

Yet, I still formed fond memories, doing all the normal teenage things, like skipping school, sneaking out at night, and drinking with friends on the weekends.

After high school, I moved on to Mississippi State University, believing that's what I was supposed to do next. During my freshman year, I took my newfound freedom and ran too far with it: I ate out frequently, drank, and went to fraternity parties. I still felt like the odd one out, and I struggled to fit in.

That year, I gained fifteen pounds, which emboldened the insecure voice within me. This voice grew louder every day. My drastic changes in diet, lifestyle habits, stress, and sleep patterns were to blame. We'd go out at night, drink, and eat fast food before bed. Enough college freshman experience this weight gain for it to have a name—"the freshman fifteen"—but that didn't help me feel better about my weight.

Food became my refuge and my enemy, a source of comfort and control in a world where I felt I didn't belong. No one knew about my struggles. My eating disorders, bulimia and anorexia, were silent predators, determined to keep their claws in me. Nobody wants to talk about eating disorders. They aren't pretty.

During my struggles, my mom had moved back to Tennessee, and I joined her for a few years. As my eating disorder grew worse, the crowd I spent time with reflected my inner turmoil. It was hard to live a normal life. I hid my eating disorders from everyone I knew.

Eventually, I got into drugs to suppress my appetite. I hung out with the wrong people and partied. Deep down, I knew if I didn't make a change, something bad was going to happen. I was well aware that doing drugs and drinking could result in addiction. You can overdose or go down a path where you do not work, and the ripple effect of these decisions can be tragic.

As I started mapping out a way to escape this crazy pit I'd dug, my mom transferred to Indiana for work, my sister was moving back to Las Vegas, and my grandmother was going to Michigan. With our whole family parting ways, it was time to make a choice. I moved back to Las Vegas with my sister. That was the turning point to a new chapter of my life.

If I could say anything to my younger self, I'd tell her, "Have fun and be yourself. You're beautiful. Your heart makes you beautiful. Everything happening to you is normal, and it's not worth risking your life for. Everyone is made differently, and everything changes. Not being able to control change is a good thing, because change itself is good. Change is the only thing we're promised."

I have many regrets. I missed out on my twenties, what should have been some of the best years of my life. Things could've been so different.

When I returned to Las Vegas, I was still consumed by my eating disorders. The **struggle to eat** consumed my world for many years, leaving me stagnant and paralyzed.

Though I grappled with anorexia and bulimia for years, amid the darkness hope remained, a tiny ember refusing to extinguish.

One day I woke up and realized I was worth more than the sum of my insecurities. That I deserved a life filled with joy and abundance. I wanted more, because either way I wasn't living. I found a new beginning and took the opportunity to rewrite the narrative of my life.

Recovering from anorexia and bulimia was a journey fraught with twists and turns, with moments of triumph and setbacks alike. I started by simply focusing on eating. Most of the time, my meals were low calorie, but as I progressed, I added more and more food to my life. With each passing day, I reclaimed a piece of myself I thought I'd lost forever. An eating disorder is not something you ever fully recover from and you always live with it, but it can get better.

I recovered on my own, without help, but I do not suggest that for most people. Fighting this addiction alone was not easy, and I faced many challenges. I failed often. It was not an overnight process, and it's something I continue thinking about and live with the memory of. If you are struggling with an eating disorder, seek professional help and therapy immediately.

Fortunately, I found a job soon after moving to Las Vegas. I worked there for a long time, which helped me get through that dark patch. I was still lost, but I knew that wasn't the right path for me.

That's where my entrepreneurial journey began. I wanted to help people, to work for myself and to build something meaningful.

One of my friends went into real estate, and that inspired me. Helping others achieve home ownership or move into their next journey sounded like the perfect fit. I quit my job and dove into real estate full-time. It was a scary but necessary leap of faith. That decision sewed my world together. I knew I was capable, because the trials I'd endured showed me my strength.

Entrepreneurship is not easy. There are ups and downs, and it's not as glamorous as it looks. Working for yourself is great, but many people go into entrepreneurship thinking they'll be working fewer hours. In reality, you work far more. However, it is fulfilling, and through entrepreneurship I'm finally finding my place in this world.

Embarking on an entrepreneurial journey, especially in an industry like real estate, is daunting at first. My strength and determination have made it easier to navigate. Having the right mindset is crucial to your business's longevity. Fortunately, I had mentors around to help. I surrounded myself with people who'd help me grow fast, and I jumped in without hesitation.

Shortly after getting into real estate, I met my now ex, who was great in sales. They helped me hone my skills. I learned how to speak professionally and how to help others overcome obstacles. Each transaction made me better. My competence and confidence in running a business bloomed.

Before I knew it, my company had one of the top producing teams in Las Vegas. For four years, not only did I have the honor of running a large real estate team, but I also coached and guided agents as they matured in the profession.

Reflecting back, I learned a lot throughout those years with my own twist on the sales industry. As I grew into the person I was created to be, so did my superpower, which is connection. Once I shed the shy girl I was during my childhood, I thrived through connections and the satisfaction of helping others fulfill their dreams, which in turn helped me fulfill my own dreams.

There were many steps that went into becoming more outgoing. I worked with coaches and invested in myself by attending conferences, networking and speaking events, and community forums to gain knowledge and boost my confidence.

I contributed a great deal of my own personal energy and pain into a four-month leadership class I was invited to. The class dove into childhood traumas. We set healing and empowerment goals, challenging ourselves to complete tasks we once thought impossible. This newfound confidence pushed me into going independent, starting my real estate team, and mentoring and coaching sales agents.

My biggest pieces of advice for anyone trying to dive into entrepreneurship are:

- Seek a mentor.
- Develop a business plan.
- Take risks.
- Educate yourself.
- Embrace failure.
- Stay focused.
- Be persistent.
- Prioritize customer satisfaction.
- **Take care of yourself.**

Entrepreneurship can be a rewarding journey, but there are many challenges along the way. Sometimes you only have yourself to rely on. Sometimes you don't know if you'll have another sale, or when the next one will come, especially if you're in the real estate industry. Buckle up and get ready for the ride.

Striking a good work-life balance and building a successful business isn't easy. Your business will require uncountable hours, focus, and sacrifice. You must adapt to change and scale your operation. Self-doubt and stress will trickle in.

Today, as I stand on the threshold of the life I've created, I am grateful for the journey that led me here. The scars of my past are a testament to my strength and a reminder that everyone can overcome their darkest days. Finding my place in this world by helping and inspiring others means so much to me.

I learned to love myself unconditionally, to celebrate my imperfections while using the strength I've built. Recovery is never easy, but it's a path worth walking.

*****

About Katie Meadows:
Originally from a small town in Mississippi, Katie Meadows made the move to Las Vegas in 2003 with a vision to make a meaningful impact in real estate. As the founder of Meadows Home Team, a real estate company specializing in residential properties, Katie leverages years of industry expertise to guide clients through the buying and selling of homes.

In addition to her successful real estate career, Katie is the proud owner of Farm To Table Farmers Market. This venture underscores her commitment to promoting local agriculture and providing the community with fresh, high-quality produce and crafts, supporting local small businesses.

A distinguished leader in the business community, Katie serves as the vice president of the Entrepreneurs Club of the Women's Chamber of Commerce. In this role, she champions the growth and success of female entrepreneurs, fostering a supportive network and driving initiatives that empower women in business.

Recently accepted into the Leadership Academy of Nevada for the Realtor Association, Katie is dedicated to advancing leadership standards and innovation within the real estate industry, reflecting her ongoing commitment to excellence.

Outside of Katie's professional pursuits, she is a fitness enthusiast. Balancing her busy schedule with regular workouts and a love for reading, she finds inspiration and enrichment that positively impacts both personal and professional life.

For expert real estate advice, fresh market produce, or entrepreneurial guidance, contact Katie!

Chapter 19

Father Not Like Daughter

Skylar Wolf

"A person is a person, no matter how big or small. "
—Dr. Seuss

Hot breaths of fire direct at me by screaming in my face,
Your eyes are full of hate and rage.
Throwing your anger around to make an intimidating point,
Trust me ... I get it, all I am, is a disappointment.
I can't be who you want me to be,
Why can't you see me for who I am?
There are reasons why I am the way I am,
Partly your fault, and to admit this, I do not think you can.
The way I feel can never be spoken aloud to you,
I'm bruised and broken, both inside and out.
I wonder what you would say if you were me?
From the eyes of your daughter, you would for sure have to see.
Right?
Feeling the pain and the ways you hurt me stems from you, my father.

Many people can speak openly and freely about their childhood. Even after thirty years on this planet, I don't like talking about mine. I understand it's a big part of who I am. I can't run from the truth.

My father was often gone. He was in the navy, stationed on a submarine. During his service, he married my mother, then a single parent to my older brother and sister. While he was serving, they had me. I didn't know much about him then, but everyone said I looked just like him. I never knew if that was good or bad.

When I was six, my father got out of the navy. We adjusted to life with him in it. We learned what kind of man he, unfortunately, was. When he came home, he was a stranger to me. I had no memories of him prior to his discharge from the military. His rules and expectations were a new and uncomfortable shadow looming over the household. Things were OK for a while, but when things started changing, they snowballed.

At the start, my father was loving and kind to my mother, but that dissolved. He began working as a car mechanic while my mom worked as a cashier at a local gas station. My dad's work schedule was regular, and he'd come home around the same time every night, unless he went to the bar. My mom's work schedule was irregular.

On a night when my mom worked later than expected, my dad was at home, glued to the TV and drinking beer like it was water. That was his routine. Dad didn't talk to my siblings or me much. His moods were painted on his face, so often mean and angry.

By observing my siblings, I learned how to stay out of Dad's way. I sat at the kitchen table, coloring, waiting for Mom to get home. When she walked through the door, I jumped up immediately and ran to hug her.

Mom was my favorite person in the whole world. She'd pick me up and wrap her arms around me so tightly. That night, she gave Dad a kiss after hugging us kids. He stared at her and said, "What's with all the makeup and perfume? Why are you coming home late?"

She said, "I always wear makeup, and I told you, someone called out sick."

Mom went to her bedroom to pick out a pair of pajamas, and I followed, sitting on her bed. "Will you read this book I got from the school library?" I asked.

"After I shower, baby," she said.

Dad stormed into the room, looked at me, and screamed, "YOU! You are not supposed to be in here. GET OUT!" He pointed at the bedroom door. Startled and scared, I ran out as he redirected his screams at my mother. It lasted a while. He stomped into the kitchen and opened another beer, then sat on the sofa and continued watching his television shows.

After my mom showered, my sister and I settled into bed. Mom had only gotten through the first page of my book when Dad came into the room, stood beside my bed, and said, "I'm ready for bed. Meet me in the bedroom."

Mom said, "After I read her book, I will."

He snatched the book out of her hands, tore up the pages, and yelled, "NO. NOW."

I cried.

She yelled, "Now look at what you've done."

He bent down, grabbed Mom's arm, and dragged her away. I grabbed on to her so tight he pulled us both off the bed. He yanked me away from her and shoved her out of the bedroom. Standing in the doorway, he turned to me. I screamed out for my mother. He said, "You want to cry? I'll give you something to cry about."

Mom tried to stop him, but he pushed her out of the bedroom, slammed the door shut, and locked it.

Curled up on the floor against my bed, I heard her banging on the door, screaming my dad's name. "David, no."

He grabbed my shirt collar, put his forehead to mine, and said, "You've got ten seconds to stop crying, or else."

I gasped for air. Tried to stop crying but couldn't. He counted. "One … two … three … four …," as my mom continued pounding her fists against the door. Dad removed his belt. "Five … six … seven … eight …," he said through his teeth. I shook.

He made it to ten.

The belt clasped in his fist, he raised his hand high in the air and hit me as hard as he could. Curled into a ball, I screamed out to my mother. Again and again, he hit me. "The more you scream, the harder it'll be."

With every hit, another scream tore through me.

The belt turned into a whip, the metal buckle injuring my fragile body.

Somehow, Mom got the door open. She cried, rushing over to shield me with her body, and yelled, "That's enough, David."

He threw the belt down and took a sip of his beer. Wiping the sweat off his forehead, he said, "Now put her to bed and get into the bedroom."

After he left, she comforted me, pulling me into her arms, crying, kissing my forehead and whispering, "I'm so sorry, baby." She ran her hand down my back. I cried out in pain. She lifted my shirt and saw the marks he left, then gently picked me up and put me into bed. Every part of me ached. My back and arms were on fire. Mom kissed my forehead one last time, turned on my night-light, and rushed out of the room as the sound of his calls rang through the house.

I kept wondering, what did I do wrong? I'd been in trouble before, but Mom had never punished me like that.

Everything happened so fast that I didn't realize my sister had witnessed every second of the scene. She was frozen in fear.

My sister climbed out of bed and came over to me. "Are you OK?"

I wiped my tears. "I am OK."

She hugged me. "I love you," she said.

I said it back and turned away to stare at the wall until I cried myself to sleep.

The next morning, it hurt to move. Mom checked on me. She made my father look at the bruises he'd inflicted.

"Well, keep her home from school, then. I bet she wouldn't mind that. Would you, kiddo?"

I stayed home from school that day and took a warm bath to ease the pain. Mom sat next to me on the toilet, holding her head in her hands. It killed me to see her upset, so I reached out and touched her leg. She grabbed my hand and wiped the tears from her eyes. "I love you. Let's get you out of the bath. Mommy has to go to work soon."

As she laid out my clothes, there was a knock on the door. The babysitter, a next-door neighbor, had arrived. Miss Rosa always smelled like her pet birds. She wore glasses and had a wooden walking stick shaped like a candy cane. I didn't like her much because she was lazy, watched soap operas all day, and I had to beg for her to feed me. Eventually, I grew so tired of asking that I'd make myself cereal or a peanut butter and jelly sandwich.

I wished Mom could stay home. I couldn't go to school until Dad said it was OK, and I didn't know why. I stayed on my best behavior, entertaining myself with toys and coloring. When he came home from work, I was nothing less than the perfect child. If his beer was empty, I brought him a new one right away. I'd sit next to him and quietly watch TV, even if it was something boring like NASCAR. Maybe if I spent time with him and liked what he liked, he would like me more.

Terrified as I was, I did everything in my power to earn his approval. He disregarded my attempts at conversation, shut me down, and found ways to shut me up. He always had time to talk to my siblings, but not me. Why was there such disparity in how we were treated?

*****

My siblings and I had fun together growing up. We played together all the time, but we argued too. Once, we played a game called "lava," where the floor was lava, so if you touched it you lost. We leaped from couch to couch, walked on the coffee table and chairs, waiting for someone to fall.

During one game of lava, I broke something important. Terrified of punishment, I tried hiding it. A few days went by before my father discovered it. He called the three of us into the living room, lined us up, and said, "Who broke this and tried to hide it?"

We never told on each other. We always stayed silent. No one pointed a finger. I never liked lying, and I was bad at it. Dad would say, "Look me in the eyes. Did you do this?" and I'd try to talk my way out of it, but he'd yell over me. I'd stutter. Later in life, I needed speech therapy to overcome the stuttering.

When he asked a second time, I nodded. I was in big trouble.

Days prior, my father had made a paddle with holes in it. Named it Corporal Punishment. He made sure to show me the paddle. The next time I acted up, I knew what I was in for.

My siblings were forced to sit on the sofa while he grabbed Corporal Punishment. He instructed me to pull my pants down, looked at my siblings, and said, "Let this be a lesson to you both."

I still can't explain how badly that beating hurt. The holes made the paddle stick to my skin. He beat me until it snapped in half. Spanking a few times wouldn't have been enough to prove his point. When he wanted to hurt me, he did just that.

I lay on the floor behind the sofa, sobbing. Dad didn't say I could move, so I didn't. My brother and sister were dismissed. He sat on the sofa, turned on the television, and said, "Marissa, you may get up now."

My legs felt like jelly. The pain struck me as I stood. "While you're at it, kiddo, bring me another beer," he said, his tone casual, as if nothing had happened. I looked at him, confused, tears running down my face. He looked back and said, "Today would be nice."

I ran to the kitchen as fast as my legs would carry me and brought him a cold beer. Questions surfaced in my mind. Why? Why does he hate me so much? Why does he do this to me? He's my dad. Isn't he supposed to love me?

Why couldn't Mom come home already? At least she loved and cared about me.

That night triggered the first of many nightmares where I'd scream in my sleep.

The first time my mom woke me during a night terror, I had frightened my sister so much that she ran to wake Mom up. By the time she got into my room, I was screaming out, "Please stop it."

She shook me, and the moment I opened my eyes, I threw my arms around her. She didn't look like she knew what to say or do. "Are you OK? What's wrong?"

I had no idea how to explain it, but I did not feel OK. How do you tell your mother that you're having nightmares about your father harming you? I felt helpless. If I tried to speak, I'd stutter, so I never said a word. Mom calmed me down. Told me it was all a dream, that none of it was real. She tucked me back into bed, then left the room.

I couldn't fall back asleep, so I crawled into my sister's bed. "Sissy, can I sleep with you?"

Without saying a word, she made room for me next to her, my favorite wolf stuffed animal tucked under my arm.

The following day, Mom was off work. She and my grandmother took us kids out to eat at a local buffet. During our meal, Mom said, "Kids, there's something I want to tell you."

We stopped eating and gave her our full attention. She took a deep breath, placed a hand on her belly, and said, "You're going to have a new baby brother or sister."

My brother said, "Please let it be a boy."

My sister said, "No, I want her to be a girl."

Mom and Grandma looked at me. "You don't have anything to say?"

I said, "Do-do-does Daddy know?"

They laughed. Mom said, "Yes, baby, your daddy knows."

They carried on talking while I finished my plate.

Dad was in a good mood that night. "So, kiddos, I heard that your mother told you the news."

The smile on his face was uncharacteristic. Was he going to treat the baby the same way he treated me?

My brother said, "I wonder if the baby is going to look like you because you'll have the same dad."

I said, "W-w-we do not all have the ... the same dad?"

My brother looked at my parents like he'd said something wrong. Mom picked me up, put me on her lap, and said, "Your brother and your sister have different dads, but your dad agreed to be their dad before you were born."

Taken aback, I started crying. "So, they're not my brother and sister?"

My father was irritated now. He told Mom not to baby me and explained how half siblings worked. Then he said that since he was raising my siblings, he asked my mom for a child of his own, and that's why they had me. He ended the conversation, turned on the stereo, and said, "Let's have some fun."

Dad picked up my sister, tossed her over his shoulder, and began a wrestling match with my siblings. I watched them climb over him, watched him playfully toss them on the sofa. Mom said, "Go join in and play with your daddy."

He gave my sister a piggyback ride, came over to me, and said, "Come on, hop on, kiddo!"

I smiled and climbed on. He ran around the room acting like a horse. I wished he was always like this.

Another nightmare came to me that night. This time, Dad came into the room. He pulled me out of bed by my ankles and screamed, "How dare you wake me up with your crying."

I curled into a ball, and he wrapped his hands around my throat, picked me up, and held me against a wall. His eyes were lifeless as he said, "If you don't shut up and go to sleep, I will put you to sleep," and threw me on the floor. "You don't want me to come back in here."

Before he left the room, he smashed my night-light. "Thanks for waking me up. Now go to sleep."

He knew I was afraid of the dark. Why was he so cruel? Why did he punish me like that? What did I do to be treated like this over and over? My stuffed wolf was my only comfort that night.

My mom called us out for breakfast the next morning. Half-asleep, I rolled out of bed and met my family at the table. Before I could pull out my chair, Dad walked past me and slapped me on the back of the head, the way he always did if I didn't do or say something correctly.

Mom asked, "What was that for?"

Dad said, "Waking me up in the middle of the night with one of her crying fits."

"Sorry," I said.

"What was that? You look at me when you speak to me."

I picked my head up, looked at him, and apologized again.

After breakfast, I approached my mother. "Can I go pl-pl-play outside?"

Asking for anything was nerve-racking. Even though my speech was getting better, I stuttered when I was nervous.

She said, "Wait. Come here and let me look at something."

As she examined my new bruises, I asked again if I could play outside. She said I could.

My favorite spot was high in a tree. I watched the neighborhood kids play at the park. I pretended the tree was a watchtower I needed to protect. I was a spy, a superhero, a monkey. The tree was magical, a secret escape from reality.

When the streetlights came on, it was time to go home. I was never ready to go back home. I learned to pause outside the door and listen, to read the moods of everyone inside, before heading in. Even on nights devoid of screaming, tension hung in the apartment.

My parents often gave each other the silent treatment until Dad got fed up and went to the bar. Mom cooked dinner that night while my sister and I bathed, and by the time we were dressed, food was ready.

While we settled into bed, Mom asked where my night-light was. "Broken," I said.

"Did you break it and not tell Mommy?"

I shook my head.

"Daddy?" She tucked us both in. "I'll leave your bedroom door open and keep the hall light on, so you're not scared. Good night. I love you."

"I love you too," we said.

I was glad she left the hall light on, but I still couldn't sleep. Scared of another nightmare, I lay there while my sister slept. The front door rustled open. Dad was home.

"Why is this light on? You kids don't pay the bills," he yelled. My heart pounded in my chest. Once he reached our bedroom, I closed my eyes, pretending to be asleep. He knew better.

He grabbed my ankles, ripped me off the bed, and dragged me into the living room. As soon as he let go, I attempted to run. Couldn't get away from him.

Dad backed me into a corner. Inches from my face, he said, "You … You're the reason your mother hates me."

I made the mistake of breaking eye contact, and he took the opportunity to grab my throat and pin me to the wall. Tightening his grip, he looked me in the eyes and said, "I brought you into this world and I can take you out of it."

He squeezed so hard I almost passed out before he finally let go. My knees hit the floor. I gasped for air.

"Don't you ever forget it. Get up and go to bed."

I never spoke a word about what happened. This was my life. This was my father.

*****

Months later, when Mom was far along in her pregnancy, I couldn't wait to be a big sister. I talked to her bump as though the baby understood me. I didn't know anything about pregnancy, so I didn't understand Mom's hormonal mood swings. I thought she was mad like how Dad got mad. The days where they were both angry became more frequent.

One night, Dad came home from work, and they got into an argument in their bedroom. We were in the living room watching a movie while they screamed at each other.

Then there was banging. Shattered glass replaced the yelling.

I looked at my siblings, then got up and went down the hall. I opened the bedroom door. He was on top of her, both hands wrapped around her throat.

Without thinking, I yelled, "GET OFF MY MOMMY!" I punched him and tried to pull his hands away.

He let go and turned toward me. I tried to run away, but before I'd made it halfway through the hall, he snagged the back of my shirt, grabbed my neck, and smacked my face into the wall. I hit the floor. Blood leaked from my nose. He flipped me over and pinned me down, his knee jammed into my chest. I fought back.

My mom yelled out to my siblings, "Go to Miss Rosa's and call 911."

She tried getting him off me. They bolted out the door.

Dad stopped. Didn't say a word. Grabbed his keys and left.

Mom made us wait at Miss Rosa's while she spoke to the police, who pulled my dad over and took him to jail for domestic violence.

He was released the next day. When he came home, he dropped to his hands and knees and cried for forgiveness, swore he'd change and do better.

Mom must have really loved him, because she agreed to give him another chance.

*****

My mom gave birth to a little girl. Dad put on a loving father act. Called her his little princess. Made sure she had nice things.

I was jealous, but I pushed past it and promised myself I'd protect her from him as she got older. Mom went back to working crazy hours, so we were stuck with Miss Rosa often. She ignored my sister's cries. I did my best to take care of her, but I didn't know how to make a bottle of formula. To force Miss Rosa's hand, I had to be disruptive, annoying, disrespectful. I'd unplug the TV so she'd have to get up and notice my sister crying.

One day I unplugged it, and she pulled out a book instead, ignoring us entirely. When she wasn't looking, I stole her cane and hid it in a jacket in the coat closet, figuring if she didn't want to move to take care of us, I'd make it so she couldn't move when she wanted to. Unfortunately, she never ended up wanting to move that night, so she didn't notice her missing cane. I forgot about it until my dad came home and it was time for her to leave. "I can't find my walking cane," she said.

"Kids, did one of you touch Miss Rosa's walking cane?"

My heart fell to my stomach. My siblings said, "No, sir."

I rushed to the closet to grab it without him seeing, but he caught me red-handed. "What have I told you about touching things that aren't yours?"

I tried to explain myself, but my stutter came out again. He ripped the cane from my hands, brought it to her, and walked her to her apartment. Dad returned with the cane, stood by the front door, and glared at me. I sat on the love seat. He raced toward me. I leaped over the back of the couch and ran to my room.

But I couldn't hold the door closed long enough to lock it. Dad burst through. Before he could hit me with the cane, I grabbed it. We wrestled to the floor, both of us gripping the cane. He pressed it across my chest and shoulders. "You think you can beat me, huh?"

My legs weren't strong enough to push him off me.

"You think you're so tough? You're nothing without me. Without me, you wouldn't be breathing," he screamed as he overpowered me and began beating me with Miss Rosa's cane.

I must have passed out. I remember being hit, but I don't remember the beating stopping. The cane was another weapon used and broken on me.

*****

Soon after, my parents split up for good. I wish I could say that part of my life ended there, but it didn't. Things got darker. We played musical parents, mixed with drugs and alcohol, before life improved.

Even when things got better, I struggled through my teen years. I hated looking at myself in the mirror. I didn't see me. I saw him. I remembered everything he said and did to me. I held on to so much pain and anger, even though he wasn't around to physically beat me up or mentally beat me down anymore.

I replaced him and abused myself in his absence. My pain, inner chaos, and hopelessness dragged me down so far, I attempted suicide. That's when I finally got the help I needed and deserved.

Therapy was hard at first. I didn't know how to express my emotions. My therapist was understanding and let me write things down until I was comfortable talking. Journaling became my outlet. Eventually, I realized that writing and journaling had a positive, healing effect on me and my life. I finally recognized myself.

Now when I look in the mirror, it doesn't hurt as much to see him. I cannot change him or my childhood.

I can, however, change the direction of my life. I choose to not be like him, a bitter, angry person who hurts the people they claim to love, a person who chooses to live in darkness and hide behind cowardice. I choose to release my anger, to be a better person despite the trauma I suffered through. I choose to see the light in my soul instead of following in my father's footsteps. I choose to love myself in the absence of his love, and I choose to accept myself knowing he never will. I wish someone would have told me to not punish myself, that it will only keep his cycle going.

You cannot be enough for someone if they are not enough for themselves. It may not take the pain away, but that sentiment helps me push forward. I had to really dig deep to find myself and learn how to make myself happy. This is when I found out what I was really passionate about and what brought enjoyment to my life: dogs.

I spent more time running around with the neighborhood strays than kids my age. I wanted them all and to save them all and as a kid, I was always happy around a dog. It was later in life I found out that being around animals is a form of therapy. I suffer from depression and anxiety, so I decided to get a dog for emotional support and motivation. As an adult, I now have gained more knowledge and have a career working with dogs and I am proud of what I do.

The best thing you can do is find something that makes you feel good about yourself and do something that makes you want to get up every day. You're in control of your life and your own happiness now. You may not be able to change the past, but you can decide to have a better future.

*****

About Skylar Wolf:
I have always had a passion for writing, ever since I learned how to spell. I love writing poetry and collecting poetry books. I have a huge love for animals, so I work at a training facility for dogs as their agility trainer/ kennel manager. I also come from a huge family who love spending time together. If I'm not working or writing, I'm making new memories with friends and family.

Chapter 20

The Power of Closure

Theresa Reyes

Broken to blessed.
Psalm 34:18: "The LORD is near to the brokenhearted; he saves those crushed in spirit"

Some young girls dream about the Cinderella story—finding their prince someday, just like in the movies and fairy tales. I was one of those little girls.

My father worked full time and my mother was a homemaker. My dad would get home from work and my mom would meet him in the driveway with a hug to welcome him home. Then she would take his lunch box in to wash for the next day, and of course, dinner was already on the table, always ready by five o'clock. It was almost a fairy-tale upbringing.

The story I'm about to share is not a fairy tale. It's also far from being a scary story. My story is one of triumph and victory. My story references God, and what He has done for me. The happy ending of my story was only possible because of God.

I believe that most people want to do better, live better, become better. Doing so takes strength and determination. Changing yourself for the better is hard work. You can choose to do that hard work with God on your side, or you can try to do it on your own. I will share my story of how I made my choice, how it changed my life, and how it made me forever grateful.

Far From Cinderella
At the age of nineteen, I met a man. He was thirty-one years old. We dated for five months. The relationship developed super quick, and before I knew it, I was in college and newly married. I thought that's how the story was supposed to go.

At twenty-one, I became pregnant. Everything seemed to be wonderful … until it wasn't. When I was five months pregnant, my husband came home late from work, and I could smell alcohol on his breath. I asked him where he'd been, and he answered, "None of your business." We got into an argument. That night, I got my first slap across the face.

The next morning, my husband returned with a dozen long-stem roses, apologized profusely. He said it would never happen again. He seemed so sincere, and I believed him. Things were good for a while. However, a few months later, while we were driving home, he did not like the way I spoke to him, and once again, I got a quick backhand across the face. Of course, it was followed with apologies, flowers, and hugs. The cycle had begun.

Our marriage started to go downhill. My husband was drinking regularly and a lot. We stopped attending church. Looking back over these years of abuse, I had a dark cloud over my life.

Abuse was not something I was used to. Growing up, I only saw my parents fight once. They had disagreements and arguments, but these always took place behind closed doors. They never happened in front of me. I remember as a little girl taking a glass and sticking it to the wall so I could hear what they were saying. It was always about finances.

I grew up poor in finances but rich in family. I watched my parents' healthy relationship. To them, family was the priority. When things started to sour in my own marriage, my parents said, "You made your bed, now you have to lie in it." I'm sure a lot of people have heard this before, but what they really meant was that my husband and I should work things out to create a house and home like they had.

They didn't know what was really happening. I didn't tell them the full extent of what went on in my house until years later. Every year, I would move back to my parents' home for at least a month at a time. My husband would promise he would change, that things would be better. I'd move back home, and the first few months would be awesome. Then slowly, things would go right back to the way they were, and the abuse would restart.

His abuse and control were financial, mental, emotional, and physical. He held a gun to my head on multiple occasions. I was picked up and thrown across the room so many times. Sometimes at night, he would throw me outside and lock the doors so I couldn't get back into the house. I would have to walk to a pay phone to call friends to see who could pick me up. The street we lived on was listed as the third-worst street in the city for crime, but that didn't seem to matter. He would even take the distributor cap from my car, so my car wouldn't run.

Daily I lived with the meanness of the playground bully. His abuse was so bad and so persistent that I decided I didn't want to live anymore. I had two beautiful children who were my world. Even though I loved them, I just couldn't take the abuse. I prayed and asked God to take me out of this world. Following that prayer, I got sick with walking pneumonia.

After four weeks of severe illness, I started having asthma attacks. I required a rescue inhaler at least ten times a day. I was extremely weak and could hardly get around. My mom and sister came over every day to help me. They would make dinner and clean my house and watch my girls. I remember the night my husband came home and was mad that I was still sick. We argued, and he slapped me across the face. That slap ruptured my eardrum.

I went back to the doctor to treat the pneumonia. My doctor saw blood inside my ear. He asked me how it happened, and I said that I had fallen. He was not fooled and told me that he knew I did not fall. He said, "This only happens when somebody slaps you in the head. The cup of the hand acts as a plunger and breaks the eardrum."

He told me to take classes and speak to a counselor at SAVE (Safe Alternatives to Violent Environments). He said if I didn't agree to go, he would have to report it to the police. So, I started attending group classes with a counselor and began to get a clearer view of what was happening.

One night, I had a dream where I saw my grandfather, who'd passed away the year I was born. We were up on a balcony, and I gave him a big hug. While I was hugging him, I heard babies crying. I looked over the balcony and saw my children below. They had all these amazing toys around them, yet they were crying out, "Mama! Mama!" over and over. I looked back at my grandfather, and said, "They need me, don't they." He never said a word but just nodded as if to say, "Yes." I could see that my children needed me.

I woke up the next day, Tuesday, with a clearer perspective. I asked my sister to have her pastor come and pray for me. He did. After he prayed, I felt stronger, but I was still not able to breathe clearly.

On Wednesday, I had another doctor's appointment. Six weeks into my illness, I was on my fourth round of antibiotics. Nothing seemed to be working. The doctor who examined me did not have good news. He said my left lung was ready to collapse. He then told me that the lung specialist was out of town, but he would be back on Friday. My doctor then made an appointment for me to be hospitalized on Friday.

As I was leaving, he said that I needed to get my affairs in order. We all know what that means. I went home crying and thought, "Well, this is what I prayed for, so I got what I prayed for."

That night, a family member called. They told me there was a revival in a church in San Jose and they invited me to go. In the past when someone asked me to go to church, I was always too busy. I had things to do, or I would make up some excuse to not attend. This day was different. I knew what I had to do. I immediately said yes.

At the service, we sat in the very front row, an unusual choice for me. The service started, and the guest evangelist stared right at me. He asked my name. Then he told me in front of everyone, "Theresa, God has something for you tonight." I had no idea what he meant. I was a little nervous, but every word the evangelist spoke seemed like it was just for me. It was like God was using him to speak directly to me. In fact, the whole service seemed like it was orchestrated only for me.

We were at a United Pentecostal church. This church believes in the Holy Ghost and speaking in tongues. (If you don't know what that is, you can look it up in the Bible under Acts 2:38.) I grew up Catholic, and at age twelve, I was introduced to Pentecostal and Apostolic teachings.

When the service was almost over, it was time for the altar call. In the past, that would've been my time to sneak out to the bathroom so no one would invite me to the altar to pray. This time however, I was asked if I wanted to receive the Holy Ghost. I said yes, and when I stood up in the front row, I was already at the altar.

While I prayed, a minister came up to me and said in my ear, "Someone has been making you feel worthless." I replied, "Yes."

Then he said, "Someone's making you feel inferior. I said "Yes."

Then he said something that totally shocked me. "You have been contemplating suicide lately." No one knew this about me—not my closest friends, not even my sisters. Nobody knew how I felt.

At that moment, he told me, "God just revealed those things to me. He wants you to ask Him for forgiveness." When I raised my hands and asked God for forgiveness, I felt a warmth come over me and I started speaking in another language. That was my confirmation that God was in full control.

I was at the altar for probably half an hour. Afterward, I was asked, "What did the minister say?" They couldn't hear a word he was saying, even though they were standing right next to him. The words he spoke that day were for my ears only.

Once I finished praying, I told the minister "I've been sick for six weeks with pneumonia and asthma. Will you pray for me?" When he prayed for me, I felt a heat go down to my waist. When the heat lifted, I inhaled deeply—and breathed clearly for the first time in weeks.

The following day, I called my doctor. He said, "I can't see you. There is nothing more I can do for you." I persisted and finally, he said, "Fine. Come in at 11 a.m."

When I arrived at his office, I walked all the way in. Previously, I had to stop or even sit down several times in the parking lot to catch my breath. When the doctor came into the exam room, he looked puzzled. On prior visits, I'd been slouched over, but this time I was sitting upright.

He sat on his wheeled stool and listened to my lungs. All at once, he quickly pushed away and hit the wall behind him. He kept saying, "This is not possible," repeating it over and over. I asked, "Don't you want to know what happened?" He looked at me and said, "Yes."

I told him that I'd gone to church, a minister prayed for me, and God had healed me. Without speaking, the doctor wrote in my chart, and put down his pen. He silently got up and walked out of the room. That day Dr. Barrie witnessed a miracle. I'm sure he has never forgotten it. I've since wondered many times what he wrote in my chart that day.

This started a whole new journey for me. I had a renewed purpose. I needed to be there for my children. The peace, strength, and joy I now had, was like a light shining brightly around me.

While my husband's abuse didn't stop, I had a new strategy to battle it. When arguments started, I would walk away, singing. Things that bothered me before, no longer bothered me.

Fast-forward ten years: One day in the middle of an argument, my husband was screaming in my ear. He was so close, the pain was unbearable. I put my hand up and pushed him away. I went to my room and started packing my things. Then I thought, "Why should I move out? He needs to go." I went into the other room and told him he needed to leave this time.

He got so mad, he called the police. Two officers arrived—an older officer and a rookie—and my husband asked them to remove me from the apartment. They asked who I was. He responded by identifying me as his wife. Then the cops said, "We can't remove her unless there's been a physical altercation. Has there been one?"

He said, "Yes, she scratched my face." When one of the officers came back inside to ask me if I had scratched his face, I said I may have because I'd pushed him away with my hand. They took pictures of his face, and there were no signs of scratches. The older officer said, "I can see what's going on here," whereas the rookie wanted to book me for domestic violence. As the officers argued in my living room, the rookie asked the older officer, "Are you going against the law?"

He said, "No, I can just see what's going on here. She is not the abuser."

Sadly, a new law had recently passed that stated if anyone admits to touching another, it's an automatic arrest and domestic violence charge. The older police officer said he was going to take me down to the station and book me. He said he wouldn't handcuff me in front of my children, but he did so in the car.

I spent a whole day in jail until my dad came to post bail. One of the captains came back to my cell and said, "Your dad is not going to pay your bail unless you go straight to the courthouse and file for divorce."

After I was released, my dad and I headed over to the courthouse to file divorce paperwork. Then I moved back home with my parents. Because I'd been arrested, charges were filed. After suffering years of abuse, I was the one being charged with domestic violence.

My case passed through to the court system. I was a woman charged with domestic violence, and I felt they wanted to get a conviction to make an example of me. If I were convicted of domestic violence, the punishment could be up to a year in jail. They wanted to prove a point that not only men commit domestic violence. However, they didn't realize that, in this case, I was the true victim.

During the criminal case, while I was in court, my ex-husband filed for full custody of our children. The judge asked where I was and the lawyer said, "She's upstairs in another courtroom fighting a domestic violence charge." The custody case was dismissed, and this judge sensed something was off and stamped *Denied* all over the paperwork.

For the criminal case, I had three public defenders who all quit. I was on my last public defender. When he came to meet me, I remember looking out the window as he walked up the driveway. I thought to myself, "Great. What is this guy going to do for me?" We spent several days gathering evidence. He ridiculed me, saying he didn't understand why women stayed in abusive relationships for so long. He was convinced that my church must've had something to do with me staying for as long as I had.

Then the day came when we had to interview jurors. One young man, around nineteen years old, started to cry and said his parents were in a violent relationship. He said it would be hard for him to sit through the trial. I remember the words he spoke as he stared at me: "Only God can be her judge." The public defender wanted to keep him on the jury, but I said, "No, let him go." That poor boy had already been through enough in his life.

Once the jury trial started, it lasted five days. To my dismay, they had my eleven-year-old girls testify against me.

This was one of the worst times of my life. I could handle all the abuse, but this trial was among the hardest things I'd ever gone through. My girls said the exact same thing, word for word, like they'd been coached.

During the trial, my ex-husband provided a poster board of photos that consisted of damage done to walls and doors of our shared apartment. Some of the photos were very old. I didn't know that since the beginning of our marriage, he'd been setting up a case. One photo was of a plastic shower door that had broken while I was cleaning the ceiling. He'd taken a photo of it and saved it. Had he been planning to make it seem like I was an abusive wife for years?

During the trial, I got a phone call from one of the public defenders. He asked, "Your ex-husband's prior domestic violence charge—was it against you?" I didn't know what he was talking about, but wanting to find out more, I said, "It could've been," and I asked for details.

When he shared the details, I almost passed out. I never knew my husband had a prior domestic violence conviction.

On the last day of the trial, I had my head in my hands. My public defender asked if I was praying. I told him yes. And he said, "Good, keep praying." I looked up at him with disbelief, because this was a man who didn't believe in God.

When the jury returned their verdict, I got a full acquittal.

After we were dismissed, we stepped into the hallway. My public defender told me that when he got up to give his closing argument, what came out was not the argument he'd written. He said it was like something had taken over and spoken through him.

His family was present in court that day to watch the trial. He told me that being a public defender was a hard job, and he rarely got a good night's sleep. But during my trial, he slept like a baby. My family all pitched in, and we bought him a nice Bible. The following Sunday, he and his wife showed up at our church.

New Beginnings
My ex-husband always told me that I would never make it on my own, that I would end up on welfare, and that he would take my children away from me. These were all threats meant to control me. I am here to tell you that I am thriving. We all have strength inside of us. We need to reach down and pull it out. God has opened many doors for me, and I am successful today because of God.

If you are someone who is experiencing domestic violence, I won't lie and say that every day since getting out has been amazing. I will say to you, that you're going to have days when you feel down. No one will be there to pick you up, and you'll feel alone. That is the time when you must step up and encourage yourself. Speak words of life TO YOURSELF. Find that inner strength that I know you have. We all have it.

Many days, I've had to step up and encourage myself. I'd say,

"I'm strong, I'm confident, I'm beautiful, I'm ready."

"Put on your smile and watch God open doors for you."

"I am a great mother. I listen, I love, and I protect."
"I WILL be greatly used by God."

I went on to earn my certificate to become a domestic violence advocate through S.A.V.E. I have since remarried a wonderful man who loves my children as his own. Life has been amazing.

My ex passed away from cancer a few years ago. It was a very sad time for my children. Closer to his last days, I prepared some of his favorite meals, and my husband and I delivered them to his house. I thought this would be a great way for me to heal. Over the years, I still harbored resentment, unforgiveness, and hate toward this man.

But I'd kept it all buried deep. I had to focus on empowering women who were going through similar situations. I would even teach about forgiveness.

My ex-husband was not a bad man. In some areas, he had a big heart. He was a diligent worker. Growing up, he'd learned bad habits. He was abused and had seen abuse and thus became an abuser. He saw things that carried over into his adult life. He never broke the cycle.

Domestic violence is a learned behavior, and it carries through generations. It affects everyone in the family. You owe it to yourself and to your children to break the cycle.

One Sunday after church, I got my ex-husband a prayer blanket, which is a blanket that is prayed over during the church service and then gifted to someone who is sick. My ex never took my phone calls. Our conversations happened through our children. I called my daughter and told her that my husband and I were going to drop off the prayer blanket for her dad. She said he didn't want it. Then she said he wanted to see me, but only me, not my husband. This upset me, so I decided not to go see him. But when I got home, I had this feeling that I needed to see him one more time. I asked my husband if he minded, and he said, "No. Go ahead."

When I arrived at my ex's house, his longtime girlfriend had gotten there before me. My daughter came outside and told me the girlfriend said I could not go inside. My ex passed away the next day. The prayer blanket was given to my daughter to keep in her dad's memory.

We never got the closure we needed—the closure *I* really needed. Whenever his name was mentioned, an ugly feeling would rise up inside me. I only remembered the terrible things he did to me.

One night, I had a dream, and in my dream, I saw him. He was a young man again. We hugged and asked each other for forgiveness. When I woke up, all the feelings of hate and anger toward him had gone. There was just love, a brotherly love, a selfless love. Now when I share stories of our life together, I only remember the good times. I am able to share those stories with my children and grandchildren.

God gave me a gift. How could I teach and share with others who are going through domestic violence, if I harbored resentment and anger in my own heart? It was like God had wiped it all away. My journey has just started, and I am here to help others stop the cycle.

The Power in Forgiveness
Domestic violence is hard to talk about, but it's reality. It crosses all boundaries—financial, racial, and social—and persists unless the abuser seeks help.

I've seen broken marriages restored through God's grace, but only if the abuser is willing to change. It's tough work, but necessary to break that cycle of violence: love, tension, explosion—over and over. You must stand up, shake it off, and make changes. Someone else may need your story to make their own change. Your children need you to break the cycle.

We all make mistakes, but recognizing and correcting them is key. If we've hurt someone, we must seek their forgiveness. Holding on to pain can cause sickness and stress. Forgiveness sets us free, not just from others, but from ourselves. Past mistakes are just that—in the past. Don't let that past define you. You have a present and future purpose—embrace it.

Forgiveness is powerful. When we forgive, we release the anger and pain and begin anew. Remember: "You will never be victorious if you are always a victim."

You can overcome anything. Let today be your new beginning. You're worth it! My story is meant to encourage you—change your story for yourself and your family. No one will see your potential until you see it in yourself. You're amazing—start living and loving your changed life!

*****

About Theresa Reyes:

Theresa Reyes is a certified domestic violence advocate. She has been empowering and speaking to women at group homes and churches around the bay area since 2005. She spent fourteen years as the director of the children's junior department at the Union City Apostolic Church and has taught youth at summer camps for fourteen years. She is a John Maxwell Leadership certified public speaker as well as a patent and trademark paralegal. She is the author of many children's lessons and is writing a faith building book, soon to be published. She is mom to many and grandma to many more.

Chapter 21

Unto Shore

Kendra Trần

"Boat!"

My mother, Nga, had escaped a communist regime, and though she was far beyond its reach, her dissidence did not go unpunished. Her 4'11" frame knelt in prayer on the stern of her wooden boat, a weary vessel in the expanse of the South China Sea. Behind her, crewmates burned scraps of clothing, fanning the smoke plume to draw the eye of salvation moored on the horizon.

For thirty-six days, my mother and twenty-five others had drifted on the water, their boat's motor dead on day three, their rations spoiled by day four, and water supply short—amounting to a couple of wet mouthfuls a day. On that thirty-sixth day, in the breath before that discordant shout, my mother had reached the nadir of her endurance and was ready to surrender herself to the ocean. Her fate hung on the whims of the far-off ship's captain, whose barge appeared a mere speck on the water, likely deciding whether to rescue her insignificant dory or leave it to its fate, as several had done before.

Then, a miracle. "We're saved!" the cry pealed, a lifeline of sound that haled my mother back from the azure. The ship was no longer a speck but a staggering colossus, a merciful terminus.

It was 1981, and the aftermath of the Vietnam War had left my mother's home in the southern province of Trà Vinh a shadow of its former bustling state. The ensuing collectivization of agriculture, censorship, and erasure of heritage combined with the paucity of rice, electricity, and international support were especially paralyzing. Amid this desolation, my mother, along with an estimated million others, fled their country by boat, becoming part of diasporic history as the "boat people."

I wouldn't be born for another fifteen years to learn of her perilous journey, but the story of what transpired in her early adulthood is so emblazoned in my psyche that I can see the crouched boatman's moonlit face as he motioned for my mother's silence while briskly guiding her onto his craft. I can visualize the weathered panels of the wooden hull, the frightened children who cleaved to their anxious mothers, and the determined fathers whose hope outweighed their trepidation—eight of whom would never see the inside of the Dutch *Nedlloyd Tasman* freight ship that eventually rescued them. I feel the caustic irony of being surrounded by so much water and yet be dehydrated. I smell the acrid smoke of flaming polyester as they signaled for help.

My mother is a reticent woman, so I've often wondered how she lasted at sea. How did she reconcile the wasting of her country and of her family from whom she parted in haste? Where was her refuge when the first storm approached, its darkness from above and below threatening to engulf her fragile vessel? How did she cope with witnessing numerous deaths? I imagine the voice inside her head: "You're doing this for your family, Nga. You must reach America."

And she did. Despite starting anew in California, those harrowing moments, along with others etched deeply into her memory, continue to affect her in many ways. This is the story of my mother, Nga Lê, and her embarkment for healing at sixty-eight.

Mère came of age during an era of war both inside and outside her home. Her mother, my *bà ngoại*, was a porcelain vendor. Her father, my *ông ngoại*, was an intelligence officer for the Army of the Republic of Vietnam (ARVN). Now that both grandparents have passed on, I remember them longingly for their laconic natures—bà ngoại reserved and ông ngoại austere. It was only as I grew older that I understood the rarity of their joy.

Long ago, ông ngoại both suffered and inflicted pain. Almost nightly, he would arrive home in a stupor, the scent of whiskey preceding him as a herald of chaos. Mère describes his eyes as different from the discerning ones I knew, clouded by the haze of spirits. Before her three sisters and five brothers were born, Mère and bà ngoại knew too well the script of his nightly torment, which took place on the edge of bà ngoại's wooden platform bed.

"Do you think you're better than me?" he'd slur. "Your family, they never wanted you with me. You, with your airs and graces, always looking down on me." He'd sway, his fists clenching and unclenching. "I'm not my dad. I wouldn't hit my wife." His fist would lash out, rapping the bed instead. Sleep deprivation was his weapon.

Sober, perhaps, ông ngoại might have wordlessly gone to his room upon returning from work. But having packed away half a dozen pints, he would raise his voice at bà ngoại, and she would tolerate it. The hours would stretch as he paced and ranted, lost in the labyrinth of his insecurities.

Mère, from the age of ten, would huddle beside bà ngoại during those interminable nights, as if her presence alone could shield her mother from the barrage of resentment her father hurled. Notwithstanding her unease, she never showed defiance. In a deeply patriarchal society that placed filial piety above all, Mère's role was to bide in silence. By being there, she hoped to vicariously absorb the sorrow from bà ngoại's heart. Attuned to the venomous content of her father's monologues, she would waver between straining to understand who was at fault for the generational abuse and attempting to drown out the noise by silently chanting Buddhist mantras, repeating them as many times as it took for the din to subside. Only then could mother and daughter steal a few remaining hours of the morning before bà ngoại needed to set up shop and Mère set off to school.

This cycle for Mère continued until she was twenty-four years old, only halting briefly when ông ngoại was sent to a reeducation camp.[1]

Soon after annexing Saigon in 1975, the communist regime enacted retributive policies against families throughout southern Vietnam. Notably, the Việt Cộng administration employed a personal dossier system to evaluate an individual's amenability to communist ideology. This system recorded such identifying information as the individual's name, ethnicity, religious affiliation, and vocation to dichotomously classify him or her as "good" or "bad." Those with family members who worked with the French, American, or Southern Vietnamese government during the war were categorized as "bad." Similarly, having a relative who owned a business or property labeled the entire family as capitalist, subject to reprisal.

Under this policy, ông ngoại was compelled to intern in a reeducation camp. Bà ngoại's porcelain business was suffocated by exorbitant taxes and subsequently went bankrupt, leaving her with meager resources to support Mère and her eight siblings. Because of their affiliation with the ARVN and capitalism, Mère and her siblings were barred from continuing their schooling. This edict was especially heartbreaking for Mère, who had just completed her first year at university and dreamed of becoming a teacher. Deprived of educational and

---

[1] See Hiroto, D. S., & Seligman, M. E. P. (1975). "Generality of Learned Helplessness in Man." *Journal of Personality and Social Psychology*, 31(2), 311-327. https://doi.org/10.1037/h0076270

economic prospects, my mother resolved to be the first of the Lê children to find freedom.

According to psychiatrist Bessel van der Kolk (2014):

Trauma is not just an event that took place sometime in the past; it is also the imprint left by that experience on the mind, brain, and body. This imprint has ongoing consequences for how the human organism manages to survive the present. Trauma results in a fundamental reorganization of the way mind and brain manage perceptions. It changes not only how we think and what we think about, but also our very ability to think.[2]

Even after experiencing domestic dysfunction, war, and displacement, my mother flatly repudiated the word *trauma*. Trauma, to Mère, was not an apt descriptor for what she faced—she who lived through war but wasn't a veteran, who beheld her father's alcoholism but was physically unscathed, who was a refugee but reached shore. To the fighting woman who is my mother, acknowledging trauma and its overwhelming stress meant conceding defeat.

While she never showed that her past affected her, its impact on me became apparent in my early twenties.

Inherently, Mère is selfless to a fault, always putting others before herself. However, during times when I expressed my young adult Vietnamese American angst, her complaisance toward me fell short. In particular, when airing my grievances about the microaggressions felt living outside the California bubble, Mère would reprimand me for what she perceived as entitlement and emotional fragility. Instead of acknowledging

---

[2]Van der Kolk, B. A. (2015). *The Body Keeps the Score: Brain, Mind, and Body in the Healing of Trauma* (1st ed., p. 21). Penguin Books.

the deep sense of isolation prejudices can evoke, she dubbed me *da giấy*, meaning "paper skin."

Granted, growing up under traditional Vietnamese parents meant adhering to cultural norms of stoicism, as emotional vulnerability is interpreted as weakness and an inability to cope with life's challenges. However, Mère's responses often focused most on the shame she feared my private outbursts might bring. It was incomprehensible to me that she couldn't relate to my culture shock. Didn't she experience similar challenges when acclimating to life in the West? This dilemma exacerbated the already significant generational, cultural, and linguistic differences between us.

Mère's past blocked her from grasping not only my perspective but also that of my father. Unbeknownst to her, she came across as fiery, headstrong, and defensive toward him. When he vented about work, her reproachful replies led him to begin working weekends, leaving home earlier, returning later each day.

Over time, her fretting became chronic. Underneath her taut veneer, the worrying compounded the chemical stresses humans naturally face: bacteria, viruses, hormones in food, heavy metals, and blood-sugar levels. Altogether, Mère's stress compromised her immune system and hindered her ability to properly digest food and efficiently eliminate toxins.

Beyond the reactions caused by her trauma-induced stress, Mère's physical health began to change. In late 2019, she developed rheumatoid arthritis, a chronic autoimmune disorder where cells attack their own, causing her finger joints to deform. In early 2020, she received a diagnosis of Parkinson's disease, a neurodegenerative disorder that impairs movement coordination, leading to tremors and imbalance. In 2023, she learned of a lung nodule that had tripled in size within three months. Since the causes of Mère's illnesses remain unknown to medical science, we initially attributed them to past occupational exposure to toxins during her employment as a nail technician.

Fortunately, Mère's lung cancer was operable, and we were assigned a skilled thoracic surgeon. However, the surgeon's impersonal statistics and grim prognoses exacerbated my fears. Moreover, due to the precarious location of her lung nodule, what initially seemed like a routine surgery escalated into a far more invasive lobectomy. The procedure, involving opening her chest to remove half of her left lung, was scheduled for May 5, 2024.

Following, she would face a prolonged and arduous recovery, relearning how to breathe and coping with postsurgical cognitive decline. I blanched at the thought of repeating any of this to Mère. Ultimately, I chose not to, convincing myself that keeping her in the dark would spare her further worry.

With so much happening inside her body and no clear answers, Mère withdrew, believing it unjust to burden others with her troubles or allow them to express pity for her. As a result, her siblings remained unaware, my father was prohibited from confiding in his, and I shouldered the weight of her cancer alone.

For the first time, I understood the helplessness Mère must have felt when she sat beside her own mother through dark times. Once again, I felt like a child, missing her even when we were inches apart. I missed her most when she turned casual conversations into life lessons, as though she sensed an urgency to impart final wisdoms before some unseen end. She reminded me to receive others compassionately, to respect my elders, to harmonize with everyone, and to exercise equanimity. I was never prepared to hear any of it—her lessons, her farewells.

One June afternoon, I parked in a Starbucks lot, cut the engine, and was immediately overcome with wistfulness. *It's not fair for someone who has already experienced so much grief to fall ill because of it. How is it fair for it to happen to someone as forbearing as Mère? And why, when people can fly to the moon, do we still not have a cure for cancer?* I spiraled until I was interrupted by a glimmer. *Miracles exist. Maybe I can earn one by May 5.* My miracle was for the lung nodule to disappear.

What followed was a ten-month journey of healing. In the latter half of this chapter, I share everything my mother and I did with the intention of showing readers that miracles can be willed. Please note that I am not a medical practitioner, and the chronicle of my mother's healing is not intended as medical counseling.

A Cure
Conventional medicine predicated on the work of René Descartes and Isaac Newton views the body as a device containing organs with buttons and levers that need fine-tuning. According to this view, any irregularity is the consequence of a problem in the mechanics of the physical machine, and a doctor's drug prescription is meant to troubleshoot that issue. While pharmaceuticals are indispensable in treating injuries and infections, I believed that the sort of medicine Mère needed was more holistic in nature—a regimen that involved changing the diet, releasing suppressed emotions, increasing positive emotions, and deepening one's spiritual connection.

<u>Body</u>

"Tell me what you eat and I will tell you what you are." An aphorism from the 1820s on culinary reminiscences on the craft of cookery and the art of eating has evolved into an admonishment to those entranced by the allure of modern foodie culture.

This truism prompted me to inspect whether my family's food preferences could have been contributing to Mère's illnesses. From my father's enthusiasm for barbecued meat and Mère's staple of white rice and braised pork to my own dwindling stash of instant Vietnamese coffee, I deemed it highly likely. In a chastened response to "you are what you eat," our diet was imbalanced, and so were we.

The health risks of our victuals were overlooked in favor of its cultural significance. Vietnamese cuisine, abundant in grilled pork and fried favorites like *bánh xèo*, but scarce in whole and raw greens except as aromatics, symbolized our connection to a lost home. Herein, the potential harm from our dietary habits felt negligible compared to the sense of belonging that our food provided. Furthermore, food was a medium of love. The labor-intensive nature of Vietnamese cuisine, with *phở* taking over a day to achieve the right flavor depth and lotus root salad requiring hours of picking, pickling, and julienning, was a testament to this love. Mère was the maestro of our culinary quests, and the comfort of an authentic dish accompanied by a side of neatly cut fruit after a long day was a love my father and I linked to Vietnamese food. To ask Mère not to make her usual dishes was tantamount to having her renounce her identity.

Nevertheless, every medical essay and nutrition documentary I encountered made me view our food as enemy supply lines that needed to be cut.

Out of obligation, I became executive chef, and my first order was to eliminate meat, sugar, dairy, ultra-processed snacks, and eggs. This decision was based on various epidemiological studies that highlighted the following:

- There is a positive association between high red meat consumption and cancer risk; certain compounds in meat increase DNA synthesis and insulin-like growth factors (IGFs), affect hormone metabolism, and promote free radical damage.[3]
- Excess sugar consumption leads to cancer development and disease progression via inflammation, glucose, and lipid metabolic pathways.[4]

---

[3] Genkinger, J. M., & Koushik, A. (2007). "Meat Consumption and Cancer Risk." *PLoS Medicine*, 4(12), e345. https://doi.org/10.1371/journal.pmed.0040345; Farvid, M. S., Sidahmed, E., Spence, N. D., Mante Angua, K., Rosner, B. A., & Barnett, J. B. (2021).

[4] Epner, M., Yang, P., Wagner, R. W., & Cohen, L. (2022). "Understanding the Link between Sugar and Cancer: An Examination of the Preclinical and Clinical Evidence." *Cancers*, 14(24), 6042. https://doi.org/10.3390/cancers14246042

- High dairy consumption raises concentrations of IGF-1, a hormone that promotes cell growth and proliferation. Experiments yield a strong correlation between circulating levels of IGF-1 with cancer development.[5]
- High consumption of ultra-processed foods increases the risk of cancer and cardiometabolic multimorbidity (i.e., cancer, cardiovascular diseases, type 2 diabetes, etc.). Non-nutritional mechanisms through which ultra-processed food could be hazardous for health include alteration of the food matrix, inclusion of certain food additives during processing, and contaminants from packaging material. Any of these may affect endocrine pathways or the gut microbiome, contributing to disease risk.[6]
- Eggs are high in choline, which is metabolically converted to trimethylamine (TMA). Once

---

[5]Trasias Mukama, Bernard Srour, Theron Johnson, Verena Katzke, Rudolf Kaaks. "IGF-1 and Risk of Morbidity and Mortality From Cancer, Cardiovascular Diseases, and All Causes in EPIC-Heidelberg," *The Journal of Clinical Endocrinology & Metabolism*, Volume 108, Issue 10, October 2023, Pages e1092–e1105. https://doi.org/10.1210/clinem/dgad212

[6]Cordova, R., Viallon, V., Fontvieille, E., Peruchet-Noray, L., Jansana, A., Wagner, K.-H., et al. (2023). "Consumption of Ultra-Processed Foods and Risk of Multimorbidity of Cancer and Cardiometabolic Diseases: A Multinational Cohort Study." *The Lancet Regional Health* – Europe, 27, Article 100771. https://doi.org/10.1016/j.lanepe.2023.100771

oxidized, the substance may promote inflammation and result in cancer progression.[7]

In place of meat, sugar, dairy, ultra-processed snacks, and eggs, I introduced a medley of cruciferous vegetables, legumes, and Ayurvedic herbs into Mère's diet, crafting meals that functioned to starve the cancer inside her. Each morning, we enjoyed a breakfast of almond matcha lattes, pennywort juice, or avocado smoothies. My lunch menu featured two items: soup of the day and salad of the day. Our beloved phở was replaced by a vegetarian *hủ tiếu* in shiitake, daikon, and pear stock. Coconut curries were substituted with lentil soups spiced with turmeric and cumin. Sweet sticky rice desserts were set aside for berries. And evenings ended with a steaming cup of moringa tea in her favorite Demon Slayer mug.

At first, Mère found the new vegan fare alien and unsatisfying. While my novice cooking and lackluster plating skills might have been to blame, she politely cited the unfamiliar textures and earthy notes as the reasons for her reduced appetite. Feeling guilty, I offered her companionship, and we suffered my concoctions together. I traded my own indulgences—milk tea, egg tarts, and ramen—for bean stews and colorful salads.

Over several weeks, our palates adjusted, and we began to appreciate simpler, more natural flavors. Food was no longer sought for its taste but for its power to nourish. Eventually, food

---

[7]Zeisel, S. H., & DaCosta, K. A. (1994). "Formations of Methylamines from Choline and Lecithin." *Nutrition Reviews*, 52(10), 327-339. https://doi.org/10.1111/j.1753-4887.1994.tb01374.x

became even more an emblem of love, now embodying solidarity in the pursuit of health.

Mind
Familiarity with the writings of Sigmund Freud, Carl Jung, and Judith Herman underscored the imperative to treat the mind as the source of ailments. These psychiatrists studied how the psychological consequences of trauma manifest in symptoms and disorders, and their research is often cited in literature on mind-body connection. Influential publications in this area include Bessel van der Kolk's *The Body Keeps the Score: Brain, Mind, and the Body in the Healing of Trauma*, Babette Rothschild's *The Body Remembers: The Psychophysiology of Trauma and Trauma Treatment*, and Peter Levine's *Waking the Tiger: Healing Trauma*. Drawing from their insights, I sought to aid Mère in healing her mind, despite the fact that Vietnamese culture has an inclination to repress emotional suffering rather than confront it.

      Processing trauma often requires making associations, interpreting visual information, articulating feelings, and working through both positive and negative feelings. Dr. Adrienne Heinz of the National Center for Posttraumatic Stress Disorder at the US Department of Veterans Affairs and Stanford University states, "Across all the different trauma-healing approaches and strategies, the unifying theme is that you do have to go back to the trauma in some way. You have to walk through it to get past it."[8] So, we walked.

---

[8]Borges, A. (2022, February 24). "Processing Trauma." *SELF*. https://www.self.com/story/processing-trauma

There is a profound relationship between the mind and one's step.[9] The rhythm of walking can influence the internal cadence of thoughts and emotions, and vice versa. While walking, one engages in optic flow, where constant lateral eye movements update the brain on spatial positioning. This bilateral eye stimulation quiets the amygdala, the cerebral region that processes threat responses. By inducing a calmer emotional state, optic flow enables the brain to clear traumatic blockages and derive meaning from past events, thus aiding in moving forward.

As we strolled along a port trail, among ground squirrels, sandpipers, and grasses, Mère and I talked. I listened as she reflected on her gentle mother, her father's imprisonment, the poverty-based discrimination she and her siblings faced, her in-laws, the passing of her parents. Between my questions, I watched her remember with sorrow and then relinquishment, becoming aware of her inner experiences and befriending her inner self. It was during our walks at the port that we transformed toxic thoughts into tonic thoughts.

<u>Spirit</u>
My meditation class at a monastery serendipitously coincided with my family's period of uncertainty. At Buddha Gate Monastery, I learned about causality, or *karma* in Sanskrit. Karma is a fundamental aspect of nature; every phenomenon

---

[9]Zhu, Z., Chen, H., Ma, J., He, Y., Chen, J., & Sun, J. (2020). "Exploring the Relationship between Walking and Emotional Health in China." *International Journal of Environmental Research and Public Health*, 17(23), 8804. https://doi.org/10.3390/ijerph17238804

arises from various causes and conditions. Applied to human life, we are responsible for the outcomes of our own actions. Augmented onto a continuum beyond birth and death, I began to ponder Mère's sickness as an outcome of not just stress but also of accumulated bad karma through past life actions. Interestingly, this concept isn't limited to Buddhist cultivation; the Hawaiian practice of *Ho'oponopono*, meaning "correction," poses that a person's errors cause illness and that prayer, self-accountability, and seeking forgiveness would release negative experiences in past incarnations and resolve traumas.[10] Therefore, I reasoned that acts of contrition should be part of Mère's recovery journey.

As Mère and I meditated, I kept Mère at the forefront of my mind. I sat in stillness, reciting:

To those who bear unfavorable karmic bonds with my elders—those who have shown them enmity or whom my elders may have wronged or resented, including foes from past lifetimes: The Buddha taught, "Hatred does not cease by hatred, but only by love." I fervently seek to transform the adverse karma between my elders and their adversaries into positive, fruitful karma. I extend my forgiveness to all who have wronged my elders, and for any harm my elders may have caused, I dedicate my merits to ease their suffering. With a sincere heart-mind, I embrace them as no longer enemies by extension. By

---

[10]Kretzer, K., Evelo, A. J., & Durham, R. L. (2013). "Lessons Learned from a Study of a Complementary Therapy for Self-Managing Hypertension and Stress in Women." *Holistic Nursing Practice, 27*(6), 336–343. https://doi.org/10.1097/HNP.0b013e3182a72ca4

offering all my merits from acts of charity and meditation, I pray to extinguish their greed, anger, and ignorance; to clear their karmic obstacles; to help them hear, practice, and uphold the Dharma; to grant them blessings and wisdom; to bring forth the Bodhi mind; and to ensure they never regress until perfect enlightenment is attained.

On the road of cleansing, we turned to energy healing, which suggests that every physical ailment has an emotional and energetic component. Growing up Buddhist, I was naturally receptive to the metaphysical and intrigued by its connection to quantum physics, which posits that everything in the universe consists of energy fields that interact with one another. It made sense to think of the human body as having an energy field too.

Trauma, according to this perspective, creates blocks in the energy field that need to be released for true healing to occur. Energy healers work to dissolve these blocks, facilitating the body's innate ability to heal itself.[11] Embracing this interconnectedness, Mère opened herself to receiving from a healer who claimed to have "removed the cancer from the template of her life." We ended the meeting with incredulous stares because at the time, we didn't know energy healing could go beyond chelation, but out of desperation, we were willing to stretch our minds to believe this remark.

Lastly, we practiced philanthropy. Our fight against cancer illuminated the immense difficulties of overcoming

---

[11] See Bruyere, R. (1994). *Wheels of Light: Chakras, Auras, and the Healing Energy of the Body*. Touchstone. See also Brennan, B. A. (1988). *Hands of Light: A Guide to Healing Through the Human Energy Field*. Bantam Books.

sickness. Our good days were few and far between, and our bad days were especially pronounced. Taken together, the financial strain of numerous CT and PET scans, the exhaustion from radiation exposure, the disorientation caused by biopsy hemoptysis, and the soreness from repeated needle prodding were overwhelming. So was the helplessness that loved ones feel.

Acting on this sentiment, we donated to lung cancer research institutes, hoping to fund developments that would provide respite to others living with lung disease. In giving, we thought of those awaiting surgery, undergoing chemotherapy, and those recuperating after surgery—wishfully thinking that there'd be no May 5.

May 4
The morning air was heavy with a somber hush, the kind that clings to the skin and whispers of uncertainty. The clock ticked incessantly, each second drawing us closer to the surgery that suspended over us like a dark cloud from summer to spring. Mère sat across from me, her eyes reflecting both the strength she fought to maintain and the fear she couldn't quite mask. Her battle with lung cancer had been an exacting journey, one that had stripped away many things, including her spirit, which I fought hard to recover.

As she folded her clothes for the hospital, her hands trembled slightly, partly from her Parkinson's and partly from unease, betraying the expressionless facade she wore. I wanted to say something, anything, to ease her worry, but words felt inadequate against the enormity of what lay ahead. We had done what we could, embracing a holistic path that transformed her diet, mindset, and spirit. Organic greens, herbal teas, and mindful meditation had become the pillars of our daily life. It all assembled an atrium of healing around her, though we dared not believe it could be enough.

My phone trilled, slicing through the silence, and I reached for it with an erratic heart. The voice on the other end was professional, fatigued from his heroic vocation—the surgeon. His words flowed, first with a clinical detachment, then with a wonder that mirrored my own. *The lesion in her lung is gone*, he said, replaced by a linear scar. The energy healer's words hearkened "removed the cancer from the template of her life." There would be no surgery tomorrow.

For a moment, I couldn't speak or think. Relief surged through me, a wave that crested in my chest and unfurled outward, ebbing my shock. I looked at Mère, who had paused mid-fold, her eyes searching mine for the truth of what I was hearing. When I nodded, tears welled up in her eyes, and she crossed the room to my outstretched arms in an instant.

We hugged, the weight of the past months falling away like chains unshackled. Gratitude and awe flooded our hearts. This miracle, this inexplicable healing, was a testament to the path we had chosen—a restoration of the body, mind, and soul.

This is the story of my mother reaching the other shore, first in her twenties and again in her sixties. In Buddhist tradition, the shore symbolizes freedom from suffering. Conversely, the water that one crosses to get to the shore symbolizes the obstacles and delusions encountered in life. Through perseverance, we seem to have reached a shore that granted not just spontaneous remission, but also profound understandings: unresolved trauma can result in chronic diseases; the body has innate healing abilities under the right conditions; good food nourishes beyond taste; and connection to the higher self is transformative.

My mother says, "Each day since reaching this shore is a chance to live by these principles and inspire others to do the same." Hence, this chapter.

Our journey would not have been possible without invaluable friends who supported us along the way. Their consistent acts of kindness and unwavering support, whether they knew of my mother's sickness or not, sustained us. The few who were aware guided us through medical jargon, offered remedies with pure intentions, brought us homemade meals and lovely flowers, encouraged mindfulness, and held space for us. Without them, we would not have the tools to persevere. On the other hand, those who were unaware couldn't offer solace, but they radiated kindness through friendly nods and small talk that distracted the mind. Their genuine support shone through our dark days and was a balm for our souls.

In the same way our friends extended compassion and encouragement, Mère and I hope to cheer you on through these pages. The notes section provides resources we found helpful.

Today, my mother is cancer-free, and I no longer sit by myself in Starbucks parking lots. Nevertheless, our path of holistic healing continues—we eat mindfully, cultivate positive thoughts, deepen our spiritual practices, and extend kindness knowing others are on their own journeys. Believe in a positive outcome and maintain positive emotional states to attract a healthful outcome.[12] We have full confidence in your ability to reach your shore.

*****

---

[12]See Byrne, R. (Producer and Director). (2006). *The Secret* [Motion picture]. Prime Time Productions.

About Kendra Trần:
Over years of serving crime survivors and incarcerated individuals in the American criminal justice system, Kendra discovered her advocacy was most effective and rewarding when integrated by Yogacara principles. The profound transformations she witnessed in her clients inspired her to examine the connection between mental and physical health, and she strives to improve access to mindfulness practices, particularly within underrepresented communities.

Beyond her professional endeavors, Kendra volunteers at a Buddhist monastery, where she coordinates a meditation course. Her debut memoir chapter, "Unto Shore," explores her mother's illness as a reflection of trauma and presents the way she confronted this affliction in someone who saw trauma as a taboo subject.

instagram: @captainpkhanh

Chapter 22

Rebirth: Naked and Unashamed

Tiffany Winn

Dedicated to my four amazing children and the little orphan girl in me who was wounded, neglected, abandoned, and rejected.

I loved life when I was growing up. Like most children, I played jacks on the front porch, along with hopscotch, kickball, Barbies, and so much more. My morning alarm clock rang as the sun shone through my bedroom curtains. I was the most excited little girl because I loved my teacher. Somehow, I thought I was her favorite, even though there were twenty other students. She made me feel special.

As happy as I was playing outside and going to school, my home and family life were difficult. If dysfunction were a picture, it would be my family's portrait. I lived with my grandma since my mom was incarcerated and was not being released anytime soon, and my aunts and uncles all had substance use disorder (SUD) and opioid use disorder (OUD).

Going home from school was often unpredictable. My grandma was quite the hostess, so we always had a lot of company. One night a man I considered an uncle entered my room like a thief in the night and left with my identity. That night, I saw life in a fearful, painful, twisted, dark, and distorted way. As I lay still and stiff in my bed, my body parts felt detached. I screamed in silence while trying to understand what was happening to me. Why me? Why him? Why now? What do I do? Suddenly, the eight-year-old girl who had so much excitement saw the world for what it really was: painful.

Before that night, like most children, I trusted everyone around me—I'd never had any reason not to. After that, my life was turned upside down. My regularly scheduled life was interrupted by the reality that evil has and will always be present.

It wasn't just my life that changed that night. My body parts, my attitude, and my mindset were altered. Eventually, I started to think I was the poster child for sexual perversion as two more men were added to the list of my abusers. I wish I could say that I woke up from this nightmare, but the truth is I never was asleep.

    I let my teacher know about the abuse. As a mandatory reporter, she had to tell the authorities what was going on in our home. I was removed into the state's custody, placed in and out of different homes because my grandma never came back to get me. I believe this was the beginning of my feelings of abandonment and rejection. When those feelings aren't understood as a young child, you begin to act unseemly and long for acceptance and attention. It doesn't matter what kind or where it comes from.

    By the time I was sixteen, I was completely reckless. I was homeless, fighting on the streets, selling drugs, hating myself, and hating my life. I got shot in my femur and ended up in a wheelchair, relearning how to walk all over again.

    At seventeen, I was pregnant, with another child at home. I worked at McDonald's by day and as a bathroom attendant at a strip club at night. My grandma had passed away and my mom was living a Christian lifestyle, so I wanted to connect with her and see where we would go from there. We didn't know much about each other and instead of trying to learn, we assumed that it would all come together because she's my biological mom, right? I knew by birth I was hers; however, I knew very little about this woman I call Mom.

    I just wanted my life to make a little sense. Life was already a roller coaster ride, and I wanted to get off and be normal, whatever that looked like. I wanted her to accept me, but we were like acquaintances. I had so many questions—what was her favorite color? Why was she a lesbian? Why didn't she want me or my brother? Who was my father, and does he know I exist? All the questions I'd buried in my heart would never come out of my mouth.

I'd been with the father of my two kids since I was thirteen and he was sixteen. Now I have no comparison of how a man should love and protect me or as a young woman how I should be loved or treated, so I cleaved to my children's father and accepted what I thought was love.

By that time, I was seventeen and he was twenty. He was incarcerated. At that point, I knew I needed a spiritual awakening, plus I had a bone to pick with God. My life was so different from what I pictured most young girls' lives were. I saw girls my age going to dances, homecoming, and prom. My world was real, with no fairy tales, fairy godmothers, and no glass slippers. Just survival and no weaknesses.

I'd been so innocent at one time in life. Why, God, why was my path so hard and hurtful? These thoughts plagued my mind often and when they did, tears would roll down my cheeks. Then, suddenly, I would hear another voice say, "Stop being a damn crybaby and grow up!" I would dry my tears and get back to regular programming.

An Elder's Abuse
Trying to make sense of everything, find relief, and remember normalcy, I went to church. For a moment, I was on the right path. I was seventeen, getting ready to be a mom again, working, and striving to be someone. I met a church elder who eventually became my godfather. Within a few months, he overstepped boundaries, and I was a victim of circumstances again.

To add to my injury, after withstanding his abuse in silence, I told my mom (who was now the wife of the pastor in the church I attended). While I was not alone this time, as there were several other women he abused, I am the only one who came forward. Somehow, this made me feel bad. But why? I was so distorted by trauma and rejection, I kept wondering if I'd done something wrong.

    I always thought about the story of Adam and Eve. Shame has a way of making you feel afraid, and that fear opens so many other phobias in our minds. Genesis 3:7 NIV says, "Then the eyes of both of them were opened, and they realized they were naked; so they sewed fig leaves together and made coverings for themselves." I imagine how they both felt in the garden, pure and free until they ate that forbidden fruit. In a moment, their lives changed. What if they'd never realized they were naked? What if they'd never eaten off the tree? Would we have a story so profound today about the first fall of humans?

    These are the same questions many of us have when we are naked, uncovered, and ashamed. Remember before that, they had always been naked and not ashamed. What changed that? Genesis 3:10 NIV says, "He answered, 'I heard you in the garden, and I was afraid because I was naked; so I hid.'" I didn't understand then why Adam or Eve ran and hid, but today I know why.

    In 2 Timothy 1:7, it says, "For God hath not given us the spirit of fear; but of power, and of love, and of a sound mind." I was acquainted with pain. Pain was one of two constants in my life. I began looking at it as a companion. Fear will grip you and teach you to hide the truth about who you are and where you come from. Fear causes more inadequacies through your experiences, so somehow hiding becomes your new normal and truth is shameful and makes you feel guilty. Twisted, huh? That's most of us in this world right now. It might even be you.

    After I came forward about the church elder's abuse, other victims were forced to come clean as well, not willingly but forcefully. You would think I'd be happy, but the truth was I was ready to run away from it all. I was ashamed, my life was closing in, and I had no one to pull me out of this dark hole. I wanted to die!

After my life drama, the church drama caused even more trauma. I felt there was no way out. I stayed and faced my demons and my predator with courage while anger, resentment, rejection, abandonment, and fear boiled inside. I was a ticking time bomb.

I relate to Eve in the story in Genesis 3. She was easily manipulated because she was familiar with the snake in the garden, but not the spirit that had entered him. Eve had no reason not to trust anyone; she was immature and inexperienced. She only knew what she was told by God, and she was easily charmed. Adam and Eve were still learning who they were, who their Father was, and about their places in the garden.

I think about the relationship they had with their creator. Was it strong and secure enough? For me, it was not. Although they were created first, they hadn't been in the garden long enough to have a strong bond with the Lord. Before they could, it was interrupted by deception, and their innocence was stolen. Oh, how I can relate to their relationship with the creator. My identity was stolen, and the deception distorted my perception on what a loving God was or even felt like. I didn't trust something unseen or someone who allowed me to be hurt without even understanding life yet.

My relationship with God started off rocky. I didn't understand why someone who made sure my mom birthed me would allow me to go through so much pain. Have you ever asked yourself that?

For many years, I was lost in the wilderness of life. My anger evolved into rage and released itself through lawlessness. I was a drug addict. My kids' father was murdered. I was barely surviving, so I turned to crime and became a felon. I was charged with assault with a deadly weapon, which later turned into battery with bodily harm.

Hearing those words from a judge changed me: I had hit rock bottom. If I inflicted pain and trauma on others, evidently, I didn't care anymore. I was numb.

But someone did.

At thirty-one years old, I was sentenced to two to eight years in a women's correctional center, and by this time, I had four children.

I was still a child inside, but because I'd made choices with significant consequences, I had to face them as an adult. My life flashed before my eyes. I hadn't been away from my children since I was fifteen years old.

The other constant in my life was motherhood. My first child arrived when I was fifteen, my second when I was seventeen, my third when I was nineteen, and my fourth when I was twenty-six years old. My children are my greatest accomplishment. I was lost without them. I have nothing but them.

Life has a way of dealing you a hand you never imagined possible, but you still try to play the deck, wishing the dealer would shuffle again.

Getting Closer to God
While incarcerated in 2011, now thirty-one years old, I sat on my bunk. I'd been crying for what felt like years, asking God to speak with me. I prayed as I waited for the officers to conduct a head count. I asked God what my purpose was and why He created me in my mother's womb. Jeremiah 1:5 says, "Before I formed you in the womb, I knew you before you were born; I was appointed as a prophet to the nations."

When I was violated by the elder at my church, it tainted the relationship I was trying to build with God. I did not trust Him because I assumed He had allowed me to experience so much pain. I felt like He hated me. What did I do to deserve parents who did not want me and a grandmother who abandoned me?

I cried for almost a year. Sometimes I didn't know why I cried. I missed my kids while in prison, but I didn't miss life: bills, pains, relationships, everything that overwhelmed me in the outside world. I realized I didn't want to sit in this madness that had attached itself to me for so many years. I knew it wouldn't be easy; however, I was ready for a divine appointment with the creator. It was my turn to be heard, seen, and accepted! I was desperate for answers.

Later, I realized it was the little girl inside me, the orphan, the one who'd been mishandled her entire life. She was lost and hurting. She wanted to be free from pain, anger, and suffering.

The real work began then. Peeling away the concrete walls around my heart and working out the negative energy associated with lifelong trauma.

During my incarceration, I attended anger management classes and Toastmaster classes to build confidence with public speaking and leadership skills; I received my high school diploma, attended church services regularly, and maintained employment. These activities made my heart happy and kept me busy, with the added benefit of shortening my sentences. I kept my head down and avoided trouble.

I got closer to God. I felt Him. I spread His word to the other inmates, and although I was locked up physically, I was freeing myself mentally, emotionally, and spiritually.

One night, I heard a small voice. It said I would heal and that I would heal others through my testimony and love. I felt a presence hover over me, and I wept. There was a sense of peace I'd never felt before.

After that, I hungered for the presence of God. I woke up praying and went to bed the same. I read spiritual books and the Bible constantly. I wanted to know the Father and His word.

I no longer wanted to be naked and ashamed.

A Taste of Freedom
In 2014, at thirty-four years old, I was released from prison. Thank God almighty, I was free at last!

But on the inside, I was scared. So much had changed. How would this new-and-improved version of me fit into this world? My heart beat faster and faster as I approached what we call in prison, "THE FREE WORLD."

Though intimidated, I was determined to face it with my creator by my side. I recalled the many conversations I had with Him from my bunk bed throughout my journey. I knew every tear was held in a bottle. As Psalms 56:8 says, "Record my misery; list my tears on your scroll, are they not in your record?"

A fresh start isn't easy or smooth. I laugh now because I'm no longer the little girl with a victim mindset, but that journey scarred me, nonetheless. I'm reminded when I see my many scars—some from battles lost, but others from battles won.

After three and a half years, I was excited to see my family. I felt the Lord had redeemed me and given me another chance to get it right. No shame and no guilt. I wore my past as a badge of honor on my heart. I was ready for life and whatever came with it, because I knew Jesus. I was ready for motherhood, to advocate for transformation, reformation, and grace.

When I started over, I had nothing. My house and car were gone, and my children were scattered because my mother couldn't handle them. Then my mom kicked me out. I took my kids and slept on the floor of my cousin's house until I formulated a plan. I job-hunted. I didn't care how much it paid or what it entailed. I needed stability.

I got a job as a sales associate, making minimum wage until I was blessed with a second job. Finally, I had income and, as the Bible says, "Never despise small beginnings."

As I got back on my feet, there was turbulence along the way. I thought God and I had come to an agreement. I learned agreements come with opposition. My mother and I were like enemies. We still struggle to this day. My criminal background prevented me from getting my own place. The walls were closing in again, but this time I was determined to come out kicking.

I no longer asked, "Why me?"

The question instead became, "Why *not* me?"

I asked God for guidance and direction. Every detail mattered.

A thought came to mind. My daughter, now eighteen years old, was employed. She applied for an apartment in her name. We prayed and waited patiently.

Three weeks later, we were approved for the apartment and ready to move in. My children and I were overjoyed.

I thought, "I can finally breathe."

We didn't have much to move in with, but I didn't care because we were no longer sleeping on the floor at my cousin's house. We had our own floors to sleep on, if we so chose. We just wanted something to call home.

I continued working and attending church. My kids were in school. We were focused on life. I rekindled a relationship with an ex-boyfriend. Everything was great—or so it seemed.

Life was going well because I was ignoring the red flags. I'd forgotten why this man was an ex in the first place. I stayed in a toxic and abusive relationship with him for eleven years. I gained and lost so much in this relationship because I didn't know what love was. We got married. Unsurprisingly, I turned to something familiar and was fooled by a different mask on the same face. A person who has false intentions can't hide for long; the seed of deception growing on the inside will harvest soon, and when it does never glean in their garden.[13]

Surviving a Bitter Place
When I thought my journey couldn't get any more complicated, this marriage dragged me into a bitter place. We married because my church preached about fornication and the pressure overwhelmed me. This may have hurt me in ways that could not have been love. As 1 Corinthians 13:4-8 says, "Love is patient and kind; love does not envy or boast; it is not arrogant or rude. It does not insult; it is not irritable or resentful; it does not rejoice at wrongdoing but rejoices with the truth. Love bears all things, believes all things, hopes all things, endures all things. Love never ends."

I have never felt that.

In 2016, now thirty-six, I planned my escape. I had been abused, cheated on, and he had gotten someone else pregnant.

---

[13] In ancient Israel, God instituted the practice of gleaning as a way to feed the poor. A farmer would leave some of his crop in the fields, and afterward the poor (the fatherless, widows, foreigners) would gather the leftover crops for their own sustenance.

We had no children together. He wasn't financially stable. Also, he was a drug user and alcoholic.

I conversed with God. "I married this bum, and I thought I was doing the right thing because the pastor said so." (That's how my Father and I converse). "If I have made a mistake, let my suffering not be in vain. Give me a way out," I said. "If you can fix this marriage, change me, because I hate this man."

Eventually, I went behind his back, applied for housing assistance, and informed the staff that I was in an abusive relationship. Two months later, they had an open spot for my children and I to move to.

One day, while he was at work, I started moving out. He found out eventually and came home to argue. The argument escalated into him pulling a gun on me. Still wearing my pajamas, I ran to my neighbor's house. They didn't answer, so I hid behind a grill on their porch. He never found me. I returned to his home to find him gone. He thought the police were after him, so he didn't return. I got the clothes I had with me and never went back.

That was the last straw. I was done.

God answered my prayer by giving me a way out, so I stayed out. My separation and healing journey began.

Afterward, I turned my back on religion. It was false. It had added to my trauma. I had an adventurous fling with the young man next door. Didn't care anymore. I felt like the rules were too hard to live by. The church gave rules they didn't follow. I needed something real, honest, and trustworthy, and religion wasn't it.

Life was good. I was financially stable, and I was going to school, working, dating, and enjoying my newfound freedom. But in the back of my mind, conviction visited periodically. "Do you want to make your marriage work? Do you want a divorce?

Should you go back to church?" These thoughts wriggled in at the wrong times. To drain them, I turned to alcohol and marijuana, which intensified them. I prayed less, cried less, and my heart hardened.

1 Samuel 6:6 says, "Why do you harden your hearts as the Egyptians and Pharaoh did? When Israel's God dealt harshly with them, did they not send the Israelites out so they could go on their way?"

There was no one to talk to like I could talk to God. People can only give me surface-level answers. Your creator can give you all the answers. Genesis 2:25 says, "Adam and his wife were both naked, and they felt ashamed."

Why did I feel ashamed again? Why was I back where I started, going in circles? For the first time in my life, I didn't know what to do or how to get out, but I was tired of praying, tired of surviving, and tired of being tired.

For the first time in a long time, I was vulnerable. I'd been raised in a family where women dominate, and men are few—where vulnerability meant weakness and recklessness. But this was so far from the truth that I needed because, as 2 Corinthians 12:9-10 says, "But He said to me, 'My grace is sufficient for you, my power is made perfect in weakness.' Therefore, I will boast all the more gladly of my weaknesses, so that the power of Christ may rest upon me. That is why, for Christ's sake, I delight in weaknesses, in insults, in hardships, in persecutions, in difficulties. For when I am weak, then I am strong."

The truth is, vulnerability was a risk because it allowed others to see my weaknesses, and not just God. However, it has given me a power I never knew I had. I have found that in being vulnerable, my understanding for hardship and hurts are not biased. I have learned the wisdom that comes from learning my weaknesses.

We all have weaknesses, but when we hide them, it feels safe. It keeps us from interacting with life. We tend to disconnect from individuals and things that bring us life and liberty. We can keep our walls up and separate ourselves from emotions, people, decisions, and existence.

Eve's vulnerability made her a target for Satan's manipulation, but the same vulnerability gave her blind faith. If we want to step out and move forward, toward God, we must take that risk. With great risk comes great reward.

It'd be easy if I stayed comfortable inside and maintained my walls. This time, I sought help, and I realized I needed someone—not someone who'd already hurt me, but someone who'd show me the truth without ulterior motives. I wanted trust, love, and belief again.

I wanted to be naked, but this time unashamed.

*****

About Tiffany Winn:
Tiffany Winn is a community health worker who uses her expertise and compassion to strongly advocate for those in need. She is a business owner, a passionate speaker, a life coach, and a servant of Yahshua, who pulls hearts out of the darkness and into the light through His word.

Known for her witty remarks, forthright and unwavering commitment, and contagious smile, Tiffany suffered much hardship as a youth. She grew in West Las Vegas, Nevada, an impoverished area overrun by drug use and drug dealers, a disproportionate number of single parent homes, and extreme health disparities. As a product of this environment. Tiffany was desperate to get out, and through His grace and mercy was able to do so. She has vowed to return to help others to reclaim and recover what was stolen from those forced to live in those types of areas worldwide. She makes zero apologies for her passion and compassion for humanity! "Love Still Winns" is her motto.

Tiffany Winn

Chapter 23
Libertad!

Lisbet Perez

For immigrant women everywhere, I share my story with love and vulnerability, hoping it resonates deeply with you. I hope my journey inspires you to discover the incredible strength within you and guides you on a path of self-love and healing. Remember, your voice is precious. Connecting with other women who understand your story is liberating, and together, our voices form a powerful force for change. ~ Lis

I was born in Mexico and raised in San Diego County from the age of nine. My parents and oldest sister worked tirelessly to provide for our family. As the youngest child, I felt pressured to excel academically, but in my junior year of high school, I learned I was an undocumented student. This shattered my dreams, as I thought it meant I had no chance of getting accepted to a university because I did not fully understand how the admissions systems worked, and I had no one to advocate for me.

    Discovering my undocumented status also helped me understand why my family never had access to health care. I vividly remember as a child having a horrible toothache that wasn't relieved with painkillers or home remedies. My parents took me to see a dentist who, to my surprise, worked out of a small storage room behind a liquor store. And still this visit was a financial burden for my parents.

    Depressed and discouraged, I quickly fell into an abusive seven-year relationship. My boyfriend and I met as children, and we had familial connections that established trust. When we first got together as teens, he was kind, hardworking, and charming. His behavior soon changed, however, and between my depression and the cultural normalization of abuse I'd witnessed, I ignored all the red flags and ultimately married a controlling and abusive husband.

    During our marriage, he humiliated, disrespected, and mistreated me in ways invisible to others. It started with subtle control: questioning my outfits, friendships, and choices. I mistook his abuse for love. The verbal jabs, gaslighting, and emotional manipulation crept in like a thief in the night and suffocated me. Gradually, he isolated me from friends and family. I lost myself in the relationship until I became a shadow of my former self, walking on eggshells to avoid his wrath.

During those years, I was blessed with three beautiful children, adding on to the pile of reasons I feared leaving. He held legal status, controlled our finances, and threatened to take our children from me and have me deported.

The fear and shame consumed me, but my parents' unwavering support ignited my courage. One day, they visited unannounced. They sensed something was wrong. Though I pretended everything was fine, my parents knew I was not okay. My father said, "We know what's happening. You and your children don't deserve this. We'll help you if you decide to leave him. You're not alone." His words marked the beginning of my long healing journey.

Leaving my ex-husband was neither easy nor safe. I still loved and cared for him and wanted my children to have their father in their lives, and I was terrified of calling law enforcement. Eventually, his threats escalated, and he began trafficking firearms and drugs, and I reported the abuse and found refuge at the San Diego Family Justice Center, where I met the detective assigned to my case, and my children and I finally found physical safety. I believe that the detective's immediate intervention and safety plan saved my life.

New Beginnings
At the San Diego Family Justice Center, I learned about the California Victims' Compensation Program, one of the few resources I could access. This program became my lifeline, providing free therapy for myself and my children. Through therapy, I started untangling the complex web of abuse, learning

to recognize its subtle forms, acknowledge my emotions, and develop coping strategies.

Growing up, I mistakenly viewed extreme jealousy and control as signs of love, romanticized by societal norms and cultural influences. For instance, when my husband was overly possessive or dictated my clothing choices, I saw it as affection. In fact, I thought these behaviors were charming and romantic. However, through therapy, I learned to recognize these actions as red flags. Rewiring my brain has been challenging but transformative. By intentionally exposing myself to healthier relationship models and practicing mindfulness, I've become more adept at identifying red flags and teaching my children about healthy relationships. This journey has empowered me to break free from toxic patterns and foster positive connections.

As I embarked on this healing journey, I realized that my restoration was essential to becoming a better mother. My children deserved a joyful, healthy parent, and I was determined to fulfill that role. Support groups connected me with fellow survivors, allowing us to share our stories, tears, and triumphs. We found solace in one another's company, deeply understanding our struggles. Still, my depression, anxiety, and insomnia were relentless. Seeking medical help felt daunting due to my undocumented status and lack of health insurance.

Fortunately, a close friend recommended an affordable family clinic. There, I met a compassionate family care doctor who was astonished that I had survived so long without treatment for my depression. After hearing my story, he offered to treat me, accepting any payment I could manage or deferring payment until I qualified for health insurance. His generosity and kindness still bring tears to my eyes.

While I found hope in the doctor's care, I did face other setbacks. To be able to stay in the US with nonimmigrant status, I needed to obtain U-Visa under the Violence Against Women Act (VAWA). My immigration attorney mishandled my case and delayed my U-Visa and VAWA process. The waitlist for nonprofit support exceeded a year, and I could not afford to wait. My children depended on me.

However, another ray of hope emerged: an immigration attorney who accepted my case with no deposit, allowing for monthly payments.

Thanks to her compassion, I received permanent residency within two years. During that time, I worked toward obtaining my GED, volunteered at a refugee resettlement agency, and enrolled in community college to pursue a degree in business management and administration.

As I immersed myself in supporting refugee communities, I discovered the profound beauty of connection through shared stories that transcended background, religion, and culture. Despite language barriers, we found common ground through tears, smiles, hugs, and gentle handholds—gestures that spoke to our shared humanity.

In this sacred space, I realized that our differences dissolve, revealing our essential oneness. I witnessed the universal language of resilience and love and realized we are all threads in the same intricate tapestry, woven together by our memories, joys, and struggles. My journey also deepened my gratitude for the Violence Against Women Act, a lifeline that offered me protection and support.

Raising Awareness

Around 2012, a psychiatrist named Dr. Lass invited me to join VOICES, where I met fellow survivors using their powerful stories to raise awareness about domestic abuse and educate professionals from the survivor perspective. Joining VOICES was a pivotal moment in my healing journey.

Initially, I struggled to disclose my undocumented status, but meeting Casey Gwinn and Gael Strack, co-founders of the Family Justice Center movement, changed everything. Their leadership, expertise, and compassion inspired me. Casey's visionary work in Camp HOPE America and Gael's dedication to domestic violence prevention and passion for VOICES resonated deeply. Their words of encouragement—"Your story is powerful, and it can make a difference. No one can argue with your experience"—empowered me to share my truth. With their support, I found the courage to speak out, overcoming shame and criticism. Discovering my voice has been liberating, and now I'm committed to helping other survivors do the same. Casey's and Gael's unwavering belief in me has been a blessing.

I vividly remember the first time I shared my story. On February 7, 2014, I received a call from the Alliance for HOPE team, asking if I could speak at a press conference where Assembly Majority Leader Toni Atkins was announcing new legislation aimed at offering victims confidentiality at family justice centers in California. Many survivors hesitate to come forward due to their undocumented status, criminal activity in the home, or substance abuse concerns, fearing they might lose their children. The proposed legislation, AB 1623, ensured that information disclosed while seeking help would remain private. Although I didn't fully grasp the implications at the time, I wanted to support the cause, so I agreed to participate.

When I arrived at the center and saw the press, cameras, and people in suits, I felt overwhelming anxiety. However, before the press conference began, Toni Atkins sat next to me, shared her personal journey, and held my hand. Her humility made all the difference. She validated my anxiety, acknowledged the importance of my experiences, and reassured me that I was not alone. Recognizing the privilege of accessing these resources, I felt compelled to pay it forward by amplifying the voices of immigrants, refugees and those who remained silenced.

Another significant milestone began with the introduction of Camp HOPE into my life in 2014. Camp HOPE America is the leading year-round camping and mentoring program in the country for children and teens impacted by domestic violence. Its mission focuses on creating hope and healing-centered pathways through collaborative, trauma-informed care, empowering youth exposed to trauma to believe in themselves, others, and their dreams.

My children and I were fortunate to participate in the early stages of this program, initiated by Casey Gwinn and his wife, Beth Gwinn. They sought to provide children and teens who had received services at the San Diego Family Justice Center with something to look forward to as they embarked on a positive path toward safety and healing. Casey, Beth, and their team welcomed my son and, a couple of years later, my two daughters with open arms. We desperately needed Camp HOPE in our lives.

For a few years, the Alliance hosted a weekend camp for parents and children, which provided an incredible healing experience for our family. We glimpsed what a healthy family trip could look like, surrounded by wonderful friends in beautiful campgrounds nestled in nature. I realized that I needed support to facilitate my children's healing. I will always be grateful for the significant positive impact Camp HOPE had on my children's well-being during their formative years.

Around this time, my father lost his job after working for over a decade at a cleaning business. His depression worried my sisters and me, prompting us to start a commercial cleaning company. My oldest sister's employer gave us our first real break by providing a contract with his wholesale flower business. I named our company RCL, using the initials of my children: Rodolfo, Cristina, and Lizbeth.

From the outset, accessing capital proved challenging. As a single mother seeking a visa and lacking any credit history, I faced significant hurdles with traditional banks. Fortunately, I received support from friends and mentors. Casey, Gael, and the Alliance for Hope team stepped in again, providing a small business loan and eventually becoming one of our clients. Several agencies that had previously assisted me during my crisis also became clients.

The most meaningful partnership was with the Center for Community Solutions, where I provided services for their Project House Shelter—the same shelter where I had stayed with my children after leaving their father. This full-circle moment deeply humbled me, and I felt grateful to support their efforts to provide shelter for survivors in crisis. Later, I joined their Project Safe House Board, helping to raise funds for the shelter.

While seeking additional funding opportunities, I met Maria, a loan officer who connected me with the Eva Longoria Foundation's microloans. These loans helped me establish RCL's credit as well as my personal credit, opening doors previously locked to me. The everyday opportunities that many take for granted—such as securing a cell phone contract or a car loan—were precious to me. With the support of my loan officer, my business established a solid reputation in the community.

I was fortunate to find an incredible co-working space for female entrepreneurs called Hera Hub, where I had the opportunity to learn from and connect with powerful entrepreneurs from diverse backgrounds. Their guidance allowed me to manage my business and significantly boosted my confidence as a woman and business owner. My goal during that time was for RCL to employ victims of domestic violence within immigrant and refugee communities, providing them with mentoring and resources to help them regain their footing. This vision combined my passion for community service with my entrepreneurial goals.

In 2015 I experienced another breakthrough. After five years of therapy with my psychologist, Dr. Diane Lass, I began to rediscover myself and be a more present mother. I met an incredible person, Candace, the director of Counseling and Residential Services at CCS, while volunteering with the Center for Community Solutions. When I shared my story and my plans for my business, she expressed her excitement and suggested I participate in the Leap to Confidence Program.

When I received the email about the program, I was impressed by Leap to Success, an organization dedicated to empowering women through self-confidence and leadership development. The program teaches women to reframe negative self-talk into positive communication, manage stress and anxiety, improve communication skills, recognize their strengths, and build healthy relationships.

After I completed the Leap to Confidence program, Candace invited me to her Christmas celebration at Hera Hub and said I would be an excellent candidate for the Leadership Program, which honored me.

A year later, I graduated from the Leadership Program, achieving my goal of learning self-nurturing habits. Despite overcoming many challenges—being a single mom, sharing my experiences from small groups to national conferences to raise awareness about domestic violence, and starting my own business—I struggled to enjoy my success and often felt overwhelmed. This program and amazing self-nurturing coach, Kelley Grimes, helped me learn to love, respect, acknowledge, and forgive myself.

Amid the Leap to Success Transformation Leadership Program in 2016, Casey and Gael invited me to manage their first after-crisis program for the Latinx community, "Proyecto Esperanza," funded by the Avon Foundation. This marked the beginning of a new chapter in my life. My passion for this work grew daily as I witnessed the personal and professional growth of the Latinas I supported through Proyecto Esperanza. The love and affection I received from their children were priceless, and the dedication of my team at Alliance for HOPE International inspired me. The knowledge I gained from professionals working with domestic violence and sexual assault victims worldwide was invaluable. I felt blessed and grateful, living a dream better than I had ever imagined.

Unfortunately, the grant concluded a year and four months later, but we worked hard to keep our VOICES community connected.

In October 2017 I was invited to speak at the Eva Longoria's Foundation Gala in Los Angeles to share my story. I got the opportunity to meet the fearless Eva Longoria and other celebrities. Raising awareness about domestic violence and the importance of supporting empowering Latina entrepreneurs through access to capital and training to foster income stability, growth, and economic mobility was incredibly empowering. Most importantly, I got the opportunity to invite my son and share this special accomplishment with him.

A few months into my journey, I received an invitation to join the San Diego District Attorney's Office on a pilot project supporting individuals experiencing homelessness. Working directly with women in crisis was both heart-wrenching and rewarding. My colleague and I worked tirelessly to provide exceptional support, launching the first-ever peer support groups across three shelter locations. Although the pandemic halted in-person support and group facilitation, it presented an opportunity to join the San Diego Domestic Violence Council. I was honored to establish the pioneering Binational Domestic Violence Committee, fostering collaboration with Tijuana agencies to support survivors on both sides of the border.

In 2022 I became a founding member of One Safe Place, the North County Family Justice Center in San Diego. Initially serving as VOICES director and Welcome Ambassador supervisor, I later transitioned to VOICES director and care coordinator. Additionally, I led and coordinated the survivors' retreat for Latina survivors at Alliance for HOPE's Retreat Center in Allenspark, Colorado. These experiences have profoundly impacted my commitment to supporting vulnerable populations and fuel my continued efforts to drive positive change.

Liberation

These years provided incredible personal and professional growth. However, I faced an unexpected challenge when the father of my children sought to reconnect in 2021. I knew I had to prioritize their safety and well-being. Fortunately, the restorative justice training I had received equipped me with tools to navigate this process, prioritizing safety.

With the guidance of a psychologist, we navigated a process that allowed us to confront the harm and heal. I created a safe space for my children to meet with their father, with the accompaniment of my sister and her partner.

Through this process, I found closure and liberation. I realized that my children and I didn't need their father's validation or apology to heal. We had the power to create our own narrative and forge a new path forward.

Restorative justice isn't a one-size-fits-all solution, but it can be a powerful tool for survivors. In our case, the criminal justice system ensured our physical safety, while restorative justice facilitated our emotional healing. As we work toward creating a more just and compassionate society, I believe restorative justice will play an increasingly important role.

During my healing journey, I had the privilege of meeting inspiring and humble survivors, including Rosie Hidalgo. Rosie is the first Latina appointed as the director of the Office on Violence Against Women (OVW) and the first Senate-confirmed director to lead OVW since 2012. I had the pleasure of collaborating with her virtually during the pandemic in her role as senior director of public policy for Casa de Esperanza: National Latin@ Network for Healthy Families and Communities, which focuses on training, research, and policy advocacy to prevent domestic violence and sexual assault.

In April 2024 I finally met Rosie in person at the 24th Annual International Family Justice Center Conference. Later, Rosie and the OVW team invited me to commemorate the 30th anniversary of the Violence Against Women Act on September 12 and 13, 2024. This event reflected on achievements in the field and reaffirmed our commitment to enhancing community and federal responses to domestic violence, sexual violence, stalking, dating violence, and other forms of gender-based violence (GBV). I also participated in a panel titled "Survivor-Centered Change: Driving the Evolution of VAWA through Lived Experience and Advocacy" at the Robert F. Kennedy Main Justice Department Building in Washington, DC, presented to 300 in-person attendees and online viewers.

A highlight of the event was receiving an email invitation from President Biden and Dr. Biden in celebration of the 30th Anniversary of VAWA at the White House. Words cannot express the joy and gratitude these experiences brought to me, my children, family, friends, and fellow survivors. It was an honor to share my story, highlighting the protections VAWA provides to immigrant women while also addressing existing challenges.

One of the most memorable moments was expressing my gratitude to those who advocated for the inclusion of immigrants when President Biden first introduced VAWA in 1994. Their passion and dedication made my journey possible. I also had the opportunity to meet President Biden, known as the father of VAWA, and the mothers of VAWA, while celebrating the leadership of my dear Rosie Hidalgo.

Ever Onward

As a former undocumented immigrant and survivor of intimate partner abuse, my story exemplifies courage and resilience. I never imagined I would become trapped in a relationship with my light slowly fading, but I did. And I know I am not alone. Intimate partner abuse affects millions of immigrants, refugees, and asylum seekers worldwide. It's a silent epidemic, hidden behind closed doors and masked by shame.

Thankfully, my journey is one of healing and hope. My story is not unique, but it is mine. I share it to inspire hope, encourage healing, and remind others that they are not alone. My intention is to communicate to people who are immigrants and those who are experiencing intimate partner abuse that your voice matters, and your message resonates with others. Supportive relationships are crucial for personal and professional growth.

Embracing authenticity is key to building trust and credibility. Self-care is not selfish; it is essential for sustaining your passion and purpose. Every setback presents an opportunity for growth and refinement. Setting boundaries and learning to say no are vital steps in this process, as is rediscovering personal interests and passions.

Practices I will always value include:

- Mindfulness and meditation: Techniques for calming the mind and focusing on the present.
- Reframing negative thoughts: Challenge negative self-talk by viewing it in a positive, realistic light.
- Gratitude practice: Focusing on your accomplishments and blessings shifts your perspective.

- Support network: Surround yourself with encouraging loved ones, mentors, and peers.
- Self-compassion: Treat yourself with kindness, understanding, and patience.
- Journaling: Writing down thoughts and feelings helps process and release emotions.
- Positive affirmations: Repeating empowering statements can rewire your mindset.
- Celebrating small wins: Acknowledge and celebrate your achievements.
- Seeking constructive feedback: Embrace constructive criticism as a tool for growth.
- Embracing imperfection: Accept that mistakes are opportunities for learning.

These practices have become essential tools in my journey toward healing and empowerment, and I hope they can help you too!

*****

About Lisbet Perez:
Lisbet Perez turns her personal experience with domestic violence into a powerful force for change, empowering fellow survivors and advocating for immigrant women and families. Through her advocacy and public speaking, she challenges systems and agencies to develop programs that are inclusive, diverse, and guided by the insights of survivors.

Chapter 24

Life After

Brenda Grisham

Life has its twists and turns, you just have to ride it out and stand tall at the end!

Trauma is a word that carries immense weight, but what does it truly mean? How does one navigate the aftermath of such an overwhelming experience? These questions have haunted me ever since December 31, 2010—that fateful day when I lost my son. To understand trauma, one must delve into the emotional and psychological scars left behind by an event so catastrophic that it disrupts the very fabric of one's existence.

My name is Brenda Grisham, and I am the mother of Deshonda (Shonda), Christopher (Chris), and Janiesha (Niesha), and NuNu to Laini, Kaori, and Khatari. I never imagined my life would take such a tragic turn, but New Year's Eve, 2010, will be forever lodged in my mind as if it were just yesterday. Every time I close my eyes, I am sitting back in my car, reliving that day. How could such unthinkable events have happened to my beloved Christopher?

The day started like any other, with my children making plans and going about their activities. Chris was supposed to go to his dad's house, but those plans changed around 1:00 p.m. Chris instead decided to tutor his mentee, a young man who was learning to play the drums. The young man often came to our church to watch Chris play, eager to learn from him.

"Mom, since I'm not going to my dad's, I called Grandpa [who was not his grandfather; that was just his name for him] and asked him to pick me up. I'll take my sister and go for a few hours, and we'll be back at six to get ready for church," Chris told me.

Chris returned home at six, and by six thirty, he was murdered. It felt like a matter of seconds. One second, everything was normal. Let me say that one more time: It was only a matter of seconds. Chris put his baby niece in the car—which I didn't even realize he'd done. I got in the driver's seat,

Shonda was outside the passenger's door, and Chris got in the back seat. My daughter Janiesha was locking up the house.

Just then, I looked up and saw flashes and heard bullets hitting our car. Shonda yelled, "I'm hit!" I went into mommy mode, shouting, "Run!" Shonda got into the house, Niesha was screaming, and Chris, who had exited the car, said, "Mom!" and turned toward the car again. I ran to him, throwing my 5'3" frame against his 6'3" body and pushed him to the ground. But it was too late. He had been shot in the temple and jaw.

From that point, all I remember after that is hollering, screaming, people jumping over fences—just sheer terror. Over seventy shell casings were collected.

I never thought Chris would die. He was a strong boy, and I knew he would make it. I had just pushed him down and was sitting on his back when Shonda came out of the house screaming, "Where is my baby?" Then she said, "Someone is hit!" You could see that puddle of blood spreading. What was most likely a matter of minutes went by like seconds. Everybody and everything was moving so fast.

Janiesha was crying and calling people, Shonda was telling the 911 operator off. I heard all of that, as well as my neighbor calling from the sidewalk, "Is everybody OK?" My next-door neighbor had hopped the fence and used her jacket to try to stop the blood. Fire trucks, police officers, and the ambulance waited at the corner because they needed to secure the scene. How did this happen? I had two children who were shot and needed their mom, and my youngest was traumatized. When I look back, the memories play in my head like I'm standing on my porch that very day, navigating those around me. Chris would not be coming back home with us.

People called people, my phone was ringing, and I answered every single call as I made my way to the hospital to check on my children. I was met with a waiting room full of familiar faces. How did they all get there so fast? I talked to people, hugged them, and checked on the girls. Shonda had been shot, so she was in the back, and my friends had Janiesha until her dad got there. What was taking so long? I should be hearing something about Chris—they never said he was in surgery, so what was going on and why hadn't I heard anything?

Then someone said, "Here comes the doctor." She took me to that room and told me they could not save Chris. I screamed. The pain was indescribable. What was that feeling? I may never be able to answer that—it was at least five emotions rolled into one. When I returned to myself, I was under a chair. Everyone in the waiting room had heard my screams, and when I walked out of the private family area, people were holding one another and crying while others just sat with their heads in their hands in disbelief.

As heartbroken as I was, I made sure everyone was OK. What was I supposed to do? I felt lost, hurt, and a bunch of other emotions I can't describe. My daughters were devastated, to say the least. As I stood in the emergency room after being told I could not see Christopher due to hospital policies, I was about to leave when two sheriffs walked up and told me to come with them. They took me in the elevator and never said a word. We stopped on the bottom floor, and the doors opened. The coroner stood on the other side. She said the chaplain was adamant about me seeing my son. She called a board member, and he gave permission for me to see him. She said, "I am going to open the curtain. You will not be able to touch him, and we have not cleaned him up. Then we will take him to the coroner's office."

The curtains were pulled back, and he was lying on top of that bag on a table, just like you see on TV. He had blood on his face and the tube still in his mouth; he had an identification tag on his toe. I placed my hand on the glass and told him I loved him, and they zipped him up in the bag and took him away. From that day on, I did not sleep. Fourteen years later, sleep is still not a constant in my life. I shed tears more than anyone knows. I saw my son gunned down right in front of me.

The days that followed were a blur. Funeral arrangements had to be made, and my house was filled with so many people who loved Chris and loved us. I shopped for his clothes so everything he would have on would be brand new. I took care in picking out his final outfit. Christmas had just passed, and he had a room full of new stuff, but nothing in his room stood out to me.

I walked the mall, going from store to store, finding nothing in the same place, but I loved every single garment I bought for him. One of the most important men in my life passed away before Christopher, and I asked for one of his ties so Chris could wear something from his "Gpa," as he called him. I dropped his clothes off at the mortuary.

Later, the director called and said Chris's body was ready and he was going to pick him up personally. The next day would be as traumatic as the day he died. I gathered those who wanted to go with me to the mortuary to do his hair. I walked into an empty room where Chris was in the middle, lying on a gurney, wrapped in plastic.

I rubbed the bruises on his face from where he slid when I pushed him; I talked to him as I washed his hair and twisted every single dread for the last time. I told those in the room the first person who started to cry would have to leave, and of course, it was my sister. I gave the remaining people something each to hold—the gel, a comb, the dry shampoo, the clips. We got through it, and I went home and waited for them to put him in the casket and came back for a final look.

The funeral came and went. I still don't remember everyone who was there, but I know I did not want to go. The thought of saying a final goodbye to Chris was unbearable.

We buried my baby in a grave on a hillside. I didn't need a marker to tell me where he was; I felt him over there in Acadia Garden. Standing by his grave, I felt a sense of emptiness that words cannot capture. Healing—who said there would ever be any of that? I watched them lower my baby into the ground and knew nothing would ever be the same. I never thought I would bury one of my children, but then again, most of us never do.

The Impact on My Family
The death of a child is an unimaginable loss. Each member of our family has had to cope with their grief in their own way. Shonda, who was also injured in the shooting, has struggled with survivor's guilt. She often wonders why she survived when Chris did not. Janiesha, who witnessed the horror unfold, says Chris comes to her in her dreams and they talk and she doesn't want to wake up because then he'd be gone. The girls grieve differently because they both had a special relationship with their brother.

As a mother, it is heartbreaking to see my children in pain. My grief is from the place of a mother who birthed a son who is now gone, and theirs is from the place of sibling love. This chapter is being penned almost fourteen years after his death, but the same emotions exist.

The Process of Grief
Grief is a journey, and it is different for everyone. In the early days after Chris's death, I was in a state of shock. I went through the motions of planning the funeral and taking care of my

family, but it all felt surreal. It was as if I were watching someone else's life unfold.

As the shock wore off, the reality of my loss set in. I was engulfed by waves of emotion and I despaired at the thought of living the rest of my life without him.

Grief is not a linear process. There are good days and bad days. There are moments when I can smile and laugh, and there are moments when the pain is so intense, I can hardly breathe. Over time, I have learned to live with my grief. It is a part of me now, woven into the fabric of my being.

I have offered hours of support to families who have lost a loved one to violence, and I don't regret one minute. Part of my healing comes from helping others find a way back to a somewhat normal life.

Steps Toward Healing
Healing is a gradual process, and it is different for everyone. For me, the journey toward healing has involved both personal and communal efforts. I have sought solace in my faith, finding strength and comfort in my belief that Chris was here for a reason, he served his purpose, and now he is watching over us all.

The support of my family, friends, and church has been a crucial part of my healing process. In the immediate aftermath of Chris's death, friends, family, and neighbors rallied around us, providing emotional and practical support. They helped with daily tasks, such as cooking and cleaning, allowing me to focus on my family and our grief. Their presence and kindness were a reminder that we were not alone in our sorrow. We sat, we ate, we told stories, and we cried a whole lot for months.

Over time, this support extended to a broader network. I became involved with local organizations dedicated to preventing gun violence and supporting families affected by it. These groups provided a platform to share my story and advocate for change. I found comfort in knowing that my experience could help others and contribute to a larger cause.

Through these organizations, I met other parents who had lost children to gun violence. We formed a close-knit community, bonded by our shared pain and determination to create a safer world. We attended conferences and workshops and worked together on initiatives to raise awareness and promote legislative changes. This sense of purpose and camaraderie has been instrumental in my healing journey.

The loss of Chris ignited a passion for advocacy within me. He was a giver right up until the time he was murdered. I realized that while I could not change the past, I could work toward preventing similar tragedies in the future. I became actively involved in efforts to address the root causes of gun violence and promote safer communities.

One of my primary focuses has been on supporting anyone and everyone in our community who needs me, and that has turned out to be a lot of people. Chris was a mentor and role model for many young people, and I wanted to honor his legacy by continuing his work.

I often say I want to be just like Chris when I grow up, and I refer to myself as Chris Jones's mom—and then there is Brenda Grisham.

Months after Chris's death, I advocated for policy changes at the local and Federal levels. I have collaborated with lawmakers and community leaders to push for stricter gun control measures, improved mental health services, and increased funding for community-based violence prevention programs. I have assisted families at hearings, participated in public forums, and used my platform to amplify the voices of those affected by gun violence.

While these efforts cannot bring Chris back, they give me a sense of purpose and hope. I am determined to make a difference and ensure that no other family has to endure the pain we have experienced. Every step forward, every life saved, is a tribute to Chris's memory.

Coping with Anniversaries and Milestones
One of the most challenging aspects of grief is coping with anniversaries and milestones. Each year, as December 31 approaches, I feel a familiar knot of dread in my stomach. The anniversary of Chris's death is a painful reminder of what we have lost. On this day, I allow myself to fully experience my grief. I visit his grave and his statues and reflect on the beautiful moments we shared.

Other milestones, such as birthdays and holidays, are also difficult. Chris's absence is acutely felt during family gatherings and celebrations. To honor his memory, we have established new traditions that include him in spirit. On his birthday, we have done community activities every year. The main activity is Help the Homeless, an all-day event for which we prepare for months by gathering toiletries to distribute to unhoused members of our community.

These rituals help keep Chris's memory alive and provide a sense of continuity. They remind us that he is still a part of our lives, even though he is no longer physically present. They also offer a way to channel our grief into acts of love and remembrance.

Maintaining Chris's legacy is a driving force in my life. I want the world to remember him not just for the tragedy of his death, but for the joy and light he brought into our lives. To honor his memory, the Xperience is an event we participate in every year for the families of homicide victims. This is a two-day event in which we host a gala for the families, and the next day we host a conference that deals with the traumas and triggers of violence.

What I learned from Chris's death is that the world needs more people like him. Chris never argued, he always smiled, and he loved to show affection. If Christopher saw you once, he would never forget you.

This chapter was especially challenging for me because I didn't go through therapy—I was the therapist. I didn't reach out to others, even though they wanted to know how I, as Chris's mother, coped after seeing my son murdered right in front of me. As tragic as December 31 was and will always be, I still found the strength to sit, talk, and reminisce about him as a person. I reflected on the values I learned from him, even though I was his mother.

Grieving the loss of a child is an immense emotional burden, and it is essential to prioritize mental health during this journey. After Chris's death, I encountered countless complex emotions and trauma. I learned the most crucial part of my healing process would be providing a safe space to express my feelings and develop coping strategies. I found safety and space in helping others.

Moving forward after such a profound loss is a continuous process. There are days when the pain feels as fresh as it did on that fateful night, and there are days when I find moments of joy and peace. I have learned that healing does not mean forgetting; it means finding a way to live with the loss and honoring the memory of my son.

Chris's death has reshaped my life in ways I never imagined. It has tested my strength and resilience, but it has also revealed the depths of my love and capacity for growth. I have found purpose in advocacy, healing in community, and solace in Chris's memory. My main focus is to help families navigate the system and grab onto the parts that will make them functional citizens at some point in time.

The clock ticks differently for each and every family. Some reach a level of functionality while others are overcome with the grief and loss, to the point where they can't see their way out. Still others just don't want to find that light at the end of the tunnel. I have met thousands of victims in my over thirteen years on this journey, and the experience is unique to every survivor.

I am committed to making a difference in the world. I will continue to fight for safer communities, support those affected by gun violence, and keep Chris's legacy alive. My love for him fuels my determination and guides my path forward.

In sharing my story, I hope to offer a message of hope and resilience to others who are grieving. While the pain of loss never fully goes away, it is possible to find meaning and purpose in the aftermath. By honoring our loved ones and working toward a better future, we can create a legacy of love and change.

*****

A note from Brenda:
My name is Brenda Grisham

I am from Oakland, CA where I was born and raised by a single mother, I have three children, Deshonda, Christopher (deceased), and Janiesha. I am the grandmother (Nunu) of Laini, Kaori and Khatari.

I am the proud owner of three businesses and two nonprofits and the minister of music for the Seventh Ave Baptist church, where I have been a member for fifty-eight years.

I am a community advocate, providing services for victims of crime, and advocating for families that are going through the court system. As an advocate, I assist families with the VOC application after they have lost someone. If they qualify for the services, they need to navigate this most traumatic time.

I am the executive director of The Christopher Lavell Jones Foundation, Inc., the executive director of Their Lives Matter, Inc., the owner of Tru Blendz Beauty Bar, Upscale Financial Solutions, and Independent Financial Solutions. I provide support for human trafficking as a therapist for Love Never Fails, Inc., and am an executive board member of the Violence Prevention Coalition, Family Support Advocates and the chair of the gun violence subcommittee for the Violence Policy Center (VPC. I also serve on the board of various nonprofits in the bay area.

My team and I travel to Washington every December to address gun laws and background checks.

I have received many awards, including the Live Your Dream award, the Spirit Community Service award, Frontline Warrior Keeper of the Culture award, Oscar Grant III Foundation Community Service award, Green the Church-Green Guardian award, Black Excellence Humanitarian award and the community service award from the Khadafy Washington Foundation

Safety and accountability are my focus. The work I do is in the memory of my son Christopher. I am grateful to have been his mom for seventeen years and I hope his legacy will live on long after I am gone.

Brenda F.

Gratitude and Appreciation

Thank You God

We want to give our most heartfelt gratitude and appreciation to the following supporters who, from our first meeting, believed in this book and movement. It is because of humans such as yourself, your encouragement, and your commitment that our passions and purpose are kept alive to do and be better to others. Thank you for your partnership, your support, and your love throughout this process.

Dennis Postema and the entire team at Motivation and Success Publishing; Carrie Carr, Shane Glass, Nora Richard, Jaydn Bullinger, Maria Eva Maccione Soerenson and Stephanie Bowen. For all the work done behind the scenes that we will never be fully aware of, but most certainly appreciate and thank you for. To Yolander Prinzel and our most incredible editing team, Angelique Kees (also formatting) and Jennifer Sommersby (also proofreading). You ladies have carried our voices and stories with love and integrity from the beginning. You were able to write and bring to life our stories in a different capacity but still remained true and authentic to each coauthor. From the bottom of our hearts, THANK YOU! We knew we had the right publishing team from the beginning and are pleased to continue our work together in the future.

Jason Latona with DragonetDesign.com for all the IT, website development, and other tasks you completed without hesitation. You have been a pure delight to work with and we are grateful for you, sir.

Ms. Lydia Anderson, the emotionally connected artist who understood our concept and birthed the cover you see today. We cannot be more pleased with your skill set, integrity, and delightful personality. I highly encourage others to reach out to her for all art and graphics: Fiverr profile--Lydia Anderson Graphics.

Terae Chapman with The Earl M and Margery Chapman Foundation for seeing the purpose of this book and movement to be able to bring the light others need to not only heal, but become productive and thriving members of society so they can bring and share that same goodness and kindness extended to them to others.

Marina Lewis for all the legal assistance and guidance when it comes to protecting this book and our coauthors.

Ever After Foundation for having the courage to push forward with literally nothing but this concept and our belief in God to see us through, because of the impact and opportunities this book and movement will bring for others.

Nancy O'Malley for your endless encouragement, knowledge and support on so many levels

Casey Gwinn, President, Alliance for HOPE International https://www.allianceforhope.com, for partnering with and believing in our coauthors and their ability to provide hope and healing to others.

Resources

If you or someone you love is a victim of intimate partner abuse, please contact any of these resources for help:

- **Ever After Foundation:** https://everafter.foundation/ Reach out to Ever After Foundation for valuable resources and education aimed at building financial independence and freedom. Our platform is dedicated to helping you create a meaningful space for yourself in the workforce. Whether you're seeking support in career development or tools to enhance your financial literacy, Ever After Foundation is here to guide you on your journey toward empowerment and success. Visit everafter.foundation to start your path to a more independent future today.
- **National domestic violence (DV) Hotline:** 1-800-799-7233
- **National Suicide Hotline** (Call/Text): 988
- **National Underground Railroad for DV:** 1-888-399-8385
- **National Substance Abuse Mental Health Services Administration Resources:** 1-800-662-4357
- **Department of Rehabilitation:** Please refer to your state information.
- **National Perpetrator of Violence Resources:** 1-800-799-7233
- **Manalive Men Against Violence:** 530-392-0714

Made in the USA
Middletown, DE
22 April 2025